Raging
into
Apocalypse

Raging into Apocalypse

Essays in Apocalypse IV

**Dave Breese • J.R. Church • Grant Jeffrey
David A. Lewis • Chuck Missler
Henry Morris • Gary Stearman
John Walvoord • David F. Webber
with William T. James**

New Leaf Press

The information and opinions contained in each chapter of this book reflect the views of the individual authors, and in no way are particularly endorsed by the essayists as a group.

For Jesus

Acknowledgments

To Jesus Christ, who came to earth to seek and to save those who were lost, and who is coming again to establish and reign over His kingdom of righteousness, belongs all praise, honor, glory, and worship. Life itself is an exercise in futility apart from Him. I know that each and every one of His faithful servants who contributed to this book say "Amen" to that acknowledgment.

I am deeply grateful to my wonderful friends who included in their busy schedules time to pray about and meditate upon the crucial issues and events of our day, then apply their spirit-felt thoughts to the writing process. The result, I believe the reader will agree, is a volume that sheds much light upon a world moving toward the black abyss of apocalypse. Again, my deepest gratitude to Dave Breese, J.R. Church, Grant Jeffrey, David Allen Lewis, Chuck Missler, Henry Morris, Gary Stearman, John Walvoord, and David Webber for using their gifts in the cause of Christ.

My treasured friends at New Leaf Press have once again proven their determination to follow the God-given precepts "whatever ye do, do it heartily, as to the Lord, and not unto men" and "whatsoever thy hand findeth to do, do it with thy might." I am inadequate to express to my friend Tim Dudley and his associates the depth of my admiration for them. It is a privilege to work with them on these projects and I am thankful to our Lord and grateful to them for allowing me to do so.

To Angie Peters, whose daughter-like friendship makes our work together very special and without whose gifted editorial, research, and writing talents and skills this book would have been much more a laborious exercise than the enjoyable project it has been. And to her husband and my good friend, Kurt, as well as to their wonderful little ones, Nick and Lindsey, for so generously sharing Angie's time, my love and my thanks.

To Thelma Sutton and to John and Lucy Leslie, dear friends who were a huge part of my training under Christian influence from my earliest remembrances as a child, and whose prayers and support I continue to enjoy, my heartfelt love and gratitude. How gracious our Lord has been and continues to be in surrounding me with people of such profound maturity in Christ. In this regard, a double portion of my thanks and love to my mother, Kathleen James-Basse.

To Margaret and our sons, Terry and Nathan, each of whom mean more to me than is possible to convey in any amount of space, all my love.

Finally and especially, to you the reader, my heartfelt appreciation, best wishes, and prayers that time spent in thinking upon things contained in this book help you draw ever closer to God, who so loved the world that He gave His only begotten Son that whosoever believes in Him will have everlasting life.

Contents

Introduction

by William T. James

Perilous times have come. The warning signs of our daily headlines and constant news updates by radio, television, and computer on-line services scream at this generation, "Perilous times are upon us!" The wailing of a world in acute distress shatters this late hour of human history with ear-piercing shrillness that snaps our senses into a heightened state of alert. "LOOK UP!" The tranquillity-rending warnings shriek, "BEWARE THE APPROACHING STORM OF APOCALYPSE!"

More than 200,000 men, women, and children have had life ripped from them during the course of the terrible conflict raging within the territories of the former Yugoslavia. The peace arrangement agreed to on November 21, 1995, at Dayton, Ohio, between Bosnia, Croatia, and Serbia with Secretary of State Warren Christopher looking on, has done nothing to stem the threat of war. The signing seemed only to raise temperatures in Bosnia because of the forced splitting apart of that region.

The African continent throughout is rife with bloody tribal wars of aggression, each flare-up spawning disease and famine, and creating pathetic refugees who have no concept of why the wars are waged. Asia burns with genocidal atrocities while hatreds smolder and all too often spark to life to become full-blown provincial conflagrations. China, that vast part of Asia under the tyrannical thumb of Communism, murders millions of its people, many through abortion and infanticide.

Islamic fanatics and barbarous dictators who control most

nations of the Middle East thirst for nuclear weaponry. Some of those leaders are known to be very near having such arsenals at their disposal.

Terrorism explodes on a weekly basis throughout Europe. Paris, London, Belfast, Berlin, Madrid, Rome — all have tasted the venomous bite of the terrorists who strike often after issuing boastful warnings and who almost always claim credit for their deadly deeds after they are done. Crime of every description runs rampant throughout the eastern and western parts of Europe, with gang activities — particularly those having ethnic hatreds at their infected cores — taking the statistics on violent acts to record depths. Anti-Semitism flourishes once again in Europe — especially Germany — despite that nation's sincere governmental attempts to put a lid on it.

America. Riots in Los Angeles. Rampaging barbarism, now in suburbia as well as the inner cities. The World Trade Center bombing in New York City. The devastating blast in Oklahoma City that killed hundreds, including all those little ones in the first-floor day care center. The terroristic derailing of the Amtrak en route to Los Angeles. A three-year-old girl shot to death simply because the driver of a car in which she was riding mistakenly turned down a dead-end street in L.A.

Can there be any doubt that we live in perilous times? Read 2 Timothy 3:1-7 and come to your own conclusion.

World Conditions in Prophetic Alignment

The great seas of humanity are roaring with gigantic, crashing waves of ethnic strifes. Nation against nation and kingdom against kingdom. Israel, the most significant of all nations in God's prophetic Word, is gathered again in the region that has become the most incendiary on earth. As a matter of fact, the very existence of that recently reborn state is the chief reason the Middle East harbors the greatest potential for becoming the ignition point of man's final war. Prime Minister Yitzak Rabin's assassination November 4, 1995, the first such murder in modern Israel's history, serves as a stark reminder of how quickly disaster can strike.

Japan continues to be a powerful economic force. China, with more than 1.2 billion people, has successfully struggled to its feet upon the world stage and has forged pacts with such former enemies as India, home of more than 800 million people. The Chinese government is seemingly with ease seducing the West into opening up its vaults of wealth and technology. This bloc far east of the Euphrates River is looking suspiciously like the end-time power God's Word terms the *Kings of the East.*

Magog, the last-days power predicted in Ezekiel 38 and 39 to invade the region God deeded to Israel, stirs to life out of the dead carcass of the U.S.S.R. The former Soviet republics agitate restlessly in their own ethnic turmoil, forming new alliances that collectively possess the most formidable thermonuclear arsenal on earth. Radical Islam seems to be the tie that binds Russia (Magog) to Iran (Persia) and the other avowed enemies of Israel.

The European Union, through the astonishing growth of computer technology and socioeconomic exigencies, formed with swiftness almost as amazing as that with which the U.S.S.R. dissolved. Make no mistake. The revived Roman Empire has arrived! Although it is presently a demanding, mildly troublesome youngster, its potential for exponential growth makes unpredictable the precise moment it will burst forth as the full-fledged beast-state of the Books of Daniel and Revelation.

God's Word tells further about world conditions that will signal the imminent end of this earth age. These convulsions are likened unto a woman travailing in birth during which time the contractions occur with increased frequency and intensity. The birth pangs will, the Scriptures tell us, consist of a number of specific type disasters — catastrophies not at all uncommon to mankind. What, then, will make these calamitous occurrences so unusual as to signal the soon coming end of the age?

The answer is that while earth's convulsions come more frequently and with greater intensity, individual upheavals of nature which are components of the birth pangs will be happening in virtually every geographical area of the world practically at the same time. It is most important to understand that the specific type disasters were predicted 20 centuries ago to be raging upon the earth at a time when the world's geopolitical, socio-economic, technological, and religious conditions will be aligned exactly as they are today.

Darkening Skies, End-Time Rumblings

While the storm clouds of peril boil ominously above earth's last-days landscape, the words of the greatest of all prophets echo within the pre-tempest calm. "And when these things begin to come to pass, then look up, and lift up your heads; for your redemption draweth near" (Luke 21:28).

In this prophetic passage, *"these things"* refers back to the signs Jesus said will be witnessed by a specific generation of earth's inhabitants — the generation alive at the time of His second coming. Referring to prophetic arrangements and His return, He said further, "When ye shall see these things come to pass, know that it is near, even at the doors" (Mark 13:29).

Jesus was telling that generation of believers in Him who will be alive at the time He comes to rescue them before God's judgment falls upon a depraved, rebellious world, that when the specific signs He warned about are all prevalent on the world scene at the same time, they should be intensely alert for His coming for them. Jesus Christ, who is God himself, did not say that "all these things must first come to their ultimate fulfillment" before He comes again. He said that this unique generation of believers is to know that their Lord is standing at the very doors of heaven, ready to call them unto himself when these prophesied signs *"BEGIN"* to come to pass.

Apostasy, the Tornado Warning of Apocalypse

Paul's Holy Spirit-given prophecy warns with siren-call clarity from across the past centuries, "Let no man deceive you by any means, for that day shall not come except there come the falling away first" (2 Thess. 2:3). The warning the Apostle prophesied was, in the Greek language, the word "apostasia," meaning "apostasy." In other words, the apostle Paul was predicting total turning away from the truth of God's Word. It becomes apparent upon examining Jesus' words that the "falling away" or "apostasy" will involve the turning of the truth of God into lies. He said in Matthew 24:11, "Many false prophets shall rise, and shall deceive many."

This warning from the lips of the *true* Christ ties closely into His earlier words about the *false* christs — and, of course, apostate teachings — that will clearly mark the times in which these things become blatantly operative at the very end of the age. "Take heed, that no man deceive you. For many shall come in my name, saying, I am Christ; and shall deceive many" (Matt. 24:4-5).

It is the time of the great falling away! It is the time of unbridled apostasy!

Jesus seemed to be saying with these words of warning that incorrigible, apostate religionists will be unashamedly twisting God's truth at the end of the age. The inference can be strongly drawn that the convulsions or birth pangs alluded to earlier will grow in frequency and intensity in direct ratio to the degree of apostasy earth dwellers embrace. Thus, because Jesus immediately follows up on His warning about those who will foster the last-days apostasy by individually specifying components of the end-time convulsions. "And ye shall hear of wars and rumors of wars; see that ye be not troubled; for all these things must come to pass, but the end is not yet. For nation shall rise against nation, and kingdom against kingdom; and there shall be famines, and pestilences, and earthquakes in various places. All these are the beginning of sorrows" (Matt. 24:6-8).

Assessing the Apostate State of World Affairs

"God Gets the He-ho." It is the title of an article in a recent issue of a well-known news magazine. One would be hard pressed to more appropriately describe the blasphemous apostasy of our day.

> Readers who find the Bible sexist, racist, elitist, and insensitive to the physically challenged, take heart. Oxford University Press's new "inclusive language version" of the New Testament and Psalms has cleaned up God's act. In this version, God is no longer "Father" and Jesus is no longer "Son." The hierarchical title of "Lord" is excised as an archaic way to address God. Nor does God (male pronouns for the deity have been abolished) rule a "kingdom," as the editors explain, the word has a blatantly androcentric and patriarchal character. Darkness has been banished in connection with evil because the editors fear it may remind some readers of "darkies." Even God's metaphorical "right hand" has been amputated out of deference to the left-handed. Some examples:
>
> In the majestic opening of John's Gospel, "The glory he has from the Father as only Son of the Father" becomes "The glory as of a parent's only child" (John 1:14).
>
> The Lord's Prayer now begins like this: "Father-Mother, hallowed be your name. May your dominion come" (Luke 11:2).
>
> Jesus' own self-understanding as God's only Son is generalized to: "No one knows the Child except the Father-Mother; and no one knows the Father-Mother except the Child" (Matt. 11:27).

Avoiding another traditional phrase, "Son of Man," the Oxford text reads: "Then they will see 'the Human One' coming in clouds with great power and glory" (Mark 13:26).

The editors do not claim that Jesus spoke in gender-neutral language. But they obviously think He should have. The changes they have made are not merely cosmetic. They represent a fundamental reinterpretation of what the New Testament says — and how it says it. The King James Bible never looked so good.[1]

In a strange dichotomy, at least among the American populace, mounting acceptance of and even embracing of such apostasy is counterbalanced by a heightened interest in matters of biblical prophecy.

One writer reports in an article titled, "Interest in Second Coming Is Growing with Americans:"

> The best barometer of the mood of the country may not be Rush Limbaugh and the radio talk shows, nor the November elections that overturned the Democratic majority in Congress.
>
> The key to the public's disposition may be reflected accurately in a recent poll in the *U.S. News & World Report* magazine. The poll showed that 61 percent of the American people — more than three out of five — believe in the Second Coming, the physical return of Jesus Christ to the earth.
>
> This figure fluctuates periodically but seldom gets that high. It peaks at times of social uncertainty and unrest. This appears to be such a time.

The article continues a bit further along with some thoughts garnered from evangelist Billy Graham:

> Today Graham will only say that "our Lord gave a summary of events that would signal His return. Reading them, one must be struck by their resemblance to what we see daily on our TVs and in our newspapers."
>
> Some of those Bible "signs" in Graham's opinion are

"wars and rumors of war, famine, earthquakes and multiplied lawlessness and iniquity."

Despite the revival of interest in the Second Coming, the majority of non-fundamentalist Christians probably do not believe that Jesus will return to earth in the flesh. Why don't they?

"Most of them don't put any stock in Bible prophecies or interpret them only in the broadest sense. They may accept that the world could come to a catastrophic end, but rule out the possibility of 'the Son of Man coming on the clouds of heaven' as an accompanying event."

The writer later concludes, "Whether Billy Graham and the 61 percent of the respondents to the *U.S. News* poll who said they believe in the Second Coming are right or wrong, it can be said with certainty that people are interested in the subject more than they have been in several generations."[2]

Nature Protests Mankind's Apostasy

An earthquake ranging in magnitude from 7.5 to 7.9 shook Mexico's coastal region 325 miles west of Mexico City on October 7, 1995. Within a matter of days, several more shook Mexico once again and also regions of China where the magnitudes registered 6.5 and above. On November 22, 1995, the Middle Eastern region was shaken by an earthquake estimated as high as 7.2. Israel, Saudi Arabia, Egypt, and Jordan were affected with eight killed and hundreds injured. Reports on an almost daily basis testified to the escalation in seismic activity during the months before the Mexico quake. Every geographical region of the world seemed affected by the violent shakings.

Volcanoes stirred to life during 1995, some thought not to have erupted for several millennia. Even Vesuvius threatens to once again devastate its region of influence like in the days when it buried Pompeii.

Storms packing killer-velocity winds exploded in such profusion during the 1995 hurricane and typhoon seasons that those charged with naming the storms exhausted their supply of names and were forced to go once again to the beginning of the alphabet before the tremendous outbreak of storms ended. Billions of dollars in damage resulted. The toll in human life was, of course, inestimable.

Flooding from record-level rainfalls flooded the East Coast of America while much of the central portion of the United States suffered through weeks and months of drought. The West Coast blazed with great consuming fires while almost simultaneously tornadoes ripped New York, Connecticut, and other parts of the Northeast, the latter occurrences almost unheard of until recent times. Grapefruit-size hailstones that fell in Texas were reportedly dwarfed by volleyball-size hailstones that pulverized parts of a province in mainland China.

Nature at the microbial level is on a rampage that is nothing short of terrifying. Even the always fatal disease called AIDS seems to pale when compared to the imposing specter presented by flesh-eating viruses and unstoppable bacteria that kill within days of first contact with them.

Horror stories of these viruses and bacteria inundate our daily news with increasing frequency that rivals the barrage of reports involving earthquakes, volcanoes, and violent weather. One such story makes clear the frightening prospects man faces:

"When a 36-year-old lab technician known as Kinfumu checked into the general hospital in Kikwit, Zaire, last month, complaining of diarrhea and a fever, anyone could have mistaken his illness for the dysentery that was plaguing the city. Nurses, doctors, and nuns did what they could to help the young man. They soon saw that his disease wasn't just dysentery. Blood began oozing from every orifice in his body. Within four days he was dead. By then the illness had all but liquefied his internal organs."[3] The nuns who cared for the man died within days and soon the Geneva-based World Health Organization (WHO) sent a team of experienced virus hunters composed of tropical medicine specialists, chromomicrobiologists, and other researchers equipped with bubble suits and the latest available technology in order to deal with the quickly spreading contagion.

Last week the CDC [Centers for Disease Control] announced it had linked the outbreak to a virus. It wasn't just any virus. As many experts had feared all along, it was Ebola.

If the word doesn't make your hair stand on end, it should. Discovered just 19 years ago, when similar outbreaks killed more than 400 people in Zaire and neighboring Sudan, the Ebola virus remains a gruesome mystery. No one knows where the virus resides in nature, how human epidemics get started or why they're so rare. We know only that the virus can spread from person to person through body secretions, and that 50 to 90 percent of the victims die in a matter of days. The first flu-like symptoms typically appear within three days of infection. Then, as the virus starts replicating in earnest, the victim's capillaries clog with dead blood cells, causing the skin to bruise, blister, and eventually dissolve like wet paper. By the sixth day, blood flows freely from the eyes, ears, and nose, and the sufferer starts vomiting the black sludge of his disintegrating internal tissues. Death usually follows by day nine.

Ebola is a potent emblem of the microbial world's undiminished power over us. But it's not the only one. New viruses have emerged with terrifying regularity in recent decades. Most are still obscure tropical menaces with names like Machupo and Oropouche. But because they are viral menaces, they're largely untreatable. And the AIDS epidemic has shown us what an obscure tropical menace can make of itself when the circumstances are right. Fifteen years ago, it was unimaginable. By the end of this decade, the global number of HIV infections should reach 40 million. And despite billions of dollars spent on years of intense research, AIDS is still a death sentence.

Scientists agree that AIDS won't be the last viral scourge, and that message has finally registered with the masses.[4]

An article in the May 1995 *World Press Review* reports in part, "Through numerous scientific breakthroughs, medical science has seemed well on the way to victory over infectious diseases in recent decades, at least in the industrialized parts of the world. But as we approach the twenty-first century, disturbing signs of a different picture are emerging. Reports on outbreaks of diseases once thought to have been virtually eradicated have been making headlines with increasing frequency — for example, last year's cases of presumed bubonic plague in India. And 'new' pathogens are emerging that can be even more dangerous, because we lack not only medications to combat them but also experience in dealing with them sensibly."[5]

To add to the trepidation, many scientists now predict the soon appearance of what they term "the apocalypse bug," a viral and/or bacteriological mutant against which there will be no defense. Jesus' warning that pestilence of unusual virulence will be on the end-time scene at the same time other disasters plague mankind in confluence with the unique geopolitical, socioeconomic, technological, and religious flood of events seems absolutely relevant to our generation. Mankind, through growing apostasy, demonstrates that this is a generation of people which by and large refuses to recognize Jesus Christ as Lord. Planet Earth itself, therefore, cries out that He is the soon-coming King of kings!

Today's Tribulation Technology

Revelation 13:16-17 warns of a terrible future time when all the peoples of the world will come under the control of a dictator who will ultimately demand that they worship him as God. The Antichrist's controlling technology is described as follows: "And he causeth all, both small and great, rich and poor, free and enslaved, to receive a mark in their right hand, or in their foreheads. And that no man might buy or sell, except he that had the mark, or the name of the beast, or the number of his name."

Peter LaLonde, an author and broadcaster who addresses biblical end-time prophecy, made a well-researched observation about current computer technology and governments' use of it. "The technology is there. They say that military development is seven years ahead of what we know about here in the civilian world. My goodness, we can't even imagine. . . . We are reading now about some of the sophisticated computer technology that tracks all international phone calls going across the world looking for key words: bomb, hijacking, terrorism . . . and they will flag out those conversations and record every international phone call going on in the world today, looking for key words."

Those who do the snooping say they do it for world security, according to LaLonde. He cited the example, "We live in an age when no one knows who's got Russia's nuclear weapons. Where did these things go? In the name of facing that kind of threat, people are willing to give up a bit of their privacy . . . in the name of not being blown up."

When questioned about the possibility of putting computer chips into people's bodies for the purpose of tracking them through use of orbiting reconnaissance satellites, LaLonde said, "That's already here. The European Union right now is struggling with the question of the fastest-growing area of crime . . . car theft. The European Union is talking now about tracking every car in Europe by the end of this term with satellite technology.

"At the same time in Michigan, two Indian fellows go out ice fishing, minding their own business in the back woods of northern Michigan on a dark night out in the middle of the bush. Up show the police and arrest them for poaching on illegal fishing areas because they dug their holes outside of where they were supposed to fish. And do you know how they were caught? Global positioning systems. Satellites hundreds of miles in the sky tracking two lonely Indian fishermen in the middle of a cold bush night ice fishing. This system can track people already. It's already being used."

LaLonde went on to say, "With these things, already they can track you within three meters of anywhere on the face of the earth, and that's the cheap system. There's no question that in the days ahead, this technology is going to get cheaper, easier, and they will know exactly where you are if they want to."[6] God spoke to a particular future generation of earth's inhabitants through his aged apostle, John, who described precisely a system of marks and numbers through which history's most powerful dictator will enslave that end-time generation. Antichrist's tribulation technology is here today!

Raging into Apocalypse is intended to examine in-depth our troubled times under the intense, revealing light of God's prophetic truth. Each writer presents his prayerfully considered thoughts about the likely prophetic significance of recent developments against well-defined historical backdrops cogent to the fascinating topic he addresses. This book's total effect, it is hoped, will be to explore whether this generation has entered the "perilous times" predicted by the apostle Paul in 2 Timothy 3:1.

Is ours the generation that is seeing "all these things begin to come to pass"? While these questions are under consideration, this volume at the same time invites the reader to solicit a better overall comprehension of man's time on earth from the creation as recorded in Genesis through the triumphant return of Jesus Christ at the climax of Armageddon.

Although the history of man is more often than not an unlovely thing to behold, man's future just beyond this self-destructing earth age is beautiful beyond finite human sense's ability to grasp. There is one way and one way only to God the Father and that is through one's personal acceptance of God's grace gift for the remission of sin. Jesus Christ is that grace gift. Accept Him now as your Saviour and your Lord. Then you can — with joyful expectation, through the Hope within you — embrace God's truth about the reality of your glorious future.

SECTION I

From Creation to Evacuation

1

Satan's War against God and Man's Dark History

by Henry Morris

A cosmic warfare is raging between God and the devil. Every age, every nation, has been involved, and we also are involved on one side or the other because, after all, these are the only two worldviews. Either we can explain the origin and development of all things in terms of continuing natural processes or we cannot; so the one worldview is evolution and the other one is creation. These two perspectives embrace everything in the world of sense, knowledge, and understanding. We must believe either one worldview or the other; we cannot really believe both because they are not synonyms, but antonyms. Each is the opposite of the other.

Looking at Scriptural and Scientific Proofs

The basic rationale, the foundation of this cosmic conflict, is between these two worldviews: God-centered or creature-centered. Creator or creature. Creation versus evolution. This conflict has been going on since the very beginning in one form or another. When we evaluate these two worldviews scientifically, we find that all of the genuine scientific evidence supports creation but not a single real fact of science supports evolution.

But there's also another way to evaluate this conflict, a way that the Lord Jesus himself gave us. He said, "By their fruits you shall know them. A good tree cannot bring forth corrupt fruit, neither can a corrupt tree bring forth good fruit" (Matt. 7:16-17). We can therefore evaluate these two worldviews not only in terms of their scientific validity or invalidity, but also in terms of the fruit which they have produced. When we do this, it becomes evident that the creationist worldview, the creationist tree, has borne good fruits and the evolutionist tree has borne nothing but bad fruits.

The creationist worldview has produced sound doctrine, good systems, and good practices. The evolutionist tree, on the other hand, universally has produced bad doctrine, bad fruits, bad practices. That may sound like an extreme statement, but I believe that it can be documented compellably in ways even most Christian people are not aware of.[1] That's part of what we want to take a look at in this chapter.

In support of the thesis that there is a basic conflict involving evolution versus special creation, or Satan versus God, let me mention a few verses of Scripture. The Lord Jesus Christ said himself in John 8:44 that the devil is the father of liars. He is a liar, he is the great deceiver. Revelation 12:9 reveals that Satan is the one who has deceived the whole world. In 2 Corinthians 3-4, we read, "If our gospel be hid, it is hid to them that are lost, in whom the god of this world, [that is, the devil] hath blinded the minds of them which believe not, lest the light of the glorious gospel of Christ, who is the image of God, should shine unto them." If people cannot understand the gospel, it's because their minds have been blinded by the devil. He is the great deceiver. He appears sometimes as an angel of light and he has so-called ministers of righteousness, but he is basically the deceiver. And as 1 John 5:19 says, "The whole world lies in [the wicked one]." Evolution is, in fact, Satan's great lie, with which he seeks to persuade men and women to abandon faith in their Creator.

In reference to the creationist tree producing good fruits, let me suggest a few things. Are you aware that our nation was founded upon creationism? Our American nation, with all of its tradition of religious liberty and freedom, was founded upon creationism. It's even in the Declaration of Independence, which asserts that we have been endowed by our Creator with certain unalienable rights. And creationism is implicit in the Constitution and in the writings of the founding fathers. Even men like Thomas Jefferson and Ben Franklin, who were deists rather than fundamental, Bible-believing Christians, at least believed in creation. Thomas Jefferson explicitly rejected the idea of evolution in his writings. Ben Franklin also said that he believed in a Creator who had created the world. So did George Washington and even Tom Paine. The founding fathers of our nation were practically all creationists, and our country was founded upon creationist principles built around laws which were the laws of that Creator. Our early schools — not only religious schools, but also public schools — taught creation when they first came into existence. But it wasn't long before Unitarians such as Horace Mann and others got control of the public school system. And it wasn't too long after that until John Dewey came along and established evolutionary humanism as the religion of our public school system and, with others of like mind, established the American Humanist Association with its humanist tenets. Since that time our nation and its schools, its courts, its media, just about our whole society, have been taken over by the evolutionary worldview. But the creationist worldview was our foundation.

The same thing is true with science. True science does not support evolution; almost all of the founding fathers of science were creationists. Many people think that science came out of the Renaissance, but it did not. Greek philosophy, which was an evolutionary philosophy, was restored in the Renaissance. True science came out of the Reformation when people began to have access to the Bible and to be able to read and propagate the Word of God. Then came along men such as Johannes Kepler, Isaac Newton, Robert Boyle (the father of chemistry), Pascal, Pasteur, Brewster, and most of the other great founding fathers of science. Almost without exception, these men were Bible-believing theists who at least professed to believe in creation and in Christianity. They might have been somewhat unorthodox in various ways, but they all believed in God as the Creator. They believed in the Bible, they believed in Christ, and many said — men such as Newton, Kepler, and Clark Maxwell — that they were simply thinking God's thoughts after Him as they were doing their science. But now science has been taken over by the evolutionary worldview by and large. Our scientific establishment is currently circulating the idea that science is a proven fact and everything has to be taught in the light of evolutionism. The fact is, however, that true science, true Americanism, and true Christianity are all based on the foundation of special creation.

Jesus Christ as Creator

Sometimes we hear people say, "Don't get involved in preaching creation. Just preach the gospel. It's important to get people saved, not to make creationists out of them." In a sense we would agree with that. Our purpose is to see people come to the Lord Jesus Christ. But we have to realize that Jesus Christ was Creator before He became the Saviour. And the reason we need a Saviour is because we rebelled against our Creator who is Jesus Christ. "For by Him were all things created, that are in heaven, and that are in earth, visible and invisible, whether they be thrones or dominions, or principalities or powers: all things were created by Him," it says in Colossians 1:16. "In the beginning was the Word, and the Word was with God, and the Word was God. The same was in the beginning with God. All things were made by him; and without him was not anything made that was made" (John 1:1-3). He is our Creator, and we don't really preach Christ without preaching Him as He is. We don't want to preach another Jesus who is not the true Jesus, as we see mentioned in 2 Corinthians. We want to preach Christ as He is, and He is the Creator and the Saviour and the coming King and Lord. That's the full scope of the doctrine of Christology, which is founded upon Christ as Creator.

In reference to Christ's saving in the gospel, the last time and the climactic time the word "gospel" is used in the Bible is in Revelation 14:6-7, where John says, "I saw another angel fly in the midst of heaven, having the everlasting gospel to preach unto them that dwell on the earth . . . Saying, with a loud voice, Fear God, and give glory to him; for the hour of his judgment is come, and worship him that made heaven, and earth, and the sea, and the fountains of waters." That's the final time (of the 101 times) where the word "gospel" is used in the Bible.

Remember that Paul, in Galatians 1:8, said, in effect, that even though "an angel from heaven preach any other gospel unto you than that which we have preached unto you, let him be accursed." Therefore, we can be sure that this angel of Revelation 14 will be preaching the same gospel that Paul preached and the essence of the angel's gospel is a command to worship Him who had made heaven and earth and the sea and the fountains of waters. In other words, worshipping a Jesus who supposedly comes into our experience merely through some personal feeling, or something like that, isn't the way it is. We have to recognize that Jesus Christ is the Creator of the heavens and the earth, and all things therein. In Adam, we have all rebelled against Him and He has pronounced an age-long curse on the creation because of man's sin. Death has come in because of that; therefore, we need a Saviour, and the great Creator is the only one who can be the Saviour.

There are two other creationist religions besides Christianity — Islam and Judaism, for example — that are creationist because they accept the Book of Genesis as their foundational account of creation. But they miss the boat when they refuse to acknowledge that the Creator must be the Saviour, and that He must die and rise again in order to implement His purpose in creation. Biblical Trinitarian Christianity is thus the only real creationist religion. It's basic and essential, then, that we believe in creation.

We could go on and show that all the other basic doctrines of Christianity are founded upon the doctrine of creation. A man once wrote me and said, "You shouldn't be talking about creation being the foundation, because don't you know that Christ is the head of the Church?" Yes, Christ is the head of the Church. Christ the Creator is the head of the Church. And furthermore, He is the head of the whole creation, not just the head of the Church. He is the author, the finisher, the head, the Alpha and Omega of everything. We need to preach Him as He really is.

On the other hand, the evolutionist worldview tries to explain everything in terms of an eternal cosmos which never was created, never had a creator. The cosmos, itself, therefore is the ultimate reality. That's basically what evolution is: it seeks to explain everything in terms of the cosmos and its processes and systems and properties, even though these may be personified in terms of different gods and goddesses. Basically, it identifies ultimate reality with this physical universe. That evolutionary worldview has come to dominate not only our modern world, but it has dominated the world since time began.

As far as the present order of things is concerned, let me just read a statement from Sir Julian Huxley, who might be called the world's top evolutionist of the twentieth century until he died a few years ago. He was the first director general of UNESCO, the main founder of neo-Darwinism, and, along with John Dewey, was one of the chief founders of the American Humanist Association. Having written many, many books, Huxley was a profoundly influential man. In one of his books, he said: "The concept of evolution was soon extended into other than biological fields. Inorganic subjects, such as the life history of stars and the formation of the chemical elements on the one hand, and on the other hand, subjects like linguistics, social anthropology and comparative law and religion are studied now from an evolutionary angle till the day we're able to see evolution as a universal, all-pervading process." In another place, he says: "The whole of reality is evolution, a single process of self-transformation."[2] So every subject, not just biology and the natural sciences, but the social sciences, the fine arts, and other subjects today are taught within the framework of an evolutionary premise in our colleges, universities, public schools, and unfortunately, even in many Christian schools. Evolution is a worldview which impacts every field, no matter what your field of study may be.

I mentioned the American Humanist Association. Humanism is what's really being taught in our public schools today. Most of the secular universities would not acknowledge that humanism is a religion, though some of them do. But basically this evolutionary humanism is a religious point of view. The tenets of the American Humanist Association, which were promulgated primarily by John Dewey, Julian Huxley, and others of like mind back when they formed the organization in 1933, really provide what we find being taught in our schools and also in the news media today. Whether it's explicit or not, basically these tenets of humanism have become the official doctrine of our intellectual world. The original tenets of humanism set forth in 1933 were combined with another manifesto that was given in 1973 and published more recently by the American Humanist Association in the magazine the *Humanist*. In a preface to that, Editor Paul Kurtz said that: "Humanism is a philosophical religious and moral point of view as old as human civilization itself. . . . It has its roots in classical China, Greece, and Rome; it is expressed in the Renaissance and the Enlightenment, in the scientific revolution, and in the twentieth century."[3]

Humanism: A Denial of God

And what is this humanism? First, religious humanists regard the universe as self-existing and not created. So the first tenet of humanism holds that there was no creation; the universe is the ultimate reality. It is self-existing. The second tenet of humanism states that man is a part of nature and he has emerged as a result of a continuous process.[4] There is no Creator, there is no creation; everything is explained in terms of evolution. The other humanist tenets involve a world government, complete freedom of sex, and all of the other things that we see causing so much havoc in society today. The late Isaac Asimov, who was president of the American Humanist Association and one of the most prolific science writers of our time, was a bitter opponent of creationism. He refused to debate us publicly, but he wrote against creationism vigorously in his publications. Asimov, who is said to have produced more than 500 books covering every field of science, probably knew science as well as anybody. Here's what he said, in case you have any questions about what humanism really is: "I am an atheist." Out and out, he was an atheist. Humanism is basically an esoteric form of atheism. He went on to say, "Emotionally, I'm an atheist. I don't have the evidence to prove that God doesn't exist. But I so strongly suspect He doesn't that I don't want to waste my time."[5] Now if anybody would have any scientific evidence against God, it seems like he would. But he admitted that he didn't, and if he didn't, then nobody does.

So people are not evolutionists because of science; scientific evidence does not support evolution. If anybody maintains that it does, just tell them, "Well, show me the evidence." Science is supposed to be what you can see, but nobody's ever seen evolution take place. As long as people have been looking at changes in biological organisms and other things, nobody has ever seen a new species evolve. Nobody's ever seen a new star evolve. Nobody's ever seen evolution from simple to complex take place anywhere in the whole universe in all human history, and nobody knows how evolution works.

Charles Darwin became famous 135 years ago by solving that problem, the humanists thought, with his *Origin of Species by Natural Selection.* But as Dr. Colin Patterson of England, a great evolutionist, has said, nobody has ever seen a new species come into existence by natural selection or any other way. Nobody knows how it works; nobody's ever seen it happen.[6] If you go to the fossil record, there are no transitional forms there.[7] Evolution is even contrary to the laws of thermodynamics, the basic laws of science. There is no scientific evidence for evolution whatsoever. People don't believe in evolution because of science. In spite of science they believe in evolution because emotionally they don't want to believe in God. They don't want to have this Man to rule over them, as Christ said in one of His parables in the New Testament.

Something which is based on the rejection of the very possibility of a God who creates and controls His cosmos is bound to create havoc in the universe. Charles Darwin ended his famous book, *The Origin of Species by Natural Selection,* like this: "Thus, from the war of nature from famine and death the most exalted object which we are capable of conceiving, namely the production of the higher animals, [by which he means man] directly follows." In other words, man came about by suffering and death. So suffering and death are basically good because they produce evolution, a struggle for existence, survival of the fittest, natural selection — that's the ultimate good in the world. Of course, that's exactly opposite to what the Bible says. Darwin says "By death came man." The Bible says "By Man came death" (1 Cor. 15:21). There was no death, suffering, or struggle for existence in the world until sin came into it via man. God had to pronounce the judgment of the curse on the creation, which had been given to man as his dominion. Because of this introduction of spiritual disorder, God pronounced a judgment of physical disorder on his dominion, and there has been suffering and death in the world ever since then.

Stephen J. Gould, the most articulate modern evolutionist, has insisted in many of his writings that "evolution is a proved fact of science," in one way or another. This is a litany that evolutionists repeat over and over, as if they expect everybody to believe it because they say it so often. But then when people ask Gould for evidence that proves evolution, he says that the best evidence for evolution is imperfection in the universe. For example, he cites the panda's thumb, which he says he could have designed better if he or an engineer had designed it. Imperfections in the animal world, he says, prove that God didn't have anything to do with creation because God would make everything perfect.[8] However, the fact that God *made* everything perfect doesn't mean it's going to *stay* perfect! We do have the reality of sin in the world, and mutations, disease, decay, disintegration, and death because of sin. But rather than proving evolution, these imperfections really prove that we are alienated from God because of sin.

Evolution's Destructive Impact

Of course, this idea of struggle for existence and survival of the fittest has had a terrible impact on the world as a whole. For example, laissez-faire capitalism became the watchword of England, America, Germany, and the western world back in the nineteenth century. Even many of our conservative political people today still kind of stick with evolution because they think that the survival of the fittest applies in society and in economics today. But we need to realize that all of this was based on evolution, too. For example, the great steel baron, Andrew Carnegie, whom we honor because of his charitable endowments, said, "The law of competition is here, we cannot evade it. No substitutes for it have been found and while the law may sometimes be hard for the individual, it's best for the race because it insures the survival of the fittest in every department."[9]

So let's exploit labor, let's do whatever we have to do. What's good for the corporation is good for the world. Here's what he also said in his autobiography: "I remember that the light came in as a flood and all was clear. Not only had I gotten rid of theology and the supernatural, but I had found the truth of evolution."[10] That was the basis for his actions. John D. Rockefeller said much the same thing, and so did Raymond Hill, the railroad baron. In fact, all the great "robber barons" of the nineteenth century, as many called them, were basically following Herbert Spencer, particularly with his survival of the fittest concept. Spencer didn't believe in child labor laws or anything like that because he believed the fittest should survive, and that's what would contribute to the advancement of society.

Of course, in Germany, the concept of "survival of the fittest" led finally to World War I and later to the great racist implications of Hitlerism and World War II. Let me pass along just one statement from an authority, Daniel Gasmann, who said of Adolf Hitler in his book, *The Scientific Origins of National Socialism*, "(Hitler) stressed and singled out the idea of biological evolution as the most forceful weapon against traditional religion and he repeatedly condemned Christianity for its opposition to the teachings of evolution." Hitler was a strong evolutionist. For Hitler, evolution was "the hallmark of modern science and culture"[11] He was also an occultist who was committed to astrology. But basically, he was a Darwinian and an evolutionist and he felt that in the struggle for existence among nations, the greater nations would survive. So it was justified in his mind to wage that kind of war. Even in England, Alexander Keith, who was opposed, of course, to Hitler, acknowledged that Hitler was a good evolutionist and that he was following the principles of evolution in his plan for the war.

Communism also is based on evolution. And racism is completely based on evolution, not on fundamentalist Bible teachings in the South at all. All the great evolutionary scientists of the nineteenth century were evolutionary racists, including Charles Darwin. You can see that in his book, *The Descent of Man*, in which he makes it clear that there's an ascending order of evolution among the races. Thomas Huxley said the same thing. All these men of science, evolutionary scientists of the nineteenth century, were evolutionists.

The same thing applied particularly among the anthropologists, even up to the mid-twentieth century. Men such as Henry Fairfield Osborn, the director of the American Museum of Natural History, believed that the Negro race, for example, was not even of the same species as *homo sapiens*. These men of science said some terrible things about the supposed "lower races." Of course, with World War II and Hitler's genocide and racist activities, racism lost favor among scientists and most evolutionary scientists today, of course, are not racists.

Then we come to the social practices we're so alarmed about today: the drug culture, abortion, pornography, immorality, and others. If space permitted, we could document that all of these are based on evolutionary philosophy. That doesn't mean that, for example, every young woman who has an abortion or doctor who performs one is an evolutionist. People commit sin for all kinds of reasons. But whenever anybody tries to rationalize these things on a scientific basis, they fall back on evolutionism as their rationale. For example, take a look at this quote reported in the *LA Times* from Elie A. Schneour, who says he is the director of the Biosystems Research Institute in La Hoya, California, and chairman of the Southern California Skeptics, which is an affiliate of the American Association for the Advancement of Science. Quoting Schneour: "Ontogeny recapitulates phylogeny. This is a fundamental tenet of modern biology that derives from evolutionary theory and is thus anathema to creationism as well as to those opposed to freedom of choice. Ontogeny is the name for the process of development of a fertilized egg into a fully formed and mature living organism. Phylogeny, on the other hand, is the history of the evolution of a species, in this case, the human being. During development, the fertilized egg progresses over 38 weeks through what is, in fact, a rapid passage through evolutionary history. From a single, primordial cell, the conceptus progresses through being something of a protozoan, a fish, a reptile, a bird, a primate, and ultimately a human being. There is a difference of opinion among scientists about the time during pregnancy when a human being can be said to emerge. But there is general agreement that this doesn't happen until after the end of the first trimester."[12] You see, the justification some people use for killing a fetus in the womb is that it isn't really human. If people who propose freedom of choice and abortion really believed that this was a human being, then they would have to acknowledge that killing it is murder. But they don't believe it's a human being. Their rationale for saying that is to say that it's going through its evolutionary history. But the fact is that this recapitulation theory, this so-called biogenetic law, was disproved at least 50 years ago, and no knowledgeable biologist or embryologist would still believe in the recapitulation theory because it's completely unscientific. The embryo never does go through a fish stage. It never has gills or a tail or anything like that. In fact, the DNA which programs the whole development indicates that the embryo is a human being right from the very time of conception. There's no rationale whatever in terms of real science to support the idea that it ever is anything but a human being.

Once again, that's why I say that all these harmful practices basically find their rationale in evolutionism. I think we could show that to be true of our modern drug culture. You see, Aldous Huxley, Timothy Leary, and others who were the founding fathers of the modern emphasis on drugs some 50 years or so ago said that we've done away with God. Evolution has proved that there is no God, yet we still need that religious experience. So Aldous Huxley said that we can compress an eternity of joy into just a few hours with the materials that the pharmacologists provide for us.[13] So the drug culture is based on the rejection of God because of evolution.

New Age Seduction

What about the New Age movement? You've heard of that, I'm sure. The New Age movement, in all of its multiplicity and complexity, encompasses witchcraft and astrology and spiritism on the one hand and the anthropic principal and biosystems and biogenetic fields and so forth on the other hand. Various churches, cultures, and religions now are involved in some aspect or other of the New Age movement. Every single one of them have two features in common: 1) their goal is a world culture, a world religion, a world government; and 2) they base their worldview, without exception, on evolution. The patron saint of the New Age movement is the Jesuit priest, Teilhard de Chardin.

Marilyn Ferguson, who wrote *The Aquarian Conspiracy*, the so-called bible of the New Age movement, polled the leaders of the New Age movement, asking them who had been the most influential in leading them to their philosophical position. By far, most of them answered de Chardin. What was his view? Here's what he says in his book, *The Phenomenon of Man*: "Is evolution a theory, a system, or a hypothesis? It is much more. It is a general condition to which all theories, all systems, all hypotheses must bow, and which they must satisfy henceforward if they are to be thinkable and true. Evolution is a light illuminating all facts, a curve that all lines of thought must follow."[14]

Evolution, to him, is God. Only it's not a personal god, it's a god of nature. It's a pantheistic god. And, of course, the New Age orbit generally is a restoration of ancient pantheism. It sounds a little bit more spiritual to say "pantheism," which means "all God," or "God is everywhere," than it does to say "atheism," which means "no God." But, you see, if God really is everywhere in general, then he's nowhere in particular, and there's really, therefore, no difference in terms of the practicality of God's existence and meaning.

People would ask, "But wasn't this de Chardin a priest? Didn't he believe in Christ?" Yes, he did. But listen to what he said about Jesus Christ. "It is Christ, in very truth, who saves — but should we not immediately add that at the same time it is Christ who is saved by evolution. Evolution is not only the creator but also the saviour, and now that we understand past evolution, we can control future evolution."[15] And as the Humanist Manifesto of 1973 says, "No deity will save us; we will save ourselves." A recent assistant secretary general of the United Nations, Robert Muller, who is currently one of the leaders of the New Age movement, has said: "The most fundamental thing we can do today is to believe in evolution." He says, in effect, that our whole system must be based on evolution if we are to realize the goal of world government.[16]

Thus, the impact of evolution today is worldwide; it's devastatingly harmful everywhere. I don't think we could find a single good product that has come out of evolutionary philosophy. It hasn't produced any scientific discoveries. None of the 100 outstanding contributions of science and technology each year ever have anything to do with evolution. Evolutionary theory doesn't produce anything good in science, yet it's considered to be the basic premise in science in many states. Amazing!

Well, where did this evolutionary paradigm come from? Most people think that it came from Charles Darwin's *Origin of the Species*. Yes, Darwin was a catalyst who was tremendously influential, both in his day and in our day. He changed the world in a very real way. Yet he didn't invent evolutionism. As a matter of fact, he didn't even discover the idea of natural selection. In my own reading, I have found that at least 11 men had published books or articles advocating natural selection before Charles Darwin did. In fact, Darwin's grandfather, Erasmus Darwin, did so before Charles was even born. Benjamin Franklin advocated natural selection. And so did various others. But the most influential person in this area was a man by the name of Alfred Russell Wallace. And I must tell you a little about him because it does seem more than coincidental that the time that modern Darwinian evolution came to the fore back in the mid-nineteenth century was also the time when ancient witchcraft, spiritism, and occultism were being revived in the western world. These practices had always been prominent in the world of pantheism, in other nations and in the ethnic religions of the world, but in the western "scientific" world, spiritism and occultism began to be revived about the same time as Darwinian evolution began to be promoted.

I mentioned earlier that a long war has been raging between the devil and God. Apparently because of the God-sent revivals and the Christian worldview that dominated Victorian England and our own nation at its birth, Satan determined to accelerate his war with our Almighty God. Three men are generally believed to have made the greatest influence on modern thought: 1) Sigmund Freud, in the field of psychology and human relationships; 2) Karl Marx, in the field of economics and political science; and 3) Charles Darwin, in the field of natural science. These men all seem to have had some strange occult influences behind what they were doing. Scholar Paul Vitz, in his book *Sigmund Freud and His Christian Unconscious*, gives an abundance of evidence that Sigmund Freud (whom most people believe to have been an atheist, but who really was a pantheist) based his system on the recapitulation theory mentioned earlier. Vitz explains that Freud thinks people have psychological hang-ups because they haven't evolved far enough; therefore, they can be treated by psychoanalysis. Vitz says that Freud was preoccupied with things like the devil, Antichrist, demonism, and so forth, and then he presents some rather significant evidence that Freud might even have made a Faustian pact with the devil.[18]

The same thing has been shown to be true of Karl Marx. In his book, *Marx and Satan*, Richard Wurmbrand suggests that Karl Marx was not just an atheist as we tend to think; he was a pantheist. Marx was a professing Christian through high school. In fact, he wrote a rather interesting essay that appeared in *Christianity Today* many years ago on "Abiding in Christ." It sounded like a spiritual testimony from someone who was a Christian talking about how important it was to abide in Christ. But shortly after that essay was published, he, like Freud, seems to have made some kind of a Faustian pact with the devil. He even says in one of his poems, "My goal is to destroy him who reigns above." So Wurmbrand makes a strong case for the belief that Marx was actually a Satanist.[18]

As far as Darwin was concerned, he wasn't a Satanist; he was an atheist, although there may be some rather equivocal evidence that he may have had a partial change in his thinking near the end of his life. At any rate, up until very near the time of his death, Darwin was an atheist who sometimes wavered between being an atheist and an agnostic. He firmly rejected Christianity, the Bible, and creation. He had been working on his theory of natural selection for some 20 years there in England, ever since he returned from his well-known round-the-world voyage on the *Beagle*. He was influenced then by Charles Lyell, in particular, to try to develop this theory. But Darwin was afraid to publish the theory; he didn't think he had strong enough evidence, so he kept looking for more evidence, with the intention of publishing at some point a massive tome on natural selection. But all of a sudden, he condensed his material down quickly and got his book out, because he was afraid he was going to be pre-empted by Alfred Russell Wallace.

Wallace was an interesting person. He was an anarchist and a spiritualist. In fact, he was one of the leaders in the spiritist revival in England at the time. He wrote books on the scientific evidence for spiritism and he believed that one could communicate with the spirits, just like modern New Age people believe they can do this through what they call channeling. Furthermore, Wallace had spent many, many years in the jungles, working with animist tribes who also believed in this communication with the spirits. Wallace thought very highly of these people; he was not like Darwin, who thought these were primitive people just a little above the apes. He thought very highly of them because he worked with them and he knew they were true human beings. In fact, he wouldn't go along with Darwin's idea that man's soul had evolved. He believed that some sort of a panthe-istic, cosmic consciousness had generated man's soul. Wallace was a self-educated man who had never had much opportunity to associate with the scientists of England — he had only met Darwin and Lyell very briefly, but he knew that they were interested in the origin of the species as he was. He wrote this testimony in a book called *The*

Wonderful Century: "I was then (February 1858) living at Ternate in the Moluccas and was suffering from a rather severe attack of intermittent fever, which prostrated me every day during the cold and succeeding hot fits. During one of these fits, while again considering the problem of the origin of the species, something led me to think of Malthus' *Essay on Population*."[19] Malthus talked about the survival of the fittest and human populations and he had been quite influential in Darwin's thinking, too. "It suddenly flashed upon me," Wallace said in another book, "that this self-acting process would necessarily improve the race, because in every generation the inferior would inevitably be killed off and the superior would remain — that is, the fittest would survive. Then at once, I seemed to see the whole effect of this."[20] Returning to the first quote, he said that "the whole method of species modification became clear to me, and in the two hours of my fit, I had thought out the main points of the theory. That same evening, I sketched out the draft of a paper; and in the two succeeding evenings, I wrote it out and sent it by the next post to Mr. Darwin."[21]

When he received the draft, Darwin was just astounded. He told his friend, Lyell, that Wallace had anticipated everything that he had poured 20 years of research into in preparation for his big book. So Darwin had to come out with a book right away in order to establish priority. He never did publish his big book, and probably never would have published a book at all had it not been for Wallace sending him this information stating that he had discovered the theory not during 20 years of research among the leading scientists in England, but during two hours of a fit in Malaysia jungles. Loren Eiseley, a great historian of science at the University of Pennsylvania, said in an article about Wallace: "A man pursuing birds of paradise in a remote jungle did not yet know that he had forced the world's most reluctant author to disgorge his hoarded volume or that the whole of Western thought was about to be swung into a new channel because a man in a fever had felt a moment of strange radiance."[22] Make what you want out of that, but I cannot help thinking that there is more there than meets the eye. This may well have been the beginning of the modern battle in Satan's long war.

Evolutionists Before Darwin

But then, of course, neither Wallace nor Darwin originated evolution. As we go back to consider men before Darwin (his grandfather, Erasmus, and other leading evolutionists), we find all sorts of strange influences being brought to bear on them. Le Marcq, the German rationalist philosophers, and various French philosophers had all been influenced very much by a system called the "great chain of being." This is not taught much anymore, but the ancient idea of a great chain of being was that there is a continual link between all orders of reality in the cosmos. This is not a biblical concept, but it does have sort of a religious flavor. It starts out with the divine essence, whatever that may be. Some of the medieval religionists put that into the form of the theological God, but that wasn't the way it started out. It was just the divine essence of nature. That descended in a continuous link through the spirit world — angels, demons, whatever other spirits there might have been — down to the highest races of human beings, then down to the lower races, then to the great apes, then to the other animals, then to the insects, then to the non-living things, and finally down to the elementary particles. The idea was that there was a chain of being in which there were no missing links; it was up to the philosophers to find them.

Of course, all the nineteenth century evolutionists had to do was to invert this chain of being and then put a time scale on it to come up with the evolutionary system. That chain of being was really the basis for the initial studies of comparative anatomy and comparative embryology. The idea was that everything had to go through this chain from simple to complex or complex to simple. So the development of the embryo progresses from very simple to complex. Their comparative anatomy had to be based on the idea of studying the simplest organisms on up to the most complex. Finally, when it came time to develop a geological time scale (there is no place in the world where the standard geological column is ever found except in a text book) it was developed by assuming that the simple forms of life had to be early in the chain of being and the more complex forms of life later. That was imposed on the study of paleontology, and was finally built up into our standard time scale. So the recapitulation theory, the geological column, the idea of races being inferior and superior, and the idea of human beings not having fully developed and therefore still having psychological hang-ups — all these things were based on this idea of the great chain of being.

And where did that come from? Not from the Bible, obviously. It came from the ancient philosophers, probably Plato. But it became most prominently expressed among the neo-platonists after the time of Christ.

Ancient Greek philosophers without exception were non-creationists. They did not believe there was a personal creator-god who had created the universe. They all believed that the universe was the ultimate reality and that it gradually expressed itself in terms of the chain of being. Paul dealt with some of them, you will remember, in Acts 17. The Epicureans were atheists; the Stoics were pantheists. There were also many varieties of gnostics, but they were all pantheists and some of them tried to mix Christianity with their gnostic pantheism, when Christianity became prominent. In fact, one can trace such beliefs on back through Plato and Socrates and then to the pre-Socratic philosophers back around 600 B.C. in Greece. Among these were such men as Thales, Anaximander, and Anaximenes, as well as later thinkers such as Leucippus, Democritus, and others who developed the materialistic philosophy, the evolutionary system which was prominent then in Greece and later in Rome. Evolution isn't a modern idea at all!

But where did the Greeks learn it? According to Milton Munitz, professor of the philosophy of science at New York University and one of the greatest authorities on the history of science, "Anaximander reinterprets, while at the same time retaining basically the same pattern of cosmogonical development that is to be found in the Babylonian myth."[23] This has already been partly transformed in the Greek version of Hesiod's theogony. Homer and Hesiod held a polytheistic system of gods and goddesses, but really, polytheism is just a form of pantheism. Pantheism is the all-god, expressed locally as the god of fire, the god of thunder, the goddess of the river, and so forth. The forces of nature personified represent the all-god, the whole cosmic consciousness, or Mother Earth, Gaia, or Mother Nature. They got this, Munitz says, from Babylon.

But now we have to think in biblical terms, because the Bible says that Babylon the Great is the mother of harlots and abominations of the earth. Once we get back into that era, long before 1000 B.C., which was Hesiod's time, we've stepped into the realm of mythology. We don't have very much recorded history from that far back except what we find in the Bible and a few archaeological monuments.

Many people don't want to go to the Bible for their information, but that's where the best information is, of course. The Book of Genesis, in chapters 10 and 11, tells us that Babel was the center of the first great world kingdom and that Nimrod was its founder. The beginning of his kingdom was Babel, but Nimrod also founded Nineveh and other great cities. He was the first great world emperor.

He was just the great grandson of Noah, so it wasn't very long after the flood. It had probably been 100 or more years or so, enough time to build a fairly good population. But instead of going out and filling the earth like God had told him, Nimrod wanted to make a name for himself and his people. So they decided to build a great city and a great tower — not to "reach into heaven," but rather, dedicated to the heavens, to the host of heaven, to the angels, to the stars. (The stars and the angels are apparently used almost interchangeably in the Bible. Stars are called angels and angels are called stars frequently because everything in the realm of the heavens where the stars are is also where the angels are.) So this tower dedicated to the host of heaven probably had at the apex a great shrine with the zodiac symbols and so forth. God came down and confused their languages and scattered the people across the face of the earth. They couldn't talk to each other anymore, so each little family group had to become isolated and segregated. Each group first had to develop a hunting and gathering culture and inbreed for a while. The recessive genetic characteristics in the little population could now be expressed, so that each small family group developed its own tribal characteristics (not "racial" characteristics, however; "race" is not a biblical concept).

People think of that event as having been the origin of the races. No. There's no such thing as a race in the Bible. That's an evolutionary idea. God made of one blood all nations of men to dwell on the face of the earth. There's only one race, that's the human race, biblically speaking. We're all descended from Noah and from Adam. At any rate, the family groups developed into nations, some of which became extinct like the Neanderthals, and others developed into great kingdoms like Egypt and Sumeria. That's where the different characteristics of each nation came from, too.

But where did Nimrod get this concept? If we go into the Babylonian origins myth, the Egyptian origins myth, or the cosmogonies of many other nations around the world, we find a rather amazing similarity. Although they couldn't talk to each other anymore, they all carried the same religion with them everywhere. They had different names for their gods and goddesses. They had different languages. But basically the same system of evolutionary religion was carried everywhere and the source of all this was, apparently, the Babylonian cosmogony, which I suggest Nimrod had learned, probably from Satan himself. That cosmogony was the Enuma Elish. This famous Babylonian "genesis" said that originally there was nothing but a watery chaos everywhere and out of this watery chaos two gods just appeared, and from them everything else came. One finds the same thing in Egypt, the same thing in Hesiod, in many of the African tribes and American Indian tribes, this idea of a primal chaos. But none of them tell where the creation, the universe, came from. All start with the universe in a chaotic condition, usually a watery chaos.

Now why that? Well, that immediately makes us think of Genesis, of course, where, "In the beginning, God created the heaven and the earth. And the earth was without form, and void; and darkness was upon the face of the deep. And the Spirit of God moved upon the face of the waters. And God said let there be light" (Gen. 1:1-3). Initially, there was water everywhere. It wasn't chaos; it was all perfect for that particular stage of God's created work. God created the angels as well as human beings. Angels were created first, probably on the first day of creation, and Satan was the highest of all the angels, as we read in Ezekiel 28:15-17. He was perfect in his ways and full of wisdom and perfect in brightness and beauty until iniquity was found in him and God told him that He was going to cast him to the earth. Everything was "very good" at the end of the six days of creation (Gen. 1:31), so it was after that that God cast Satan to the earth. Then Satan tempted Adam and Eve, apparently with the same temptation with which he had tempted himself. He had said, in effect: "I want to exalt my throne above the stars of God, I want to be God. I want to ascend above the Most High" (Isa. 14:13-14). In other words, he thinks he is of the same order as God.

Now where would he get such an absurd idea? When he first came into existence, all he knew was that God told him that he had been created for a great purpose, but all he could see was this watery chaos around him. That's where he was when he was created, and all the other angels had been created the same way. So he thought, perhaps, that he was of the same order as God. And it was just a matter of time before he could successfully rebel and become God himself or like God, at least. So he, at that time, initiated his long war against God. Now if Satan (or Lucifer) is going to believe that God isn't really the Creator, then he has to have some other explanation. That's why I have to say that Satan was the first evolutionist. Evolutionists ridicule me for saying that, but again, I can think of no better explanation for how this worldwide, age-long lie came to be, than through the father of liars, who is the devil. Satan is the deceiver of the whole world, but he has deceived himself most of all! And he still thinks, apparently — because he's still fighting against God — that somehow he's going to win. So he keeps on fighting. He has to use the same lie with which he deceived himself, that the universe is the ultimate reality, that it's evolving itself into higher and higher systems, and that now men think they can even control its future evolution. Men can develop human beings and other things the way they want them in the future if Satan can just get control of everything.

We who believe in the Bible know that's not the way it's going to end. But that's the way it is right now. And it looks like he's getting control pretty rapidly. But God's Word does say that we "wrestle not against flesh and blood, but against principalities, against powers, against the rulers of the darkness of this world, against spiritual wickedness in high places" (Eph. 6:12). Therefore, we cannot fight this war with bullets or even with ballots. "Though we walk in the flesh, we do not war after the flesh; (For the weapons of our warfare are not carnal, but mighty through God, to the pulling down of strongholds), casting down imaginations, and every high thing that exalteth itself against the knowledge of God, and bringing into captivity every thought to the obedience of Christ" (2 Cor. 10: 3-5). That's our commission, to fight that war. It's a spiritual battle. We have to have the girdle of truth and the breastplate of righteousness and the helmet of salvation and our feet shod with the gospel of peace. We must have the shield of faith, and the sword of the spirit, which is the word of God, and all this weaponry must be accompanied by a great aura of prayer (Eph. 6:14-18), but then the weapons are powerful and mighty through God to the pulling down of strongholds.

Finally, we can read in the Book of Revelation how it's all going to come out. There it says that all the kings in the world one day are going to give their allegiance to the great humanist man who gives his allegiance to Satan. They're all going to worship the beast, as this man of sin is called, they are going to worship the dragon who gave his power to the beast. The whole world will become Satanists then, and all the kings of the earth are going to give their power to him. They're all going to "make war with the Lamb, but the Lamb will overcome them: for he is Lord of lords and King of kings; and they that are with him are called and chosen and faithful" (Rev. 17:14).

It's going to be a lot better to be with Him than with them in that day!

2

Days of Our Lives, as the World Turns

by William T. James

Powerful forces are at work beneath the relative tranquillity that masks the true state of our nation and the world. Ours is a society that boils with turbulence beneath a veneer of sophistication. It is a society mirrored by television soap operas and hedonistic movies which have, in turn, mesmerized much of the American public. Life has indeed imitated art, while year after year morals have degenerated and the very concept of morality has been turned upside-down and inside out. We are a people given a thrill-a-minute fix to satisfy our insatiable cravings for instant gratification. We are a people all the while descending deeper and deeper into depravity.

Gleam and glitter and unparalleled technological gadgetry have procured for the American public hours upon hours of time for pleasure-seeking, and it is more than abundantly obvious, for mischief-making. While it is true that the moguls of science provide great benefits for human health, wealth, and achievement within the sphere of human potential, to see the direction in which all of this is truly sweeping us, one has only to consider any given local evening news broadcast. We are not as a society *every day and in every way, getting better and better* like the New Age evolutionary thinkers would have us believe. Feeding our voracious appetites for more exciting thrills and greater pleasures has served only to generate phenomenal growth in criminal activity. Those who perceive themselves to be the *have-*

nots ravenously desire those material things which the American propagandists flash before their lusting eyes. Because Big Brother government has, in effect, destroyed work ethic through give-away welfare programs but can in no way give this dependent class the shimmering lifestyle it lusts after, the rip in the fabric of society worsens daily as the ungovernable elements engage in the only occupation they believe can secure for them the thrills and pleasures they seek. As a result, gang members as young as seven years of age live and often die in their unattainable pursuits.

Last-Days Scenarios

Can there be any doubt that conditions and activities which God's Word predicts will be prevalent while the end of the age approaches are now being played out before our very eyes? The similarities between the biblical descriptions and the reports we witness on our nightly newscasts are stunningly evident. Man's atrocities against his fellow man are pandemic. Stories of debased human behavior are so numerous that those items which would have formerly been front page headlines now are relegated to pages farther back because even more heinous stories overshadow them.

Jesus himself prophesied about the generation that would inhabit Planet Earth at the time of His Second Advent: "But as the days of Noah were, so shall also the coming of the Son of man be" (Matt: 24:37). Jesus Christ, who is God himself, gave with that reference — based upon Scripture recorded in the past and Scripture He knew was yet to be recorded — an unmistakable characterization of the generation alive at the time of His Second Advent. Jesus said, while discoursing with His disciples on the Mount of Olives, that that generation, like the pre-flood society of Noah's day, will be "eating and drinking, marrying and giving in marriage" (Matt. 24:38). Like in Noah's day, society will be conducting business as usual, having become desensitized to the perversities going on around them and even more desensitized to any consideration of the things of God and the fact that divine judgment was already on the way.

Daniel the prophet said: "And the end of it shall be with a flood" (Dan. 9: 26), meaning a flood of incorrigibly wicked behavior and a flood of God's wrath and judgment poured upon that unrepentant, blasphemous people of the apocalypse. Jesus said that the generation alive at the end of the age will be totally immersed in doing what is right in their own eyes, as were the antediluvians of Noah's day. The people of that earlier, doomed generation were marrying, partying, and busily engaged in commerce while their perversions, debaucheries, violence, and blasphemies were simply well-accepted, even welcomed ingredients within the cultural and societal mixture of the time. Jesus said that they were carrying on as usual "until the day that Noah entered into the ark, And knew not until the flood came, and took them all away, so shall also the coming of the son of man be" (Matt. 24:28-39).

Jesus was saying that people living at the time of His return will have become so rebellious as to have rejected the notion of a Creator-God. Their thinking will have become so reprobate, their consciences so seared, that many will no doubt even forget that such a God was ever said to have existed! Christ's coming will be so swift and startling that it will be analogous to the horror of that long ago, worldwide deluge that destroyed all but those who were found righteous in God's eyes. Just prior to that flood Enoch disappeared, having been translated into the presence of the God with whom he walked righteously (Gen. 5:24). Noah and his family were supernaturally preserved upon the raging sea that engulfed the entire earth (Gen. 8).

Jesus also drew the parallel between the time of the destruction of the cities of Sodom and Gomorrah and the days that will immediately precede the consummation of the age. "Also as it was in the days of Lot; they did eat, they drank, they bought, they sold, they planted, they built; But the same day that Lot went out of Sodom, it rained fire and brimstone from heaven, and destroyed them all. Even thus shall it be in the day when the Son of man is revealed" (Luke 17:28-29).

Peter the apostle wrote about Lot's days of interaction with the people of Sodom: "For that righteous man [Lot] dwelling among them, in seeing and hearing, vexed his righteous soul from day to day with their unlawful deeds" (2 Pet. 2:8). Peter then went on to imply the type of behavior which greatly disturbed Lot — the sort of behavior that inevitably brings on Almighty God's indignation and judgment.

> But chiefly them that walk after the flesh in the lust of uncleanness, and despise government. Presumptuous are they; self-willed, they are not afraid to speak evil of dignities. . . . But these, as natural brute beasts, made to be taken and destroyed, speak evil of the things that they understand not, and shall utterly perish in their own corruption, And shall receive the reward of unrighteousness, as they that count it pleasure to revel in the daytime. Spots they are and blemishes, reveling with their own deceiving

while they feast with you. Having eyes full of adultery and that cannot cease from sin; beguiling unstable souls; an heart they have exercised with covetous practices; cursed children, Who have forsaken the right way, and are gone astray. . . . These are wells without water, clouds that are carried with the tempest, to whom the mist of darkness is reserved forever. For when they speak great swelling words of vanity, they allure through the lusts of the flesh, through much wantonness, those that are just escaping from them who live in error. While they promise them liberty, they themselves are the servants of corruption; for of whom a man is overcome, of the same is he brought in bondage" (2 Pet. 2:8-19).

God's Word speaks powerfully of His opinion about the vile activities that were commonplace during Lot's day warning all generations that His righteous judgment must and will fall on those who engage in ungodly enterprises. "Even as Sodom and Gomorrah, and the cities about them in like manner, giving themselves over to fornication, and going after strange flesh, are set forth for an example, suffering the vengeance of eternal fire. In like manner also these filthy dreamers defile the flesh, despise dominion, and speak evil of dignities. . .these speak evil of those things which they know not; but what they know naturally, as brute beasts, in those things they corrupt themselves. Woe unto them! For they have gone in the way of Cain. . . . Raging waves of the sea, foaming out their own shame; wandering stars, to whom is reserved the blackness of darkness forever" (Jude 7-13).

The Holy Scripture then rolls before the mind's eye of our imagination the awesome truth contained within the words, "it is a fearful thing to fall in the hands of the living God" (Heb. 10:31). As the Book of Jude continues: "And Enoch also, the seventh from Adam, prophesied of these, saying, Behold, the Lord cometh with ten thousands of his saints, To execute judgment upon all, and to convict all that are ungodly among them of all their ungodly deeds which they have ungodly committed, and of all their hard speeches which ungodly sinners have spoken against him. These are murmurers, complainers, walking after their own lusts; and their mouth speaketh great swelling words, having men's persons in admiration because of advantage. But, beloved, remember ye the words which were spoken before by the apostles of our Lord Jesus Christ; How they told you there should be mockers in the last time, who should walk after their own ungodly lusts. These are they who separate themselves, sensual, having not the Spirit" (Jude 14-19).

Apologies to Sodom and Gomorrah

Ruth Bell Graham is attributed to have made the statement, in the context of surveying the growing wickedness she observed in her nation, that if God did not judge the United States, He would surely have to apologize to the cities of Sodom and Gomorrah. Many years have passed since Mrs. Graham allegedly made that (in my opinion, very correct) assessment. Does the fact that the United States has not been obliterated by fire and brimstone, all of its population consumed in a thermonuclear holocaust or by supernatural fire from the heavens, mean that we, as a nation of people, are improving in our conduct to the extent the Almighty will not judge like He did those now-extinct, ancient cities? Or does it mean that Mrs. Graham was wrong?

One thing is sure. God is never wrong and thus need never apologize for His actions. He is the same yesterday, today, and forever (Heb. 13:8.) His immutability is perfectly consistent as recorded throughout His Word to His creation called mankind. Thankfully, and praise His holy name, so is His quality of mercy, His slowness to anger and wrath — else the little, though tremendously prideful creature called man, would long ago have ceased to exist.

Mrs. Graham dramatically made the frightening (but true) point that sin ultimately brings death to individuals and to nations who transgress God's laws and refuse to repent. God's judgment might, in some cases, seem slow in falling as man counts finite time, but God's judgment is certain! This brings us to the question: Where does America — and for that matter, the world — stand in relationship to sin, repentance, and God's judgment like that which consumed the wicked cities of Sodom and Gomorrah? Has the TV soap opera-like hedonism in which our society has gleefully bathed made the days of our lives, as the world turns, cleaner for all my children — and yours? Or have the filth and scum simply been loosened from the bottom of the world's bathtub and brought to the surface through glamour and aggrandizement to the point they stick to and permeate our lives while they, at the same time, provide a putrefying cesspool environment for sin-germs to incubate and for soul-destroying infection to spread?

Examination, Diagnosis of and Prognosis for a Sick World

Most adults in America today would, if honesty prevailed,

acknowledge that our culture has changed markedly during the course of the last decade. Many of those adults — especially those of us 40 years of age and older — would have to admit, if that same degree of honesty held firm, societal conditions in America and the world have suffered phenomenal degeneration despite spectacular technological breakthroughs and sometimes heroic efforts to better mankind's lot by individuals and institutions. That the human race is in rapid decline does not surprise Christians who are spiritually attuned to the prophetic warnings of their Heavenly Father's written Word.

"Evil men and seducers shall become worse and worse, deceiving and being deceived" (2 Tim. 3:13). "This know also, that in the last days perilous times shall come, for men shall be lovers of their own selves, covetous, boasters, proud, blasphemers, disobedient to parents, unthankful, unholy, Without natural affection, trucebreakers, false accusers, incontinent, fierce, despisers of those that are good, Traitors, heady, high-minded, lovers of pleasures more than lovers of God, Having a form of godliness, but denying the power of it. . . . For of this sort are they who creep into houses, and lead captive silly women laden with sins, led away with various lusts, Ever learning, and never able to come to the knowledge of truth" (2 Tim. 3:1-7).

Does any of that seem familiar? Indeed, has not the entertainment industry, even down to and including the hundreds of hours of commercial advertising productions with which our senses are assaulted daily crept into our houses and "led captive, silly women" — and incidentally — "silly men"? Are not our fallen human lusts whipped into ever-heightening frenzies while we see mankind's most wicked imaginings glamorously advertised on our television screens? Is it any wonder that our national and world societies have, in biblical terms, "gone the way of Cain"?

Paul the Apostle, in that 2 Timothy account, warned that the last days' generation will pay the price for its self-sufficient, self-centered godlessness. "For their folly shall be manifest to all men" (2 Tim. 3:9).

Manifestations of Sin-Diseased Society

Sen. Robert Dole (R-Kansas), speaking in Hollywood against what he called the moral pollution that comes out of the entertainment industry, said: "Our music, movies, television, and advertising regularly push the limits of decency, bombarding our children with destructive messages of casual violence and even more casual sex. The line of decency has been crossed. It is crossed every time sexual violence is given a catchy tune, when teen suicide is set to an appealing beat, when Hollywood's dream factories turn out nightmares of depravity."

John Gizzy, editor of *Human Events,* said of Dole's speech:

> This declaration of war on the kingpins of culture sounds familiar, a lot like Dan Quayle's Murphy Brown speech three years ago. The only difference is the reaction when the then-vice president fired his missile on Murphy, the media, the moguls generally mocked him, saying it was foolish for a national figure to criticize a fictional character. And besides, it was an election year and the economy was what folks wanted to hear about. Well, not so with Mr. Dole's speech. Although many in the press said he was harsh, and Hollywood is whining its mantra of "I'm being picked on," the Senate majority leader is also winning praise for what the majority of us have thought privately: That there is a relationship between the salaciousness of entertainment and an increasingly unpleasant America, a place where we've gone from "Leave it to Beaver" to "Beavis and Butthead" and from sons hunting with their fathers to sons hunting their fathers.[1]

Dr. James Dobson, a well-known psychologist and outspoken proponent for the concept of Judeo-Christian morality in America, brought to light in an agonizingly revealing way the extent to which America's love affair with sin has now reached the depths that her "folly" is beginning to become "manifest to all men." In a speech to the National Religious Broadcasters during February 1994 at Washington, DC, Dobson said regarding the children of America:

> There is something that is going on in their spirits and their hearts and their souls, and it is dramatic. We have had a 500 percent increase in violence among the young since 1960. The number of teenagers killed by gunshot wounds has increased 85 percent since 1980. . . . A child born and raised in the United States has a 15 times greater probability of being killed by gunshot than a child born and raised in Northern Ireland. We've become one of the most violent nations in the history of the world. And especially with the violence that we are perpetrating on children and they are passing on to one another, we have raised . . . at least a part

of a generation that believes that the way to deal with conflict is you kill somebody, you shoot somebody.

Tulane University just released a research project where they asked suburban high school students about this matter of teen violence. They asked them, "When is it appropriate to shoot somebody?" That's quite a question. Can you imagine, 20 years ago, asking a question like that — when does it make sense to shoot somebody? Twenty percent of those suburban, high school kids said it is appropriate to shoot somebody if they steal something — petty theft. It's appropriate to kill them! Eight percent of those kids said it is appropriate to shoot somebody who insults you. . . . It is an unbelievable development that has occurred in this culture.

The Rhode Island Rape Crisis Center asked a similar question. It asked, "When is it appropriate, when does it make sense, when is it right, for a boy to force a girl to have sex with him?" Now another word for that is "rape." So "When is it appropriate for a guy to rape a girl?" Another incredible question. Twenty-five percent of the boys in the sixth through the ninth grade said it is appropriate for a boy to force a girl to have sex with him if he has spent money on her. They asked them how much, and the average is $10-$15. If he spends 15 bucks on her, he's got a right to rape her! They believe this! This is what they've been taught, or at least what they've been hearing. And 67 percent of them said that if a boy had dated a girl for six to eight months, he's got a right to rape her. This is the world in which they live. This is the violence of the world of the young.

And the violence that's taking place there now . . . is dramatically different than it was a few years ago. Because it is frequently without passion. It is without anger. It is wanton brutality. It is without conscience. It is without compassion. It is violence for violence's sake. You have been reading about it in the papers and so have I.

In Virginia, there was a 14-year-old boy sitting in a car at a stop light and he got out of his car, someone else was driving, and walked over to the car next to him and shot the man sitting there. He shot him six times in the face with a 45-caliber pistol. They asked him why he did it; he said, "Because he was checkin' me out." The man looked at him and he killed him!

In Seattle, there were 12- and 13-year-old boys who decided to kill the next customer who came out of a 7-11 convenience store. So they sat there and waited randomly for who came out. It happened to be a 72-year-old man and they beat him to death with a baseball bat just to watch him die. This [sort of thing] occurred occasionally in the past, but it's an everyday happening now.

In West Palm Beach, Florida, a 13-year-old girl took a ride in a cab. There was a $6 cab fare at the end. Instead of paying it, she blew the back of the head off of the cab driver. Her own mother said, "It was frightening; she didn't shed a tear. She didn't even care. . . ."

Now, what's going on here? . . . Some of us, myself included, blame a lot of it on Hollywood, the entertainment industry . . . the Rambo-type nonsense that's going on. We've just pumped violence into the ears and the eyes of these kids . . . but that's still not the basis of the problem. When you really get down and look at it, it comes right back to the disintegration of the family and the victimization of children that takes place, especially in the inner city but throughout our society [as well]. . . ."

Dobson went on to itemize the many self-centered activities such as drugs and alcohol abuse and all other forms of selfish living that cause parents to neglect their children.

When you put all of that together, you've got an incredible number of abused and neglected children . . . the latest estimate I've seen is something on the order of 10 million abused and neglected children that are out there. And you have, not uncommonly — and social workers will tell you this — a baby who is left in the crib for two or three days with dirty diapers, and when he gets diaper rash and cries from the pain, he is slapped and hit and beaten. All of us who have been on the faculties of large hospitals have seen these kids coming in, have seen them broken and battered and bruised and wounded. There is a phenomenon that's called the "red sock syndrome." It's where parents get angry at their kids and to punish them, they get scalding hot water in the bathtub and they sit these kids down in it and it scalds and blisters their feet, and they come in looking like they have red socks on. And they put their little bottoms in it. I mean, one mother in Los Angeles cut her child's eyes out with a razor blade. It is unbelievable what is happening to children. It must break the heart of God to see what we're doing to kids, and not just a few of them — there have always been some kids that have been abused, but there are millions of them out there. . . ."

Dr. Dobson went on to say that perhaps the neglect of America's children is even worse than the abuse.

We have five and six year olds now across the country who get up in the morning with nobody to dress them or look out for them, teach them anything. They go into the kitchen and try to find for themselves something to eat, some cereal or something. They go off to school, they come home alone, they are in the house alone. *Newsweek* magazine did a cover story called "Growing Up Scared." . . . [These children] come home through these terrifying neighborhoods. *Newsweek* described it in such graphic terms: "These pitiful little forms sitting in front of the flickering television sets and the lengthening shadows of winter move up the walls and flood the corners. These kids are alone, there by themselves."

I'll tell you something else about children who are not supervised by parents. They are sitting ducks for pedophiles. A pedophile who knows his business, it's usually a man, a bedeviled who knows what he's doing can move into a setting like a video center or a place where children congregate, and in five minutes he can have that vulnerable kid under his control because he gives that child what he hasn't got anywhere else — love and attention. And then he exploits him and abuses him and destroys him.

Dobson continued by saying that tremendous sums of money have been expended by the federal government to research cause and effect within the dynamics of the tremendously increasing violence being experienced by American society today.

They now believe . . . that this generation of teenagers who have no conscience or very little conscience have been brain-damaged at birth or very shortly after — some of them, even in utero, from the stresses associated with disintegrating families. So these kids that shoot people on the streets are not like the rest of us; they don't feel. They can't feel. They can't feel for other people. They have no empathy, they have no conscience. And their brutality is a reflection of the rage they have inside, but which is not linked to the governing authority of our consciences that keep it in check.

Dr. Dobson summarized the days of our lives, as the world turns in America, by saying, in part:

Society is going to pay an incredible price for the neglect and the rejection of this generation of kids. We have become so selfish, so self-centered, so determined to have it all, that we have kids around our feet who hardly know us. . . . The generation I'm describing is like a storm cloud moving over the Pacific heading for the West Coast. It's going to be over Colorado before very long, and it's going to move on across the East Coast. That generation is going to be in charge. They're going to be the parents of tomorrow. And America is in a great deal of trouble. [One psychiatrist has] said, "We've lost one generation. We may be able to survive it. But we will not survive the loss of another." . . . Because what happens to the family affects everything else. Everything sits on that foundation. Our institutions, our government, our way of life, our faith — that's dependent on the family. You can't evangelize the next generation if the family is destroyed.[2]

To carry the analogy of our soap opera-like existence in America today a bit further, it is altogether accurate but perhaps a glaring understatement to characterize a huge and growing segment of our children as *"the young and the restless."*

World's Elevated Fever Now Accepted as Normal

The fact that we live in a world that grows sicker by the minute is undeniable except to the most ostrich-like among us. A head-in-the-sand approach to life might, for a time, provide a degree of insulation against the worsening conditions closing in on even the most isolated havens of safety. Nonetheless, the time seems to be rapidly approaching when this generation of earth's population will reach the fever pitch of that ancient generation described by Paul the apostle in his letter to the Romans. Those people, like many — perhaps the majority — of our present generation of people, apparently thought the conditions which engulfed them were merely normal for the times in which they lived. They failed to detect the rising, killing temperature of their societal fever like in the perhaps trite but appropriate proverbial story of the frog simmering, then finally boiling to death in a pot of water because the rise in temperature was so gradual he could not sense the change. Could it be that this generation of earth dwellers, like those in Noah's day, like those about whom Paul wrote, is failing to or woefully refusing to read the thermometer of our time?

Paul wrote God's thoughts to all generations — perhaps particularly to the generation of people who will be alive at the time of Christ's return — about the course of degenerate human conduct that inevitably brings the Almighty's righteous judgment:

> For the wrath of God is revealed from heaven against all ungodliness and unrighteousness of men, who hold the truth in unrighteousness, Because that which may be known of God is manifest in them; for God hath shown it unto them. For the invisible things of him from the creation of the world are clearly seen, being understood by the things that are made, even his eternal power and Godhead, so that they are without excuse; Because, when they knew God, they glorified Him not as God, neither were thankful, but became vain in their imaginations, and their foolish heart was darkened. Professing themselves to be wise, they became fools, And changed the glory of the incorruptible God into an image made like corruptible man, and birds, and four-footed beasts, and creeping things. Wherefore, God also gave them up to uncleanness through the lusts of their own hearts, to dishonor their own bodies between themselves, Who exchanged the truth of God for a lie, and worshipped and served the creature more than the Creator, who is blessed forever. Amen (Rom. 1:18-23).

God, through the apostle Paul, then sets down some very specific forms of depravity that are inescapably familiar.

For this cause God gave them up unto vile affections; for even their women did exchange the natural use for that which is against nature; And likewise also the men, leaving the natural use of the women, burned in their lust one toward another, men with men working that which is unseemly, and receiving in themselves that recompense of their error which was fitting. And even as they did not like to retain God in their knowledge, God gave them over to a reprobate mind to do those things which are not seemly, Being filled with all unrighteousness, fornication, wickedness, covetousness, maliciousness, full of envy, murder, strife, deceit, malignity; whisperers, Backbiters, haters of God, insolent, proud, boasters, inventors of evil things, disobedient to parents; Without understanding, covenant breakers, without natural affection, implacable, unmerciful; Who, knowing the judgment of God, that they who commit such things are worthy of death, not only do the same, but have pleasure in them that do them (Rom. 1:26-32).

Case Histories Then and Now

It is perhaps a misnomer to characterize this chapter with the title "Days of Our Lives as the World Turns." A more descriptive title for the darkening times might be "The Edge of Night." This generation, if our hourly newscasts are accurate indicators, is indeed raging toward a precipice beyond which lurks the black abyss of apocalypse. Certainly world society has for some time now been exhibiting all of the symptoms that were prevalent during the time of the ancients, symptoms of the sin-virus engendered incorrigibility which caused a loving God to give the patient up to its self-willed self-destruction. Notice that Paul writes in Romans 1:28 that "God gave them over to a reprobate MIND."

That generation, like the ancients of Sodom and Gomorrah who would come later, were of one absolutely unchangeable mindset. They would rather perish than change! They were all in agreement. They were all inalterably determined that each had the right to do what was right in his own eyes.

Undoubtedly, these judgment-bound societies termed doing what was right in their own eyes "freedom of choice." They pursued their own form and concept of life, liberty, and happiness totally apart from the loving God who created them. In their willful right to choose, obstinacy lay the chains of their enslavement to sin and, ultimately, God's wrath and, ultimately, destruction. It took the gushing waters of a broken earth and an angry, deluging sky to cleanse the sin-sick world of Noah's pre-flood days. It took the fire and brimstone conflagration sent by a God of righteous judgment to purify that area of the earth's surface occupied by the cities of Sodom and Gomorrah during Lot's day.

Symptoms of Degenerative Sin-Disease Then and Now

God's Holy Word speaks bluntly about the cause and effect of sin-disease that ravaged the earliest reported civilizations. Considering the Holy Spirit's words spoken through Paul's pen, it is clear that the people of those ancient civilizations flatly rejected the truth of God, although God plainly manifested himself to them. "Because, when they knew God, they glorified Him not as God, neither were thankful, but became vain in their imaginations, and their foolish heart was darkened. Professing themselves to be wise, they became fools" (Rom. 1:21-22).

Let us briefly attempt to dissect what God's Word tells us was a systemic infection within that antediluvian society, with the hope of determining similarities between the state of moral decay during their time on earth as compared to our own.

Symptom #1: Idolatry
The Antediluvian

Paul reported about the corrupted ancients that they "changed the glory of the incorruptible God into an image made like corruptible man, and birds, and four-footed beasts, and creeping things. Wherefore, God also gave them up to uncleanness through the lusts of their own hearts, to dishonor their own bodies between themselves, Who exchanged the truth of God for a lie, and worshipped and served the creature more than the Creator" (Rom. 1:23-25).

God's first statement in Paul's letter to the Romans in reference to sinful behavior that causes His anger to rise and His wrath to fall upon unrepentant mankind, whether individuals or nations, is frighteningly unequivocal. "For the wrath of God is revealed from heaven against all ungodliness and unrighteousness of men, who hold the truth in unrighteousness" (Rom. 1:18). After stating that He has clearly made himself known to humankind through the creation that surrounds them, God exposes that early generation's unthankfulness and points an omniscient finger of guilt toward their idolatrous betrayal, the particular act which seems most egregious to Him.

Those people had "changed the glory of the incorruptible God into an image made like corruptible man." In other words, this generation, although they knew that God is God, nonetheless rejected Him and His own declaration to himself, the Godhead (the Trinity, God the Father, God the Son, and the Holy Spirit). "Let us make man in our image" (Gen. 1:26.). These willful people in effect said to the Almighty, "We are not made like unto your image; rather, we will make you into whatever image we choose!" They were obviously saying further, "We, like Lucifer, choose to become gods ourselves! Even though we are creatures, we choose to worship and serve ourselves — that is, do what is right in our own eyes — rather than worship and serve You even though all creation that surrounds us are clearly witness to the fact that you are the Creator."

That generation, like Lucifer, who is that old serpent, Satan, and the devil, thereby exhibited the sinful thing which God says He hates above all others; their idolatry brought into focus their supremely arrogant *PRIDE.*

The writer of Proverbs records for us God's opinion of this most heinous sin. "These six things doth the Lord hate; yea, seven are an abomination unto him: A proud look" (Prov. 6:16-17).

Idolatry, then, springs from, then orbits the iniquitous thing called *pride.* When idolatry becomes full-blown, i.e., a state of arrogance that manifests itself through determination to usurp the very throne of the eternal God, God apparently quits dealing with that individual, with that generation, and allows their mind to become reprobate. This means the mindset is one that is darkened by the infection called sin to the point that insanity rather than rationality rules the minds of men — not only the physical minds of men, but spiritual discernment as well. When that point of incorrigibility is reached and God lets man do what is right in his own eyes, human society is very soon turned upside down.

Almighty God, using His people, Israel, to speak not only to the generation of that time but to all generations and all nations, warns of the consequences of becoming so vile as a society or as an individual that God allows reprobate mentality to have its way. "Woe unto them who call evil, good, and good, evil; who put darkness for light, and light for darkness; who put bitter for sweet, and sweet for bitter! Woe unto them who are wise in their own eyes, and prudent in their own sight! . . . Therefore, as the fire devoureth the stubble, and the flame consumeth the chaff, so their root shall be as rottenness, and their blossom shall go up as dust, because they have cast away the law of the Lord of hosts, and despised the word of the Holy One of Israel. Therefore is the anger of the Lord kindled" (Isa. 5:20-25).

God expounds further through the prophet Isaiah about such prideful nations and individuals. "Ah, sinful nation, a people laden with iniquity, a seed of evildoers, children that are corrupters; they have forsaken the Lord, they have provoked the Holy One of Israel unto anger, they are gone away backward. Why should ye be [dealt with through correction] anymore? Ye will revolt more and more; the whole head is sick, and the whole heart faint. From the sole of the foot even unto the head there is no soundness in it, but wounds, and bruises, and putrefying sores. They have not been closed, neither bound up, neither mollified with ointment" (Isa. 1:4-6).

Isaiah then continues by putting forth the terrifying fact that in God's foreknowing mind, these and all such reprobate peoples will suffer terribly. In God's thoughts, their fall is already an accomplished thing. ". . . Your country is desolate, your cities are burned with fire; your land, foreigners devour it in your presence, and it is desolate, as overthrown by foreigners" (Isa. 1:7).

When Pride Equals Death

God told Adam and Eve that if they ate of the fruit that was forbidden, they would surely die. They nonetheless succumbed to the serpent's tempting appeal to their pride — the implied promise that if they ate of the fruit, they would be "as God." So pride, the sort that causes human beings to desire to usurp Almighty God's authority, is poison to those who fall to its alluring tug just as God warned. We can say with certainty that God's warning about the fatally toxic effects of disobedience to Him was true. Every person inevitably gives up his physical existence to death. Pride, then, is not a characteristic that leads to a more desirable quality of life as those who preach self-esteem would have it, but it is a fallen human trait that has always brought and continues to bring death to all mankind.

A most tragic manifestation of humanistic pride equaling death is most clearly seen in the human historical record. Every civilization, culture, and society that has gone so deep into idolatry as to have exchanged "the truth of God for a lie" have had as a common practice in their idol worship the insane horror of child sacrifice.

History is replete with accounts of human sacrifice to pagan gods. Almost always those sacrifices involve the most vulnerable. Children, young women, and sometimes the aged were most often selected by the practitioners of those abominable acts to placate their insatiable gods. We have all read of the Incas and the Aztecs, of the ancient Hawaiians, and of many other so-called civilizations whose hearts became so sin-blackened that their foolish minds grew dark, and human sacrifice was the ultimate result. However, it is a sad truth that those heathens were not the only societies to reach that depth of depravity. God wrote through Jeremiah the prophet: "Because of all the evil of the children of Israel and of the children of Judah, which they have done to provoke me to anger, they, their kings, their princes, their priests, and their prophets, and the men of Judah, and the inhabitants of Jerusalem. And they have turned unto me the back, and not the face; though I taught them, rising up early and teaching them, yet they have not hearkened to receive instruction. But they set their abominations in the house, which is called by my name, to defile it. And they built the high places of Baal, which are in the valley of the Son of Hinnom, to cause their sons and their daughters to pass through the fire unto Molech; which I commanded them not, neither came it into my mind, that they should do this abomination, to cause Judah to sin" (Jer. 32:32-35).

The Contemporary Heathen

There is no way the people of today's world as we approach the dawn of a new millennium would do the foolish and even insane acts historically attributed to those ancient heathen! Such might be the wishful acclamation of the most optimistic among our number in today's world. Especially in America. Surely an overwhelming majority of Americans would never fall prey to idolatry that, for example, "changed the glory of the incorruptible God into an image made like corruptible man, and birds, and four-footed beasts, and creeping things." Oh no?

With the primary god of this age, *mammon* (money), have not the affluent among our ranks, individually and collectively, fashioned the idols we have chosen to worship into forms that pleasure our own imaginations? Instead of worshipping the Creator, do we of this generation not rather bend the knee to our cars, boats, and our sports teams — many of which we have named after birds, four-footed beasts, and creeping things or after signs of the zodiac? Do we not sit for hours at a time before our television sets, amused at the debased activities we see, some of which might have made even the ancient pagans blush? The debasing goings-on within our television screens draw our transfixed attention, in many cases resulting in the neglect of our children who desperately need and want nurturing. Are these not altars from which emanate the *images made like corruptible man?*

But surely ours is not a generation of earth dwellers that has reached the point God has given us over to a collective reprobate mind. We would never allow child sacrifice, which is one of the sure manifestations of a totally reprobate civilization. Really?

Since *Roe v. Wade* was upheld by the Supreme Court of the land, more than 30 million babies have been aborted. Under the auspices of the secular religion called humanism, these little ones were and continue to be judged nothing more than self-created possessions subject to disposal, should the women carrying them so choose. Abortion on demand has generated a multi-billion-dollar industry based on infanticide (some would say feticide). By far, the greater number of abortions are performed for the purpose of ridding the person and/or people involved of the child who would, they fear, interfere with their own self-centered lifestyle. The majority are abortions of convenience, contraception after the fact of, in most cases, illicit sexual activity.

If God judged Israel for turning her back on Him, rebellion that brought a mindset so darkened by sin that they offered children in sacrifice to pagan Gods, will He not judge America? No other nation has been more blessed with the light of God's Truth. Yet daily, under the full sanction of the United States government, thousands of our children are passed through the fires of abortion, sacrificed to the gods of convenience and pleasure and hedonism under the specious claim that a woman has a right to choose to do what she wishes with her own body. In this convoluted way, freedom of choice becomes the willful demand to do what is right in their own eyes. In effect, she proclaims herself to be god-like. Child sacrifice, then, is idolatry come to fruition.

Symptom # 2
Sexual Perversion

Paul the apostle, under inspiration, gave the second most pronounced manifestation of any society that has totally turned its back on the loving God who has, time and time again, called for it to turn from its course of wickedness. In spite of the liberal theological acrobatics some theologians and even secular humanists go through to try to explain away this and other accounts of sexual perversions that inevitably come to a hopelessly godless people, history attests to the truth that societal decay ends in the death throes of the basest kind of sexual depravity.

The Antediluvians

Paul writes of the decadent societal characteristic that is second only to immersion in idolatry. "God gave them up unto vile affections; for even their women did exchange the natural use for that which is against nature. And likewise also the men, leaving the natural use of the woman, burned in their lust one toward another, men with men working that which is unseemly, and receiving in themselves the recompense of their error which was fitting" (Rom. 1:26-27).

Historical accounts of Greece and Rome, and to a lesser extent of other civilizations, validate and expand upon Paul's brief but graphic description of the sexual cesspool in which these ancients ultimately became mired. There can be no rational denial made of the fact that Paul reported homosexuality to be the most glaring manifestation of that society's incorrigibility.

We should take note of God's account through Paul of the fact that these people so submerged in sexual prurience — particularly the male homosexuals — were "receiving in themselves the recompense of their error, which was fitting." It is an appropriate speculation to make that this must have been AIDS and/or hepatitis or something similar. It is interesting, too, that God said in this account that these homosexuals were receiving in their bodies judgment because of the error (the sin) of their homosexual activities. God's Word says quite bluntly that the punishment fit the crime.

The Contemporary Heathen

To review the past several decades with regard to how homosexuality has evolved from being a thing kept in our culture's closet to its acceptance now as an "alternate lifestyle" would be boringly redundant because of our familiarity with the facts. We have been fed daily doses of desensitizing hyperbole intended to convince us to accept that terrible, dehumanizing activity as not only normal, but as *"gay."* What God calls *"vile,"* modern man calls *"gay."* Perhaps nothing more need be said about how thinking in our generation has become so reprobate that evil is now called good, and good is now called evil. Not only is what God called "vile" now called "gay," but those who give a clarion call back to morality and point out the mind-darkened sin-error of such perversion are vilified as "intolerant bigots" at best or as "homophobic Nazi-types" at worst.

While AIDS and the many deadly infections spawned and perpetuated by the homosexual activity raging unabated throughout the world today are reasons for great concern, the disregard for human dignity and the sanctity of human life fostered by such permissiveness are even greater cause for alarm.

One recent case in point illustrates that a permissive society whose philosophy revolves around unbridled sexual liberty takes its people down a broad road that leads to human degradation and even death.

In an article titled, "Sex, Death, and Videotape," an account of sexual freedom taken to its ultimate extent emerged from what has seemingly become an avalanche of such reports.

In Canada, the murder trial of the year isn't O.J.'s. The two victims, innocent girls in their early teens, wept while a video camera recorded their suffering. Raped and beaten and destined for strangulation, they were held as sex slaves in a suburban Ontario bedroom. Their kidnapper forced the girls to act out his fantasies and call him master. He taunted them with their impending deaths, forcing the second girl to watch videotape of her predecessor's ordeal. And they weren't his only victims. The first was his wife's little sister, who was drugged and served up to him one holiday eve. "A great Christmas present for me," he was quoted as saying. That was the story Canadians had waited two years to hear. When the sensational trial of the alleged sex killer, a clean-cut young accountant named Paul Bernardo, finally began in Toronto last week, the prosecutor's six-hour opening statement made listeners cringe. . . . Just before Christmas in 1990, Carla [Bernardo's wife], helped him ply her sister, Tammy, 15, with liquor and sleeping pills until she passed out. Bernardo is charged with raping Tammy and forcing Carla to perform oral sex on her, recording it all on video. The unconscious Tammy later died, choking on her own vomit in what was initially ruled an accidental death."[3]

Other Symptoms of a Sin-Sick Generation

Many symptoms of systemic sin sickness boil to the surface and erupt for all to see between the time a society determines to turn its back on God and the time a people become so wicked God gives up pleading for them to repent because their hearts and minds cannot be turned again to Him. Again, the apostle Paul starkly delineates specific symptoms displayed by a society well on its way to incorrigibility and thus God's judgment. Consider carefully God's examining checklist as put forth in Paul's letter to the Romans. Recall for a moment your own experiences as you have dealt with the people in situations around you this past month while going about life's activities. Recognize any of the symptoms within Paul's description?

"Being filled with all unrighteouness, fornication, wickedness, covetousness, maliciousness; envy, murder, strife, deceit, malignity; whisperers, Backbiters, haters of God, insolent, proud, boasters, inventors of evil things, disobedient to parents; Without understanding, covenant breakers, without natural affection, implacable, unmerciful; Who, knowing the judgment of God, that they who commit such things are worthy of death, not only do the same but have pleasure in them that do them" (Rom. 1:29-32).

The Cure!

How sick is the patient? What is the prognosis for the sin sickness that courses through the life's blood of this generation? We must seek answers to these questions by first examining our own lives. Society, culture, and civilization is no better or worse collectively than its individual members. The sickness that afflicts one afflicts all. The good news is there is a cure. And the cure is **THE GOOD NEWS**! The Good News of the gospel of Jesus Christ who came to seek and to save every person from the darkness of sin. God is "not willing that any should perish, but that all should come to repentance" (2 Pet. 3:9).

Jesus Christ alone can regenerate the hearts and minds of fallen man and restore him to health and newness of life. If you haven't done so, take the cure. Accept Jesus Christ this moment as your Saviour and your Lord. Then the days of your life, as the world turns, will fill with energy and excitement while you seek to serve the One who dispels the darkness of this doomed age. Jesus is the *Guiding Light!*

3

When Millions Vanish!

by William T. James

A young mother will be walking the aisles of a Wal-Mart store, or perhaps a K-Mart or a Kroger store, her two-year-old daughter riding securely and happily in the shopping cart while they both look over all the brightly packaged goods on the shelves. A businessman will be entering an on-ramp to a freeway near Los Angeles, giving a nervous glance to his left to make sure he will have room to merge smoothly into the flow of traffic.

Half a world away, the captain of a 747, having just received permission to take off, will push the throttles fully forward and the gigantic bird will begin its roll between the runway lights that appear to come together in a sharp point in the distant darkness. A mother-to-be will reach for a ringing telephone, a broad smile on her face anticipating talking with her husband, who had promised to call once he was settled in at the airport hotel where his company is holding its quarterly sales meeting.

Then, in a mind-confounding split-second, it will happen!

A surgeon in a Boston hospital who has just started the scalpel moving along the man's chest suddenly finds the blade cutting only air. The patient is gone!

A mortician in Dallas recoils in astonishment when the suit he is smoothing to make a corpse presentable collapses. The body is no longer there! The mother pushing the cart in the store turns back toward the basket with the items she has gotten from the shelf. Her little girl is missing! Only her toddler's colorful little dress and shoes remain in the cart in a crumpled heap. The woman's scream pierces the air, joining screams of panic reverberating throughout the store.

At the same moment in time, the commuting businessman in Los Angeles sees the big semi rig directly in front of him swerve sharply right and begin tumbling down the steep embankment while the roadways ahead and on either side of him explode with violent wrecks.

Precisely at that instant, the co-pilot in the 747's right seat panics when he realizes that the huge jet, now screaming down the runway at more than 100 miles per hour, is totally out of control, its pilot having disappeared!

The young father-to-be is shouting into the telephone, wanting to know what is wrong with his wife, who he hears crying hysterically. She has fallen to the floor and is desperately groping her abdomen, nearly insane because she cannot feel the baby who is no longer in her womb.

I believe literally billions of people around the world will suffer shocks similar to those depicted above, or will awaken to find they live in a world phenomenally different than the one they knew when they went to bed the night before.

Planet Earth reels with foreboding that something unknown is poised to thrust terrifying events upon our tumultuous generation. Anxiety swells within the collective mind of humanity as the new millennium rumbles in storm-like fashion toward us across the twenty-first century horizon. While optimism abounds that the new century will produce a brighter, better world, the foreboding eerily warns that the year 2000 likely harbors within its untraveled time region and beyond, perils of apocalyptic dimension.

Although worries about the future of our world grow daily, the overwhelming majority of earth's inhabitants, if they consider these matters at all, shrug off the beginning of the third millennium since the birth of Christ as portending nothing more than a continuation of things as they have always been. "Change of any kind for the masses will be for the better" is the general philosophical mindset of the globalist thinkers elite while they wrestle with the complex factors involved in dealing with miserable Third World squalor. Still, even through the malaise caused by their often heart-wrenching, day-to-day misery, there beats within the common pulse of the billions living in abject poverty seething unrest that leads to the inescapable sense that profound rearrangement on a planetary scale is about to take place.

Doomsday Worries

Although scoffers at doomsday talk most often attribute that talk to bizarre religious thinking and more and more in our day to religious right-wing fundamentalists, such gloomy predictions by secular writers and speakers far outnumber those issued by religionists of our time. Dr. J. Vernon McGee gave us a number of quotes from secular notables in his commentary introduction to the Book of the Revelation.

> Knowledgeable men have been saying some very interesting things about this present hour. Please note that I am not quoting from any preachers but from outstanding men in other walks of life.
>
> Dr. Urey, from the University of Chicago, who worked on the atomic bomb, began an article several years ago in *Collier's* magazine by saying, "I am a frightened man, and I want to frighten you."
>
> Dr. John R. Mott returned from a trip around the world and made the statement that this was "the most dangerous era the world has ever known." And he raised the question of where we are heading. Then he made this further statement, "When I think of human tragedy, as I saw it and felt it, of the Christian ideals sacrificed as they have been, the thought comes to me that God *is preparing the way for some immense direct action.*"
>
> Chancellor Robert M. Hutchins, of the University of Chicago, gave many people a shock several years ago when he made the statement that "devoting our educational efforts to infants between six and twenty-one seems futile." And he added, "The world may not last long enough." He contended that for this reason we should begin adult education.
>
> Winston Churchill said, "Time may be short."
>
> Mr. Luce, the owner of *Life, Time*, and *Fortune* magazines, addressed a group of missionaries who were the first to return to their fields after the war. Speaking in San Francisco, he made the statement that when he was a boy, the son of a Presbyterian missionary in China, he and his father often discussed the premillennial coming of Christ, and he thought that all missionaries who believed

in that teaching were inclined to be fanatical. And then Mr. Luce said, "I wonder if there wasn't something to that position after all."

It is very interesting to note that the *Christian Century* carried an article by Wesner Fallaw which said, "A function of the Christian is to make preparation for world's end."

Dr. Charles Beard, the American historian, said, "All over the world the thinkers and searchers who scan the horizon of the future are attempting to assess the values of civilization and speculating about its destiny."

Dr. William Yogt, in *The Road to Civilization,* wrote: "The handwriting on the wall of five continents now tells us that the Day of Judgment is at hand."

Dr. Raymond B. Fosdick, president of the Rockefeller Foundation, said, "To many ears comes the sound of the tramp of doom. Time is short."

H.G. Wells declared before he died, "This world is at the end of its tether. The end of everything we call life is close at hand."

General Douglas MacArthur said, "We have had our last chance."

Former president Dwight Eisenhower said, "Without a moral regeneration throughout the world there is no hope for us as we are going to disappear one day in the dust of an atomic explosion."

Dr. Nicholas Murray Butler, ex-president of Columbia University, said, "The end cannot be far distant."[1]

Speculation about the end of the world spans the broad spectrum of both secular and religious thought. Postulation and propaganda on the subject ranges from the declaration that man is totally in control of his own destiny and therefore will always find ways to prevent doomsday, to wild-eyed fanaticism that preaches precise dates the world will end and urges followers of that preaching to engage in bizarre practices that include such things as adorning themselves in white robes and going to their rooftops to wait for the end to come. In a growing number of cases, dangerous cult leaders command their followers to go so far as to commit atrocities such as have been witnessed through the Jim Jones massacre and mass suicide in Guyana and the more recent Japanese nerve gas murder.

Thinking on both ends of this spectrum of end-time matters is dead wrong, as is easily provable by historical facts. Every peace made by man has eventually been broken by war. Conflicts grow increasingly more violent with each generation of war-making technology. Despite the incessant call for mankind to come together as one great planetary community, the divisions widen and become more numerous. Obviously, mankind cannot prevent doomsday. The fanatics who have set dates for the end of the world have time after time been proven wrong. Their antics and weird pronouncements and activities have served only to bring scoffing and derision upon themselves. Sadly, their lunacy has erected a barricade that adds to the difficulty of reaching the minds of men with the Word of God, who is the only One who knows all there is to know from beginning to end. Jesus Christ is the Living Word. To know the truth about the future, one must know Him.

One Electrifying Moment!

Based upon the only *Truth* there is, and without apology, this chapter's purpose is to proclaim with absolute confidence the fact that there is indeed coming one electrifying instant in time which will cause changes of epic proportion for all who live upon Planet Earth. That event will precipitate massive rearrangements in every facet of human existence. Those rearrangements will ultimately eventuate in what Jesus himself called the *Great Tribulation*, a time of trouble unprecedented in human history.

Jesus Christ, who is the Living Word (John 1:1, 14), inspired the apostle Paul to write, "Behold, I show you a mystery: We shall not all sleep, but we shall all be changed, In a moment, in the twinkling of an eye, at the last trump; for the trumpet shall sound, and the dead shall be raised incorruptible, and we shall be changed" (1 Cor. 15:51-52;KJV).

God, the Holy Spirit, further wrote through Paul, "For the Lord himself shall descend from heaven with a shout, with the voice of the archangel, and with the trump of God; and the dead in Christ shall rise first; Then we who are alive and remain shall be caught up together with them in the clouds, to meet the Lord in the air; and so shall we ever be with the Lord. Wherefore, comfort one another with these words" (1 Thess. 4:16-18).

That this will be an electrifying moment for the child of God is perhaps the understatement of understatements! God's Word promises that the body of each believer in Jesus Christ who is alive at the time this indescribably momentous event takes place will be converted in "the twinkling of an eye" from a body that is in the process of decay leading toward death into a body eternally indestructible and beautiful beyond imagination.

The apostle Paul writes through inspiration: "For this corruptible must put on incorruption and this mortal must put on immortality. So, when this corruptible shall have put on incorruption, and this mortal shall have put on immortality, then shall be brought to pass the saying that is written, Death is swallowed up in victory. O death, where is thy sting? O grave, where is thy victory?" (1 Cor. 15: 53-54).

That instantaneous translation from mortal to supernatural being will be exhilarating beyond anything we can imagine within the framework of our present, finite intellectual capacity. Far exceeding that exhilaration, however, will be the joy of seeing Jesus Christ face to face and at last understanding through transformed and perfected senses the width and height and depth of God's holiness and love. Christians will at last know Christ as He truly is. Each believer will be like Him in that moment and will be eternally in His majestic presence. "But we know that, when he shall appear, we shall be like him; for we shall see him as he is" (1 John 3:2).

The reason for Christ returning for true believers in Him will be achieved in less than one stunning second! All who have died in Christ since He began forming His Church at Pentecost will be made ready for heavenly citizenship on the spot, as Jesus himself promised His Bride, the Church. This includes all people who have accepted Him as Saviour and Lord since the day of Pentecost (Acts 2):

> "Let not your heart be troubled; ye believe in God, believe also in me. In my father's house are many mansions; if it were not so, I would have told you. I go to prepare a place for you. And if I go and prepare a place for you, I will come again, and receive you unto myself, that where I am, there ye may be also. And where I go ye know, and the way ye know" (John 14:1-3).

God Speaks to Us Through Contemporary Voices

Jesus Christ's sudden catching up of all living believers from the planet's surface, to meet himself and all believers who have died since the day of Pentecost, to begin the journey to the heavenly city where He has been preparing *mansions* for them, will leave earth's inhabitants gasping in fear and wonderment. That secret taking away of Christ's Bride, the Church, although termed a *mystery* by the apostle Paul (1 Cor. 15:51-58) when he penned the words under the inspiration of the Holy Spirit, needs no longer be a mysterious prophetic doctrine. Truth about this miracle of God, which will be perhaps the most spectacular of all miracles surrounding the greatest of His works — His amazing saving grace through the shed blood of His only begotten Son on the cross at Calvary — has been unveiled for clear understanding by the Christians of our day.

The prophet Daniel foretold that as the time for the end of God's plan for the present earth system nears, "knowledge shall be increased" (Dan. 12:4). That knowledge, many biblical scholars believe, while including the vast body of general knowledge, refers most particularly to revealed biblical truths. When Daniel was told by the angel of God, "Seal the book, even to the time of the end" (Dan. 12:4), it is obvious that God planned to make at least some portion of His mysteries understandable to the generation alive at the end of this present earth system. The discipline eschatology — the study of end-time matters — is a recent development in the mining of the deep truths of God's prophetic Word.

Has the book Daniel was told would be sealed up until the end now been opened for examination? If so, do the new truths unveiled through eschatological methods as men and women of God are infused with understanding by the Holy Spirit make clear the mystery that Paul wrote about in 1 Corinthians 15:51-52 when he said, "We shall not all sleep, but we shall all be changed in a moment, in the twinkling of an eye"? Does any new understanding give credence to any of the several rapture theories?

Liberal theologians, almost without exception, proclaim prophecies clearly yet unfulfilled to be spiritual concepts that have already come to pass or spiritual concepts yet to come to pass. They see no physical reality in God's prophetic Word; rather, they consider the prophesied events merely interesting ideas to be used in the exercise of mental gymnastics upon the floor of theological debate. Tragically, many otherwise fundamentalist, conservative Christian scholars fall into the same trap of rationalizing and/or spiritualizing away future prophetic events such as the 1 Corinthians 15:51-58 description by the apostle Paul of a stunning event yet to come which he, under inspiration, interpreted to be literal.

Again, without apology, this chapter is meant to examine the coming microsecond of time in which millions of people will vanish. The Rapture of all living true believers and the resurrection of the bodies of all believers who have died since the Church Age began is a prophecy as Holy Spirit-given as was the prophecy in the Old Testament that promised Jesus Christ's first advent. This book's intention is to explore the many aspects and effects of that coming moment from the spiritually based perspective that the rapture will take place before the time known as Jacob's trouble (Jer. 30:7). That era will be the last seven years of the present world system, which will culminate with Christ's return to Planet Earth to put an end to man's madness. In other words, *Raging into Apocalypse* comes from the pre-Tribulation view.

In Good Company

The pre-Tribulation view of the rapture of the Church, indeed, the belief that there will be a rapture or a partial rapture at any intervening moment in history, has increasingly come under attack by theologians who are Christians as well as those who are not. Scoffing at the notion of the translation of and snatching away of Christ's own from the planet has intensified in recent times. While many true believers are firmly convinced that Christians who are alive at the end of the Church Age will go into the Great Tribulation called *Jacob's trouble* by Jeremiah the prophet, we who are also true Christians who believe that Christ himself will keep us from the very hour of temptation (Rev. 3:10) by calling us to himself in the air above the earth (1 Cor. 15:51-58) are accused of having "Star Trek" mentality. The pre-Tribulation Rapture view in particular is disparaged as "pie in the sky" and "beam me up, Scotty" fantasy.

Strangely, a significant segment of world observers apparently anticipates some sort of cosmic disruption in which millions of earth's inhabitants will be abducted in some fashion by superior beings from other worlds. Hope, according to the scoffers, puts us in the same company as science fiction buffs and New Age dreamers of our day. Many of them, like us, believe that at some point in the near future the earth will suffer a sudden disappearance of millions of its inhabitants.

"You are known by the company you keep" is an admonition many of us received from our parents early on in our lives. Those Christian theologians and others who criticize the pre-Tribulation view or even the Rapture in general most likely agree with that admonition. It would appear at surface level that such criticism is justified. And certainly it would be justified if, as they loudly proclaim, the view of Christ's "secret coming" for those who believe in

Him is a false doctrine only recently concocted by those who preach it. So the question is: Are we in bad company with these sci-fi addicts and New Agers; or: Are we in good company — with those early believers through whom Christ began building His Body, the Church?

Beginnings of Christ's Church

Dr. J. Vernon McGee, referring to the Book of Daniel, stated in his radio program, "A great many use verse 1 to try to prove the Church is going through the Great Tribulation period. Well, if we've been following Daniel and listening to him, we understand he is talking about his people in the last days and he's not talking about the Church. The Church has already been raptured. The Church is not here. This is the resurrection of the Old Testament saints, which does not take place at the time of the rapture of the Church"

And in his commentary on Daniel, McGee continues: "Scripture clearly states that at the rapture those 'which sleep in Jesus will God bring with Him' (1 Thess. 4:14). Only, 'the dead in Christ shall rise first' (1 Thess. 4:16). We are in Christ by the baptism of the Holy Spirit which began on the day of Pentecost and will end at the Rapture. This particular body of believers is called the Church. We are told in 1 Corinthians 12:12-13, 'For as the body is one, and hath many members, and all the members of that one body, being many, are one body: so also is Christ. For by one Spirit are we all baptized into one body, whether we be Jews or Gentiles, whether we be bond or free; and have been all made to drink into one Spirit.' "[2]

Much of the disagreement involving the subject of the Rapture revolves around misunderstandings about what God's Word has to say regarding God's dealings with the nation Israel on the one hand and His program for Christ's church, or Bride, or body, on the other. The distinctions between these two separate programs are not easily or clearly discerned without a careful and prayerful study of the 70 weeks of Daniel (Dan. 9). Here, God outlines His program for "thy people" — meaning Daniel's people, Israel — and tells Daniel that there is a disruption of unspecified time between the sixty-ninth and seventieth weeks. Serious study with a heart toward understanding what this disruption is all about leads to the unraveling of the mystery called the Church in the New Testament (1 Cor. 15:51). The sixty-ninth week given in the Daniel account is history. The seventieth week — the seven-year Tribulation period spoken of by Jeremiah the prophet (Jer. 30:7) and by Jesus (Matt. 24) — is yet future. This age of disruption for God's nation Israel — this period in which you and

I are privileged to live — is the Church Age.

So are we who believe in a pre-Tribulation Rapture and a premillennial view (that is, that Christ will return literally to earth before earth enjoys a prophesied thousand years of peace and harmony called the Millennium) in good company or bad? Again, Dr. McGee provides some clear commentary in answer to the divisive question.

> I am going to give you the viewpoints of many men in the past to demonstrate that they were looking for Christ to return. They were not looking for the Great Tribulation, they were not even looking for the Millennium, but they were looking for *Him* to come. This expectation is the very heart of the premillennial viewpoint as we hold it today.
>
> Barnabas, who was a co-worker with the apostle Paul, has been quoted as saying, "The true Sabbath is the one thousand years . . . when Christ comes back to reign."
>
> Clement (A.D. 96), bishop of Rome, said, "Let us every hour expect the kingdom of God . . . we know not the day."
>
> Polycarp (A.D. 108), bishop of Smyrna and finally burned at the stake there, said, "He will raise us from the dead . . . we shall . . . reign with Him."
>
> Ignatius, bishop of Antioch, who the historian Eusebius says was the apostle Peter's successor, commented, "Consider the times and expect Him."
>
> Papias (A.D. 116), bishop of Hierapolis, who — according to Irenaeus — saw and heard the apostle John, said, "There will be one thousand years . . . when the reign of Christ personally will be established on earth."
>
> Justin Martyr (A.D. 150) said, "I and all others who are orthodox Christians, on all points, know there will be a thousand years in Jerusalem . . . as Isaiah and Ezekiel declared."
>
> Irenaeus (A.D. 175), bishop of Lyons, commenting on Jesus' promise to drink again of the fruit of the vine in His Father's kingdom, argues: "That this . . . can only be fulfilled upon our Lord's personal return to earth."
>
> Tertullian (A.D. 200) said, "We do indeed confess that a kingdom is promised on earth."
>
> Martin Luther said, "Let us not think that the coming of Christ is far off."

John Calvin, in his third book of Institutes, wrote: "Scripture uniformly enjoins us to look with expectation for the advent of Christ."

Canon A.R. Fausset said this: "The early Christian fathers, Clement, Ignatius, Justin Martyr, and Irenaeus, looked for the Lord's speedy return as the necessary precursor of the millennial kingdom. Not until the professing Church lost her first love, and became the harlot resting on the world power, did she cease to be the Bride going forth to meet the Bridegroom, and seek to reign already on earth without waiting for His Advent."

Dr. Elliott wrote: "All primitive expositors, except Origen and the few who rejected Revelation, were premillennial."

Gussler's work on church history says of this blessed hope that "it was so distinctly and prominently mentioned that we do not hesitate in regarding it as the general belief of that age."

Chillingworth declared: "It was the doctrine believed and taught by the most eminent fathers of the age next to the apostles and by none of that age condemned."

Dr. Adolf von Harnack wrote: "The earlier fathers — Irenaeus, Hippolytus, Tertullian, etc. — believed it because it was part of the tradition of the Early Church. It is the same all through the third and fourth centuries with those Latin theologians who escaped the influence of Greek speculation."

My friend, I have quoted these many men of the past as proof of the fact that from the days of the apostles and through the church of the first centuries the interpretation of the Scriptures was premillennial. When someone makes the statement that premillennialism is something that originated one hundred years ago with an old witch in England, he doesn't know what he is talking about. It is interesting to note that premillennialism was the belief of these very outstanding men of the early church.[3]

Since these great forefathers of the Christian church eagerly longed for — even expected — Jesus Christ's return during their lifetime, it should be obvious to any believer with a heart toward inviting Holy Spirit discernment that they held unwaveringly to the belief that the Lord could return at any moment. If they had believed that Great Tribulation had to first occur before Christ returned, they would have certainly and ceaselessly warned all believers within their sphere of influence to be watching for the catastrophic occurrences and for the Antichrist, both of which Scripture tells us will have to come onto the scene before Jesus physically returns to earth to judge the nations and set up His millennial kingdom. That great cataclysm has not yet occurred. That last and most vicious tyrant of all, the Antichrist, has not yet come to power and subjected all the world as prophesied in Revelation 13. Man's final war called Armageddon is yet future. Yet these early saints of the Church Age anticipated that Jesus could have returned at any moment during the time they lived. They were most assuredly believers in the pre-Tribulation Rapture!

We who hold to the belief in the imminent coming of Christ for His saints above Planet Earth to rapture them into His presence are not looking for "pie in the sky." We do, however, look for that great escape from God's coming wrath and judgment, as eloquently voiced by Dave Breese, one of the pre-eminent biblical prophecy scholars of our own day:

> The Scripture says to Christians, "Because you have kept the word of my patience, I will keep you from that hour of trial, temptation, tribulation, that will come upon the whole world to try them that dwell on the earth."
>
> Therefore, we see in Scripture that the Bible says that Christ will come for His saints before the beginning of the Tribulation and take all believing Christians up to be with Him in heaven. Spoken of in 1 Thessalonians 4:16, "The Lord himself shall descend from heaven with a shout, the voice of the archangel, the trump of God; the dead in Christ shall rise first. We who are alive and remain shall be caught up together with Him in the clouds, to meet the Lord in the air; and so shall we ever be with the Lord."
>
> Paul expands on this a little bit in 1 Corinthians 15, saying to the Corinthians, "Behold, I show you a mystery," something you could not figure out just by Aristotilian syllogism. "We shall not all sleep, but we shall all be changed, In a moment, in the twinkling of an eye, at the last trump; the trumpet shall sound, the dead shall be raised incorruptible, and we shall be changed."
>
> So we can assure every believer . . . that there will

come a moment when they will be caught up in their physical body into the presence of Jesus Christ so as to ever be with the Lord."[4]

Rapture At Any Moment!

Dr. Dwight Pentecost, in his masterful work, *Things to Come*, addresses the fact that God's prophetic Word points absolutely to the any-moment coming of Jesus Christ to fulfill His promise of John 14. This truth is termed the doctrine of imminence.

> The church was told to live in the light of the imminent coming of the Lord to translate them in his presence. . . . Such passages as 1 Thessalonians 5:6; Titus 2:13; Revelation 3:3 all warn the believer to be watching for the Lord himself, not for signs that would precede His coming. It is true that the events of the seventieth week will cast an adumbration before the rapture, but the object of the believer's attention is always directed to Christ, never to these portents.

> This doctrine of imminence, or "at any moment coming," is not a new doctrine with Darby, as is sometimes charged, although he did clarify, systematize, and popularize it. Such a belief in imminency marked the premillennialism of the early church fathers as well as the writers of the New Testament.

> Although the eschatology of the Early Church may not be altogether clear on all points, for that subject was not the subject of serious consideration, yet the evidence is clear that they believed in the imminent return of Christ. This same view of imminence is clearly seen in the writings of the Reformers, even though they have had different views on eschatological questions.

> The doctrine of imminence forbids the participation of the Church in any part of the seventieth week. The multitude of signs given to Israel to stir them to expectancy would then also be for the Church, and the Church could not be looking for Christ until these signs had been fulfilled. The fact that no signs are given to the Church, but she, rather, is commanded to watch for Christ, precludes her participation in the seventieth week.[5]

The apostle Paul tells in 2 Thessalonians 2:7-8 that there will come a startling change in the moral order for the end-time generation of mankind: "Only he who now hindereth will continue to hinder until he be taken out of the way. And then shall that wicked one be revealed."

Author and lecturer Hal Lindsey gives an excellent overview of the truth about the office of the Holy Spirit in this Church Age and what the Holy Spirit's removal in performing His restraining office will mean.

> First Corinthians 12:13 says: "For by one spirit we have been baptized into one body, whether bond or free, Jew or Greek, we have been made to drink into one spirit, for the body is not one member." So how do we get into one body? By the baptizing work of the Holy Spirit. There could have been no Church before the Holy Spirit came and started His ministry of taking each believer at the moment of salvation and baptizing into living union with Christ himself, joining us in a living, organic union with Christ, so that we are in Christ from that moment on.
>
> He takes up permanent residence in every believer. He puts every believer in union with Christ. He makes it possible for us to be sealed with His Spirit, which is God's guarantee that we will be redeemed in a resurrection body and brought into His presence. It's what is called the filling of the Spirit. . . . So these are the days of the Holy Spirit. This is the age of the Holy Spirit.
>
> What does 2 Corinthians say is going to happen before the Antichrist is revealed? The restrainer is going to be removed. You see, the Holy Spirit resident within the Church is the restrainer. So when you remove the restrainer, you also have to remove the containers in which He dwells, i.e., you and me. So, you see, it was a miracle the way the Church began; it's going to be another miracle the way it departs. And that is when the Holy Spirit resident in the Church is taken out, and we with Him.

Lindsey further brings into focus the change that will take place for mankind in that twinkling of an eye.

> God does not mix His program for the Church with

His program for Israel . . . in the Book of Revelation in the first three chapters, the Church is mentioned by name 19 times. From chapter 4 through half of chapter 19, the Church is not mentioned once by name. That is no oversight; the Holy Spirit knows better. The Holy Spirit does not mention them (the Church) because chapters 4 through 19 talk about the judgment of the earth and the spotlight is once again on Israel.

I believe the next intervention of God into human history will be that time when Jesus says, "Come up here!" And only believers will understand what the noise meant. The world will hear some noise, but they won't understand it. Then suddenly, all over the world, people will disappear. . . . I believe God is going to do it just like that in order to shake them up and let them know that something dramatic has happened. If God is going to remove His ambassadors, you can expect there will be some repercussions that will shake people up and I really believe that when every living believer is snatched out, there's going to be planes crashing, cars crashing; there's going to be all kinds of weird things happening because God wants to shake up the world and let them know that something supernatural has intervened.[6]

Dr. Charles Stanley, in dealing with the imminency of Christ's return, recently said:

Jesus said "I don't know when I'm coming back . . . not even the angels in heaven know; only my Father knows." Matthew 24: 27 and Matthew 24: 36-41 . . . remind us of His warnings. He's coming without a warning; He's coming instantly without a warning. The skies are going to break open. The shout, the sound of a trumpet. And I believe that only believers are going to hear and only believers are going to know what is taking place.

Stanley then punctuates the message about Christ's imminent return with words starkly relevant to the time in which we live.

I wonder how many of us really do watch, wait, look forward to, think that at any moment Jesus Christ could come. There's not a single thing that has to be done before

Jesus comes. There are some things that have to be done before He comes a second time back to earth to judge this earth to set up His millennial reign — there are some things that are going to take place. That's why, when He talks about the signs in Matthew 24, He is talking about His second coming to earth. There are no signs about the rapture, except this. If there are evidences, scriptural signs of His coming the second time, what should that say to you and me today? . . . If there are evidences of Christ's second coming, if things are happening in the world about us that are very evidently signs mentioned in the Scripture, what should that say to us about the rapture? Close! How close? I don't have any earthly idea and you know what? Nowhere in the Bible does it say, "You'd better be checking your clock, checking your calendar, checking the time." What does it say? Just be ready. I don't have to worry about when it's going to happen. All I have to do is be ready.[7]

Although there are many signs given to warn the nation Israel that Jacob's trouble or the Great Tribulation is upon them — signs that point directly to Jesus Christ the Messiah's return to Planet Earth in power and great glory — no such signals are given Christ's bride, the Church. Dr. David Jeremiah says regarding this fact:

There is not one single statement to warn the Christian of future tribulation or to help them get ready for it. Not one single statement. There are all kinds of statements about the kinds of problems we have now. The Bible says, "They that live godly in Christ Jesus will suffer persecution." But can you believe that the God who would warn us against false teachers and false prophets and would warn us against the serious things that will come upon this world in the future, if He knew that His church was going to face judgment in the tribulation period, is it possible that God, who gave us this Book to prepare us for things to come, would leave out any encouragement or challenge or information to help us to know how to deal with the tribulation we were going to experience?

I just want to tell you again there is not one single statement in any of the epistles directed to the Church as to how they are to endure or experience the Tribulation.

There is only one reason for that: We aren't going to be here.

Some people ask me, "What difference does it make whether you believe in the pre, the mid, the post, the pan, or whatever; do you believe that Jesus Christ is coming back? Do you believe He could come [right now]? Are you sure? [If you do], then I want to tell you that you are . . . pre-tribulational. If you say you believe [Jesus can come back right now] . . . the only way you can say that, even if you don't understand what's involved in it, is if you are pre-tribulational.

You see, if He doesn't come back for the rapture until seven years, He can't come back tonight. Can He? If He doesn't come back for the rapture until three and a half years of the Tribulation period, He can't come back for at least three and a half years. The only doctrine in the Bible which is historically proven from the beginning all the way through is the doctrine of the *imminency* of Jesus Christ. *Imminency* means He can come back at any time. And one of the reasons I believe so strongly in the pre-tribulational rapture view from the Scripture that it is the only view that is consistent with the imminent return of Jesus Christ. The Bible clearly teaches from almost every perspective that the Christian waits in hope of the return of Christ, that we are to constantly be watching for His return, that He could come [right now]. . . . If He can't come until seven years of tribulation have happened on this earth, there is no such thing as an imminent return of Christ.[8]

Dr. Renauld Showers, professor for the Institute of Biblical Studies and author of *Maranatha, Our Lord Come,* states:

The Bible makes it clear that nobody living on Planet Earth knows exactly when the Lord Jesus will come for His bride, the Church. It's an imminent event. It could happen at any moment. In fact, it could even happen today! . . . Paul tells us in 1 Thessalonians 4 when Jesus comes for His bride, the Church, He will not come all the way down to Planet Earth where His bride is living. He will stop outside the Earth in the air and wait there. And then His bride, the Church, will come out and meet Him.

After the Jewish bride would come out of her home with her bridesmaids and meet her bridegroom and his male escorts, now the enlarged wedding party would have a return torchlight procession to the groom's father's house. By analogy, after Jesus has caught up His bride the Church from the earth to meet Him in the air, we are convinced in light of this passage in John 14 that He will return with His bride from the air above the earth back to His Father's house in heaven to begin living in the living accommodations He has prepared there.[9]

What Difference Does Belief in Christ's Imminent Return Make, Anyway?

God's Word says that the time of Christ's return will be like it was in the days of Noah. Although there will be gross immorality, violence, etc., it will nonetheless be business as usual for industry, commerce, society, and all other human activity. Again, God's Word warns Christians to not be caught up in the flow of worldly pursuits to the extent their hearts and minds are diverted from their thoughts of their real home, the eternal, heavenly city where the Father dwells. It is sadly unfortunate that most Christians have their noses so down on the earthly grindstone that they never think to look up toward their hope from Heaven. It seems quite obvious from the way many Christians live today that a significant portion of Christ's body, His bride, the Church, disregards the commandment of Jesus, their bridegroom: "Watch ye, therefore; for ye know not when the master of the house cometh, at evening, or at cockcrow, or in the morning; Lest, coming suddenly, he find you sleeping. And what I say unto you I say unto all, Watch" (Mark 13:35-37).

Peter LaLonde summed up the importance of living in expectancy of Christ's imminent return.

> The Lord could come at any moment. There is nothing that has to precede [His coming]. . . . We have to be ready and living and expectant at all times. . . . Some people say why study prophecy, why study all this stuff? . . . Why get on all this rapture stuff? . . . The fact of the matter is, when the disciples came to Jesus and said, "What will be the sign of thy coming and of the end of this age?" He gave them great detail. He didn't say, "Don't worry

about it. If I come, I come." He gave them great detail. We are to be expectant at all times.

What we see now in the world today are signs of the second coming of Christ, which is seven years after the rapture. And if those signs are beginning to come to pass, how much closer the rapture must be! So that gives us a sense of urgency. [The rapture] has always been imminent since the time of Christ and we are to be excited and expectant because in a moment — if we as Christians could come to grips with this — in a moment we will be in the presence of our Lord forever. How it would transform our lives![10]

Dr. John Walvoord, past president of Dallas Theological Seminary, and one of the world's preeminent biblical prophecy scholars, whose chapter titled "Why We Watch" appears in this volume, said about the imminent rapture of the church: "I've been teaching prophecy for more than 50 years on the seminary level. It's a very precious truth and a very practical one, but it's more than just a doctrine to me. The idea of being able to see Christ — perhaps any day — face to face, is an amazing, electrifying anticipation. And that's what the Bible teaches, and I believe that's what God wants us to realize and hope for. And so as I am dealing with this subject, perhaps from a theological, biblical standpoint, it is also from the standpoint that if you really love Christ, you are going to love His appearing. And this is going to be a precious truth to you."[11] Indeed, the scriptural text is abundant within God's Holy Word that the hope of Christ's imminent return to rapture all believers to himself is not pie in the sky, in the sweet by and by fantasy, but precious truth of the coming great escape from a time of hell on earth.

From Antichrist to Second Advent

4

The Roman Empire's Greatest Caesar

by Dave Breese

One of the great calls of our time comes in the form of the insistent voice of many who say, "We must have a new world order." People are willing to respond with great enthusiasm to anyone who promises "We can bring to pass the dawn of a new age." We are close to the place where we can expect a convincing and charismatic voice to say, "Follow me, I will lead you into a bright Utopia. All of our expectations for tomorrow need now be transformed because a new and golden age is certainly coming upon us." One can certainly see that, given the mental state of our time, people are looking for a human savior and are willing to enthusiastically respond. Jack Anderson, the columnist, said, "The world is now in such a condition that everyone appears to be waiting for a rider and a white horse to pick them up and carry them off to a splendid tomorrow."

Will there be such a rider on a white horse? Can we anticipate that a world government will come to pass which supervenes its power above all of the nations of the world? Does this represent a real possibility for our time?

The answer is that it represents a possibility for our time and a certainty for a given time. That given time may well be now. Yes, the rise of Antichrist could well come to pass within our lifetimes. How do we know this? We know this because we read the Bible and attempt to become students of the Word of God. The Bible tells us, "We have also a more sure word of prophecy, unto which you do well that you take heed, as unto a light that shines in a dark place, until the day dawn, and the day star arise in your hearts" (2 Pet. 1:19). The Bible indicates that we cannot know what a day or an hour shall bring forth. Happily, however, it gives us a clear prophetic picture so that we can know the pattern of the future. Knowing this, our lives are lived with anticipation and expectation, for we know that our God presides above history.

We therefore do not believe that the world is careening along, out of control with no strong hand at the wheel. No, indeed! Just the opposite is true. One of the founding fathers said, "There is a just God who presides above the destinies of nations." This is one of the great truths on which our nation of America was founded. Other nations might well and profitably pursue the same course.

There are a number of ways in which God in His Word reveals the scenario of the future. Being aware of these, we can come to an understanding of history. One of those ways is to consider the scenario of the five kings.

During the captivity of Israel, the Holy Land and the city of Jerusalem was controlled by Babylon and its headstrong king. That king was Nebuchadnezzar and he had a very troublesome dream one night. His magicians could not explain this dream and so they sought after the person they believed might handle the problem. That person was Daniel, one of the greatest prophets in the Old Testament. Daniel appeared before the king and gave him a most telling explanation of the dream which had befallen him. Daniel said:

> Thou, O king, sawest, and behold a great image. This great image, whose brightness was excellent, stood before thee, and the form of it was terrible. This image's head was of fine gold, its breast and its arms of silver, its belly and its thighs of bronze, its legs of iron, its feet part of iron and part of clay. Thou sawest until a stone was cut out without hands, which smote the image upon its feet that were of iron and clay, and broke them to pieces. Then were the iron, the clay, the bronze, the silver, and the gold, broken to pieces together, and became like the chaff of the summer threshing floors; and the wind carried them away, that no place was found for them; and the stone that smote the image became a great mountain, and filled the whole earth (Dan. 2:31-35).

Daniel Explains

After showing the king what he had seen, Daniel then proceeded to give the divine interpretation. In substance, he said that the entire history of mankind would come to pass under the hegemony of four great kingdoms. These kingdoms were Babylon, Media Persia, Greece, and Rome. Four great kingdoms — their personal history will embrace the story of all history.

We notice quickly, upon reading this account, that considerably more space is devoted in the Word of God to the fourth kingdom, which is Rome, than the other three. Concerning the fourth kingdom, Daniel said:

> And the fourth kingdom shall be strong as iron, forasmuch as iron breaketh in pieces and subdueth all things; and, as iron that breaketh all these, shall it break in pieces and bruise. And whereas thou sawest the feet and toes, part of potters' clay and part of iron, the kingdom shall be divided; but there shall be in it of the strength of the iron, forasmuch as thou sawest the iron mixed with miry clay. And as the toes of the feet were part of iron and part of clay, so the kingdom shall be partly strong and partly broken. And whereas thou sawest iron mixed with miry clay, they shall mingle themselves with the seed of men; but they shall not adhere one to another, even as iron is not mixed with clay (Dan. 2:40-43).

Daniel then is saying that the mighty fourth kingdom will be characterized by great strength and permanent divisions, and that it will finally be destroyed by the stone cut out without hands that will roll down a great mountain and crush the kingdoms of this world, especially the fourth kingdom.

How instructive are these words from the prophet Daniel! He gives us the scenario of history in a few short verses and reminds us of the triumph of God over it all. Because of the emphasis given on this fourth kingdom, we need to think further about Rome and the role it will play as we move toward the consummation of history. In a later chapter from Daniel 9 we have another scenario that also tells us of the events of history and the completion of the divine scenario. Daniel reminds us that "Seventy weeks are determined upon thy people and upon thy holy city, to finish the transgression, and to make an end of sins, and to make reconciliation for iniquity, and to bring in everlasting righteousness, and to seal up the vision and prophecy, and to anoint the most Holy" (Dan. 9:24).

Here we have the shortest version in the entire Bible of the whole scenario of history. We do well to note that here history is interpreted in terms of its moral content. This great chapter of world history will be finished when God makes an end of sins and produces reconciliation for iniquity. Therefore, we do well to remember that history is interpreted by God, not as victorious military battles, economic triumphs, and the like. No, indeed, history is interpreted by God as a moral scenario that must be consummated by the Lord.

Remembering this, we then note with interest Daniel's very special words about a set of events that will occur toward the end of world history. He says,

> Know, therefore, and understand, that from the going forth of the commandment to restore and to build Jerusalem unto the Messiah, the Prince, shall be seven weeks, and threescore and two weeks; the street shall be built again, and the wall, even in troublous times. And after threescore and two weeks shall Messiah be cut off, but not for himself; and the people of the prince that shall come shall destroy the city and the sanctuary, and the end of it shall be with a flood, and unto the end of the war desolations are determined (Dan. 9:25-26).

In these telling statements, Daniel reminds us of two great princes with whom Israel will have to deal. One is "Messiah the Prince" and, as we well know, this is Jesus Christ. He is the prince who is the Messiah of Israel, a fact yet to be discovered by the nation of Israel.

But Daniel also speaks of "the prince that shall come." He tells us that this prince will emerge from the same cruel, conquering people who destroy the sanctuary (the Temple at Jerusalem) and the city of Jerusalem itself. Here we have one of the most instructive verses in Scripture as to the people from whom the Antichrist will spring.

Who destroyed the city of Jerusalem in A.D. 70? The answer is that Rome did. Who destroyed the Temple in that awful program of conquest? Once again, it was Rome.

Who then will be the people who will produce the Antichrist? This verse indicated that it will be the kingdom of Rome that fosters the escalation to power of this dreadful ruler.

The Coming Prince

Rome was once the greatest kingdom on earth. Its power was extended south to Africa, east to the Holy Land, northeast to Eastern Europe, and even north to the center of the land to England. Everything from Spain to what is now Russia was controlled by the Roman legions, Roman law, and Roman customs.

One of the characteristics of Roman rule that we remember with some degree of admiration to this day was its strong government. This succession of governments during the days of Rome's prosperity was controlled by Roman caesars whose names remain with us until this day.

There was the great Augustus, who was chiefly responsible for the extension of Roman law.

There was the cruel Caligula, who showed the world what decadence could do when it is brought to power. Then there was the reprobate Nero. Nero was the great enemy of Christians and was degenerate in every way.

We will recommend for fascinating reading a book on the succession of caesars in the days of their control of ancient Rome, *Caesar and Christ,* by Will Ariel Durant, who have given us helpful research in this regard. Their entire series, "The Story of Civilization," is most helpful.[1]

Gibbon gives us an additional set of insights in his classic, *The Rise and Fall of the Roman Empire.* It seemed impossible, but the imperial power of Rome slowly eroded until finally Rome fell to the barbarians attacking from every direction.

Durant suggests, however, that the power of Rome was never fully obliterated. Rather, he insists that it continued in the form of an imperious system that operated tyrannically in the world of religion just as Rome itself had operated tyrannically in the realm of politics — and also religion. This continuing system, built along the facsimile of the Roman hierarchy, is for Durant, the Roman Catholic Church. The reminder of this is at least the fact that Rome had a strong religious component in its idolatrous system, along with government power.

Realizing this, we note with greater interest the teaching of the prophet Daniel that Rome will rise again. Rome will then produce "the prince that shall come." He will become the Antichrist! He will rule the world!

Therefore, one who would understand the direction of history would do well to pay careful attention to the developments in the new

Rome, Europe. Yes, Europe and the prince that shall come are inextricably tied together. The scenario of Europe, therefore, can be observed profitably, and Daniel is properly the object of the question, "What are the prophetic implications of a revived Europe?" Let us think about the European situation of our time as helpful insight into this question.

At the end of the 1970s and the beginning of the 1980s, a voice was sounded from Europe that caught the world's attention. Europe announced that it was developing an entity, which it called the EEC. This was the European Economic Community. Europe had been rather benign since the days of World War II, but now appeared to be noticing itself once again. Europe saw alliances coming together in various other areas of the world, and also the emergence of nations out of the ashes of the war that were latent with the possibility of becoming superpowers. Japan then (and even now) is an illustration of this.

There are voices in Europe that were lifted, saying, "We risk the possibility of Europe becoming very weak unless we can put it all together." What we do not want is for Europe to be a set of Banana Republics like Latin America — divided, multi-directed, ambiguous, and without influence in the world. So it seemed that the European Economic Community was the beginning of an answer.

The Call to Unity

Europe soon recognized that if it could put together the nations of Europe, it would have an entity populated by more than 325 million people and with the largest gross national product in the world. The bankers of Europe salivated over the possibility of becoming the brokers of world commerce once again. Conference after conference was held to respond affirmatively to the call for a united economic community in Europe. The EEC became a serious thrust for power on the part of Europe. The world still underestimates the possibility of the European Economic Community. The leaders of Europe are clever diplomats, forceful financiers and adept at world diplomacy. Europe in the past has given us such individuals as Tallyrand, Mitternicht, and others — diplomats par excellence. Under the leadership of successors to these men — like Delores of France — Europe began seriously to knit itself together to become an economic union.

Out of this growing economic union a new consciousness emerged in Europe that the unification of these states would have to be characterized by more than only economics. Therefore, Europe quickly moved to face the necessity of military union. One of the truisms of life is that the person who is rich must protect his riches or someone will come in and steal them. This is true not only of individuals, but also of nations. A very good way to lose the physical riches that one possesses is for that person or that entity to be thought weak and defenseless.

"We must move toward military union" was then the call. France and Germany conducted unified military exercises on the field. Imagine — France and Germany, mortal enemies who had fought many wars between themselves now taking the lead in military unity. The program continues with a standardization of weapons, transportation systems, a standard gauge, and many other things. Military union continues to grow.

In the minds of the leaders of Europe, a third form of union has appeared to be most necessary. That is political union. Military and economic union would continue to be very difficult without a new and unprecedented political unity in Europe. Europe is strongly divided by class, race, religion, a sense of national destiny, and the like. Divisions as deep as these are not easily brought into a new and unprecedented unity. More and more talk, therefore, has character-ized Europe as to what form of government could be conceived that would produce this common political unity. What can be done to cause people to leave their narrow nationalism and march in step in the unity that is needed? We can be sure that European leadership is still very deep in thought about that set of questions.

There are a number of new developments which have affected the thinking of Europe in that regard. One of them is the dissolving of the Soviet Union. Indeed, NATO itself was formed for the purpose of inhibiting Soviet aggression to the west. The days of the Cold War saw the buildup of the NATO forces, and with American help they can be interpreted as having succeeded inhibiting Russian expansionism. At the moment one can say that the Soviet Union is no more, although we must hold our breath about the future.

So the question is duly posed in Europe, "What part will Russia play in NATO?" "Should Russia become a member of NATO as it is now petitioning?" Political unity continues then to have its complica-tions, which complications seem to be growing every day.

A second consideration affecting Europe is the endless series of wars in the troubled Balkans. Bosnia, Serbia, and Croatia seem still to be locked in a fatal embrace with one another with the "answers" to the problem escaping almost everyone. What will be the outcome of this complicated process? There are a series of "threes" which can help us discuss the question.

1. The war in the Balkans embraces three nations.
2. It also touches three races.
3. It is a confusion of three religions.
4. It is characterized by three potential backers.

But as relates to political unity, the Balkans War seems to suggest that political unity is a total impossibility when there are so many other pressures for division.

As a consequence, it is now commonly reported that Europe is facing "the bumpy road to reunification." Bumpy indeed, for the implications of European unity and its related problems approach almost the point of infinity.

Nevertheless, the pressure toward unity continues in Europe. All of these forms of union are now embraced in the simple expression, "European Union." So the "EEC" continues to be held before the eyes of the people of Europe as the goal toward which they are moving.

What will finally bring to pass European union which, as we have suggested, is predicted in the Word of God? There are two other components which must come to pass in Europe in order to realize the goal of unity.

The first is that Europe must choose an effective, forceful, charismatic, dynamic leader. In human affairs it is never really possible to put together any great program of unity without that unity being characterized by a person. Leadership means everything in all of the affairs of men. Clever ideas, fine goals, fond ambitions, and lofty hopes are so much empty rhetoric apart from their being embodied in the form of a strong man. Again and again in history, the frustrations of people were vanquished and hope was built within them by the words of a leader. Europe has seen the latest, great example of that in the form of Adolf Hitler and the Third Reich. Pre-Revolutionary France experienced that with the escalation of Napoleon Bonaparte as the emperor. Peter the Great did that for Russia and Alexander for the Grecian Empire of Antiquity. Yes, the key to unity is a charismatic leader. People cannot be beguiled to gather around a strong center unless in the epic center is a person with flashing eyes and visions for the future. He must be the "Man with a Plan."

There's one more characteristic, however, that is imperative in order to produce a vortex of history. That component is what the world calls "ideology." A plan for the future must be characterized by something great to believe, some compelling philosophy, some great truth that draws people up and out of their common, banal circumstances. Passionate unity cannot be created unless the speaker can reach into the vital core of the personality, the spiritual center of everything. Many who otherwise might have been significant leaders, forgetting this, never moved much beyond mediocrity. This quality — charisma perhaps — is found in people only very seldom. It is a one-in-a-thousand, one-in-a-million capability. The ability to press a compelling ideology upon the masses of people is the key to the control of a nation. In that day, the day of the rise of Antichrist, it will be a needed key toward world control.

Such a person will emerge out of the European situation. Watch for him.

What could possibly be the trigger mechanism that causes Europe and then the world to turn in admiration and obedience to the Antichrist? There are several possibilities for such a thing in today's world. They certainly would include the following.

1. Global Economic Collapse: The present world economic situation is on the most precarious footing in all of history. Voracious governments have raised the program of taxation to the place where they are now confiscating the wealth of individuals. This is a most shortsighted activity because it will produce depression on the part of people of substance and economic depression in the external world. Economic capability does not grow out of government manipulation. It grows out of individual confidence and individual competence.

2. The Threat of Nuclear War: Nuclear proliferation continues in our time with no assurance that it will come to a halt. Therefore, the possibility of one of the great powers or even a rogue nation of the world producing a nuclear exchange is a very real one. Iraq, with its near insane political situation, could easily decide to shoot at someone. Libya, under the mad Colonel Kadaffi, is looking for a suitcase bomb even now. Russia, savoring the old days, could decide on a fast nuclear conquest somewhere. Israel, facing destruction by a 500,000-man Arab army could begin a nuclear war.

The Man with the Plan

The prospect of this is most frightening to the people of earth. Should such a war be threatened, they could be expected to turn to the assuring voice of the great leader who promised peace and safety. We note that the Scripture says, "For when they shall say, Peace and safety, then sudden destruction cometh upon them, as travail upon a woman with child, and they shall not escape" (1 Thess. 5:3). The promise of peace has again and again been the producer of false confidence and the trigger mechanism for war.

The fact is that any kind of percolation — such as a war between small nations — could escalate into a larger conflict and the stated danger of global war. Any one of these developments could cause people and nations to take leave of their senses and opt for global unity. That's when the "Man with a Plan" will appear. We can be sure that the Antichrist will not have to shoot his way into power. Rather, he will be accepted by a grateful people as the proper custodian of the future.

We do well to note that the Bible itself states a number of conditions that will call for the rise of this world leader and make possible his acceptance by the peoples of earth. The Christians at Thessalonica were one day concerned by the possibility that the Day of the Lord had come upon them. The Day of the Lord is that period of time of divine retribution. The world is even now treasuring up wrath against the Day of Wrath and revelation of the righteous judgment of God, who will render to every man according to his deeds. This prescription given to us by the apostle Paul is in effect as of now. The vast iniquities of men are being, in effect, put in the bank and one day will be poured out upon the society. That is the beginning of the Day of the Lord, the time of the Tribulation.

But these dear Thessalonican Christians, under persecution, thought that perhaps the Day of the Lord had come. With words of assurance then, the apostle Paul speaks to them and says, "Now we beseech you, brethren, by the coming of our Lord Jesus Christ, and by our gathering together unto him, that you be not soon shaken in mind, or be troubled, neither by spirit, nor by word, nor by letter as from us, as that the day of the Lord is present" (2 Thess. 2:1-2).

So it is that the apostle Paul argues that because Christ has not come to gather us to himself — because the rapture of the Church has not taken place — the Day of the Lord has not commenced. This must have come as great assurance to these Christians who were already being subverted by those who said to them that the Church must plan on going through the Tribulation.

Having said this, the apostle Paul gives us a number of characteristics that will appear in the world in the days of the emergence of

Rome's greatest caesar. The first is apostasy, "That day shall not come, except there come the falling away first" (2 Thess. 2:3). The expression, "the falling away," means to stand away from, to betray a former loyalty, to turn your back to an earlier commitment. The word *opistimi* is the word we translate "apostasy."

So it is that the Scripture predicts apostasy as one of the characteristics of the day of the emergence of Antichrist.

Do we see anything like that in today's world? The answer is, of course. In the United States alone there are possibly 400,000 churches. How many still stand for the truth of Scripture, the deity of Christ, the premillenial return of the Lord, and other cardinal Christian doctrines? Indeed, the Church will become so depraved by apostasy as we move to the last days that it will be easily co-opted by the Antichrist. He will make organized religion a tool in his hand. Thank God that by that time the Church will be taken from the world in that blessed event of the Rapture.

A second characteristic of the rise of Antichrist will be anarchy. Paul says, "For the mystery of iniquity doth already work; only he who now hinders will continue to hinder until he be taken out of the way. And then shall that wicked one be revealed, whom the Lord shall consume with the spirit of His mouth, and shall destroy with the brightness of his coming, even him whose coming is after the working of Satan with all power and signs and lying wonders" (2 Thess. 2:7-9).

The Bible indicates that we live in a wretchedly evil world. However, the evil has not yet taken over the world in the sense of the mastery of everything. Why is this the case? It is because God has ordained a force that inhibits the rise of evil in the world. That force is personal responsibility, marriage, the family, and civil authority. That force is also the Holy Spirit of God working in the life of the Church. When these things are gone, nothing inhibits the tidal wave of iniquity that the Antichrist will actually bring to pass and upon which he will build his kingdom and influence.

A third condition that will make possible his rise is strong delusion, "And for this cause God shall send them strong delusion, that they should believe the lie, that they all might be judged who believed not the truth, but had pleasure in unrighteousness" (2 Thess. 2:11-12). By the days of the emergence of the Antichrist, the world will be so confused, deluded by the many lies that it has embraced, that it hardly knows truth from falsity. That delusion will be something on which the Antichrist capitalizes, using it to produce the emergence of his power.

In the midst of all these things, the Antichrist, the man of sin, the son of perdition will be revealed. The Scripture says that he "opposes and exalts himself above all that is called God, or that is worshiped, so that he, as God, sits in the temple of God, showing himself that he is God" (2 Thess. 2:4). Here we have the ultimate of arrogance, a mere man professing himself to be God. Be very sure that this presumption does not go unnoticed by the Lord. The Antichrist, at this point, has a very short life ahead.

The Antichrist Appears

Considering all these things, there certainly is a question that remains. That question is, "Do we see these conditions developing in our time?" We suggest that we only need to consider the daily news, check the newspapers and magazines, and involve ourselves in the acquiring of awareness about our world. With such a program we immediately begin to notice in our time the remarkable developments of those things which are consonant with the age of the rise of Antichrist. As we have seen, the Bible, via the prophets, gives us many characteristics of the time of the emergence of the beast. A quick glance across today's world must lead us to agree that there is a frightening similarity between the events of our time and those predicted in the Word of God. The Bible speaks again and again about "the latter days," "the last days," "the end of the world," and other such terminal statements. In speaking about these things, we are then given by the Lord a set of emergent characteristics, "signs" of the end times. In this regard, we have a most interesting conversation by our Lord which is recorded by Scripture.

> The Pharisees, with the Sadducees, came and, testing him, desired that he would show them a sign from heaven. He answered and said unto them, When it is evening, you say, It will be fair weather; for the sky is red. And in the morning, it will be foul weather today; for the sky is red and overcast. O you hypocrites, you can discern the face of the sky; but can you not discern the signs of the times? (Matt. 16:1-3).

The lesson of this account should be clear to all and has an even greater application in our times.

Can we discern the face of the sky? Indeed, we can. Via the amazing modern satellites, we can look at every cloud in an entire hemisphere, all in one viewing. The face of the sky is a million times more discernable to us than it was to the Pharisees of that day.

But what about the signs of the times? It seems that our generation is totally unable to draw a conclusion from the dark clouds around us. Here is a cloud of moral iniquity about to break upon us and we notice it not. The clouds of judgment gather in a more ominous fashion than ever and we take no notice. That, Jesus said, is hypocrisy. That is, we pretend to be knowledgeable about the things that are important, but we are willingly ignorant, in fact, concerning the things that matter. Signs of the times are everywhere, but a kind of spiritual blindness prevents the world from truly seeing them.

Willing spiritual ignorance produces a result predicted by our Lord when He spoke to the land of Israel and the city of Jerusalem. The Scripture says:

> And when he was come near, he beheld the city, and wept over it, saying, if you had known, even you, at least in this your day, the things which belong unto your peace! But now they are hidden from your eyes. For the days shall come up on you, that your enemies shall cast a trench about you, and compass you around, and keep you on every side, and shall lay you even with the ground, and your children within you, and they shall not leave in you one stone upon another; because you knew not the time of your visitation (Luke 19:41-44).

The things that make for your peace, "the time of your visitation," — what telling words. These warnings were addressed to the nation of Israel and we can be sure that they are addressed to us as well. Any nation, any people, which forgets that we live in a dangerous world, relaxes its guard, and says, "All Is well," is very close to judgment. Yes, the time of divine visitation upon our world may well be very close. Not to keep this in mind is surely a sin of omission. Not to be concerned with the things that make for our peace, is in the same class, a sin of omission.

What makes for peace when peace is available? It is the blessing of God and the protection of Jesus Christ. Any substitute foundation that pretends to produce peace is false. Nevertheless, forgetting this, the world will one day turn to its great leader and suppose that he can bring peace. Indeed, he will make this promise, but alas, the promise will be false. "When they shall say, peace and safety, sudden destruction will come upon them, as travail upon a woman with child, and they shall not escape" (1 Thess. 5:3).

One day, Rome's greatest caesar will promise deliverance from that destruction and the glorious result of world peace. The fact is that the result will be just the opposite of this. It will be war and destruction. Finally, Rome's greatest caesar will be deposed by the reign of Jesus Christ. We look forward to that day and, indeed, we see that day approaching.

5

Antichrist's Mistress

by Gary Stearman

> And upon her forehead was a name written, MYS-
> TERY, BABYLON THE GREAT, THE MOTHER OF
> HARLOTS AND ABOMINATIONS OF THE EARTH
> (Rev. 17:5).

The identity of "MYSTERY, BABYLON THE GREAT" has been debated for as long as there has been a New Testament. Pictured as a woman riding on a beast and holding aloft a cup full of abominations, Mystery, Babylon symbolizes the distillation of evil and is the perfect companion for the Antichrist. She is his mistress in the game of religious apostasy and despotic rule.

As we trace the ancient roots of this woman's evil power, we come to a new appreciation of her prowess. Babylon is a commercial and religious movement that has existed for millennia and that can be tracked from the past to the present day. Certain scriptural insights bring to light a historical model that reveals her true identity. After a brief historical look at her power base, we will carefully examine her character and personality.

The beast this scarlet woman rides is the creature described in Revelation 13:1 as having "seven heads and ten horns." Prophetically, this is the final world empire — the fourth beast of Daniel 7. It is global in character, with the Bible depicting this system as having web-like tentacles of control that extend around the planet.

The harlot, herself, is metaphorically referred to as a "great city" in Revelation 17:18: "And the woman which thou sawest is that great city, which reigneth over the kings of the earth."

Yet, as seen in Scripture, she reigns over a "city." She is seen both as local and global. How can we harmonize these two seemingly disparate symbols? It is not as easy as one might think.

Upon closer examination, we find that, in her own way, she is decidedly global in nature. Her description conveys the impression that she is not confined to a single location. She is a "city," but it is no ordinary municipality.

Many attempts have been made to identify the "great city." Some have said that it is the actual city of Babylon, now being rebuilt in Iraq as a tourist center. Others have insisted that it is Rome, citing among many other reasons, that even first century Christians referred to Rome as Babylon. Still others believe that it is New York City. Sometimes called "Babylon on the Hudson," this bustling city is the headquarters of various international trade and monetary interactions, as well as the site of the United Nations building.

On the latter points, they see New York City as a merchant center, pointing to Revelation 18:3 as evidence that this location fits the biblical description as no other can: "For all nations have drunk of the wine of the wrath of her fornication, and the kings of the earth have committed fornication with her, and the merchants of the earth are waxed rich through the abundance of her delicacies."

Many say that this must be a picture of New York (or perhaps revived Rome). The picture they paint is compelling, particularly as the Bible describes the destruction of the great city:

> And the kings of the earth, who have committed fornication and lived deliciously with her, shall bewail her, and lament for her, when they shall see the smoke of her burning.
>
> Standing afar off for the fear of her torment, saying, Alas, alas that great city Babylon, that mighty city! for in one hour is thy judgment come.
>
> And the merchants of the earth shall weep and mourn over her; for no man buyeth their merchandise any more (Rev. 18:9-11).

Here, the city is associated with worldwide merchant traffic. Its destruction apparently shuts down their entire operation! What a great city it must be! In chapters 17 and 18, the fate of the woman and her merchant traffic is seen as a combined event. Somehow, false religion in its final form is combined with international commerce. Again, in Revelation 18:16, these merchants lament her destruction, crying, "Alas, Alas, that great city."

This begs several questions: Where (or what) is the great city? How does it act to corrupt the morals of the entire world? What religious system has the kind of commercial connections we see here? How could such a city be so important that it would shut down the merchant traffic of the entire world? And how could such a large and important city come to an end in just "one hour"? (Rev. 18:17).

The Merchants of Tarshish

In answering such questions, the Bible is always its own best interpreter. Types and symbols extend from Genesis through Revelation, sometimes as events in the lives of real, historical people and sometimes as statements from the prophets. In their proclamations, the prophets often comment upon historical events, using the past to illustrate events of their own era as well as the future.

The topological foundations of Babylon and its merchant traffic are richly described in the Old Testament. There the archetypes are introduced, then developed through a variety of prophetic utterances, until at last, the New Testament reveals their full future development.

In answering the questions about the identity of the New Testament "MYSTERY, BABYLON" and its commercial system, it becomes very important to revisit the Old Testament. There we will find the origins of the system, then track its tendrils down through history. The merchants of Revelation 17 and 18 have their roots in Old Testament prophecy. It is interesting that there, as in the New Testament, they are seen operating in conjunction with a system of false religion. The old saying that "the more things change, the more they remain the same" once again rings true. It is especially convincing in this case, as quickly revealed in a backward glance at several ancient cultures.

We will begin with a striking prophecy found in Ezekiel 27:2. Here, we find a "lamentation for Tyrus." "Tyrus" is Tyre, the biblical model of merchant trade. These merchants of the ancient world came from Tyre and Sidon. They are the ancient traders commonly known as the Phoenicians. Their history disappears into the distant era following the great flood of Noah. Based at the eastern end of the Mediterranean in the area known today as Lebanon, they were global seafarers and merchants.

Their trade routes extended around the Mediterranean, then out through the Straits of Gibraltar to the Atlantic. From there, they ranged south around Africa and north to the lands that comprise today's Europe. Many archaeological and ethnological authorities insist that there is firm evidence they had visited the continents of North and South America by the fifth century B.C., and perhaps much earlier!

Like the Greeks, the Phoenicians were organized into rival city states, vying for power and influence. It is a well-known fact of history that the princes of the Phoenicians were the most knowledgeable businessmen in the world. Their early history is often clouded, but by the time of the Davidic kingdom and the reign of Hiram, king of Tyre, the focus becomes quite sharp. Hiram's reign was extremely long, extending through the kingships of both David and Solomon.

Ezekiel's prophecy depicts Tyre as merchants of virtually everything from wine and wood to foodstuffs and vessels of glass of metal. Spices, gold and silver, clothing and precious stones were carried to every part of the earth. Tyre traded with virtually every important nation. Most interesting, however, are the two references in chapter 27 to Tarshish:

> Tarshish was thy merchant by reason of the multitude of all kind of riches; with silver, iron, tin, and lead, they traded in thy fairs (Ezek. 27:12).

> The ships of Tarshish did sing of thee in thy market: and thou wast replenished, and made very glorious in the midst of the seas (Ezek. 27:25).

Tarshish is thought to refer to a major seaport in the territory that we now know as Spain. The Tartessus region of this ancient region may represent the origin of the biblical name. Or, *"Tarshish"* may simply be the term for the Mediterranean trading stations in various countries.

One thing, however, is certain, this term definitely refers to international trade in the marketplaces of the world. It is a title of power and far-reaching control that is associated with merchandise of great value. Furthermore, it established a biblical symbol that brings meaning to the prophecy of Mystery, Babylon.

In spite of their great professionalism and navigational know-how, Ezekiel forecasts that these merchant mariners will one day come to doom:

Thy rowers have brought thee into great waters: the east wind hath broken thee in the midst of the seas.

Thy riches and thy fairs, thy merchandise, thy mariners, and thy pilots, thy calkers, and the occupiers of thy merchandise, and all thy men of war, that are in thee, and in all thy company which is in the midst of thee, shall fall into the midst of the seas in the day of thy ruin.

The suburbs shall shake at the sound of the cry of thy pilots.

And all that handle the oar, the mariners, and all the pilots of the sea shall come down from their ships, they shall stand upon the land;

And shall cause their voice to be heard against thee, and shall cry bitterly, and shall cast up dust upon their heads, they shall wallow themselves in the ashes (Ezek. 27:26-30).

Does this prophecy speak of the ancient destruction of Tyre? In part, yes. But it actually appears to reach far into the future, to the final destruction of a global commerce system. In fact, when combined with the verses above, the final two verses of chapter 27 are seen to perfectly parallel the language of Revelation 18:

All the inhabitants of the isles shall be astonished at thee, and their kings shall be sore afraid, they shall be troubled in their countenance.

The merchants among the people shall hiss at thee; thou shalt be a terror, and never shalt be any more (Ezek. 27:35-36).

There is a clear difference between the Tyre of history and the "merchants of Tarshish," whose activities do not reach a peak until the latter days.

Historic Tyre was finally destroyed in the fourth century by Alexander the Great. But long before that, when Babylon succeeded Ninevah as the Middle East's great aggressive force, the nation had already begun to fall. Under the reign of Nebuchadnezzar, Tyre's commercial dominance was broken. With the rise of the Caesars, Rome had achieved dominance in Mediterranean marketing.

Yet in Ezekiel 38:13, we read, "Sheba and Dedan, and the merchants of Tarshish, with all the young lions thereof, shall say unto thee, Art thou come to take a spoil?"

This verse, of course, concerns the battle of Gog of the land of Magog that comes to pass at the beginning of the Tribulation. Note that the merchants are still as powerful as ever. They appear here as the world's "movers and shakers," who are upset by developing events.

We have stated before that at the time of Gog's invasion, they represent the convergence of global finance and energy policy, since Sheba and Dedan represent the oil producing countries of Arabia. The point is that the merchants have, and have always had, a central position in the formation of world power.

Jezebel as the Harlot of Babylon

But they have always set themselves in opposition to God's historical plan of redemption — and against Israel. This may be seen in the remarkable interaction between Tyre and Israel during the reign of King Ahab:

> And in the thirty and eighth year of Asa king of Judah began Ahab the son of Omri to reign over Israel: and Ahab the son of Omri reigned over Israel in Samaria twenty and two years.
>
> And Ahab the son of Omri did evil in the sight of the Lord above all that were before him.
>
> And it came to pass, as if it had been a light thing for him to walk in the sins of Jeroboam the son of Nebat, that he took to wife Jezebel the daughter of Ethbaal king of the Zidonians, and went and served Baal and worshipped him (1 Kings 16:29-31).

Here we have an amazingly compact narrative that links commercial and religious Babylon. Ahab, in a dynastic marriage of convenience, married Jezebel, a priestess of Baal and Ishtar.

Her father, the Sidonian king Ethbaal, was a grandson of none other than the great Hiram, king of Tyre. In Josephus' treatise, *Against Apion,* Ethbaal is called a "priest of Astarte,"[1] or Ishtar. He came to power by murdering his predecessor, the last of Hiram's line. This gives some idea of the corruption in Jezebel's home.

Josephus writes the following account of Ahab's infamy:

> He also took to wife the daughter of Ethbaal, king of the Tyrians and Sidonians, whose name was Jezebel, of

whom he learned to worship her own gods. This woman was active and bold, and fell into so great a degree of impurity and wickedness, that she built a temple to the god of the Tyrians, which they called Baal, and planted a grove of all sorts of trees; she also appointed priests and false prophets to this god. The king also himself had many such about him; and so exceeded in madness and wickedness all the kings that went before him.[2]

And so it was that the wealth and prestige of the Phoenician merchants was wedded to the royal house of Israel, bringing with it the corruption of false worship. Jezebel brought the adoration of the Babylonian Baal and Ishtar into the vital center of national Israel. This religion was extraordinarily corrupt, connected both with agricultural paganism and "divinely granted" political power. It was centered around fertility and sex.

Jezebel is the biblical model of the harlot riding the beast, who, in the latter days, will finally rise to corrupt all the nations of the earth. It takes but a little study to see that goddess worship is experiencing a worldwide resurgence. But for the resistance of the Church and the power of God's Holy Spirit, it could easily be the world's leading religion right now. This, of course, is every New Ager's fondest dream.

Thus, the wicked wife of Ahab represents the false religion of goddess worship, but she is also connected to the global system of merchant commerce. This is exactly the way she is depicted in the Book of Revelation.

The Phoenicians had always combined the false worship of the Babylonians with their merchant traffic. One clear example of this fact is seen in the story of Jonah. As he fled to avoid the Lord's direct order, he decided that his best refuge was to flee to Tarshish. This was the exact opposite of God's will, both geographically and spiritually:

> But Jonah rose up to flee unto Tarshish from the presence of the Lord, and went down to Joppa; and he found a ship going to Tarshish: so he paid the fare thereof, and went down unto it, to go with them unto Tarshish from the presence of the Lord (Jon. 1:2).

The Phoenician merchants had set the style of their global merchandising in the days of Babylon's rise to power. When their power declined, the center of merchant trade shifted from Tyre and Sidon to Carthage, on the north coast of Africa. This also became a headquarters for the worship of Baal and Ishtar.

Eventually, the Romans conquered Carthage and the power of the merchants was transferred to the great empire that has come down to us in the present day as Europe. But the prototype for Europe's merchant trade goes back to the Phoenicians.

The Law of the Merchants

Their religion came from Babylon, but their law was a creature unto itself. From time immemorial, these merchants based their culture on business, with profit as their number one priority. Their pagan temples served as banks, and the deities honored in those temples were their protective gods.

They were international traders who ingeniously arrived at a method of remaining neutral throughout their world travels. The secular history of the "Law Merchant," is essential to the understanding of antichrist's mistress.

Known in Latin as the *Lex Mercatoria*, this law is quite different from the Common Law, where our legal system finds its roots. Common Law dates back to the civil law of the Romans. But the Law Merchant goes back to the Roman, Greek, and Phoenician sea traders, whose special circumstances required a different sort of law. According to a text called *A Student's Course on Legal History,* by H. W. Bradlee, "The first work on merchant law in England was written by Gerard Malynes, published in 1622, entitled *Consultudo Vel Lex Mercatoria* or the Ancient Law Merchant."

In the preface to his work, he stated that he had "entitled it *Lex Mercatoria* instead of *Jus Mercatorum* because it is customary law provided by the authority of all kingdoms and commonweals, and **not a law established by the sovereignty of any prince.**" (In other words, it is not a system of justice.)

Later, the famous jurist Blackstone wrote that the proceedings of commerce were regulated by a law of its own called the Law Merchant or Lex Mercatoria "Which all nations agree in and take notice of and it is particularly held to be part of the law of England which justifies the causes of merchants and the general rules which obtain in all commercial countries."

Still later, Lord Mansfield stated that "mercantile law is not the law of a particular country, but the law of all nations." This law is defined as "the law administered as between merchants and the consular or commercial courts, some of it being substantive law and some rules of evidence and procedure."[3]

From the earliest times, its merchants of the high seas operated under an international system of law. In essence, it has always been a law based upon good faith — the belief that transactions would be conducted under terms of fair exchange. This system of exchange was not based upon the laws of any particular country, but upon the time honored word of the merchants themselves. Especially, it was based upon a kind of faith that allowed merchants to buy and sell beyond a purely cash basis. The system was developed that allowed credit to be extended, loans to be made, and title to goods to be acquired.

To these merchants — the merchants of Tarshish — national allegiance has always been unimportant. As has been appropriately noted, rather than being owned, they, themselves, actually own a number of nations, as well as kings and governments. Their form of government resembles a Chamber of Commerce on a global scale. They are almost apolitical. And the only law they recognize is the Law Merchant.

The Merchant Bankers

It is interesting that the activities of these merchants have from the first, been centered around the idea of credit. This word is from the Latin *credo*, meaning, "I believe." Many have pointed out that it is mutual trust that gives merchants their final boost up into the stratospheric regions of high finance. Both now and in the dim and distant past, mercantile traffic has proceeded within an exclusive club or society of men whose goals and desires link them together into a network that is far above the laws of any nation.

Ancient Roman London was dedicated to the cult of Mithraism — Mithra being "a god of ancient Persia whose name means 'Contract' and 'Friendship.' In the third century A.D., Diocletian declared Mithras 'Protector of the Roman Empire.' Statues of Mithras had 'rays' emanating from the crown, like the Statue of Liberty."[4]

In medieval Europe, fairs were often the centers of trade and commerce. Merchants traveled from distant countries to display their wares. They would run for weeks at a time in temporary tents, booths, and buildings. Mercantile trade came to be so valued that monarchs extended peace to merchants, even though their respective countries might be at war.

Merchant trade demanded that bills of exchange be extended, honored, and regulated. These led to the development of negotiable promissory notes, currency, and finally, to checks.

Eventually the system produced the secret fraternity that included the Hambros, Mattioli, Barings, Rothschild, Abs, Warburg, and Lehman families. Referring to the latter family in the book entitled *The Merchant Bankers*, Joseph Wechsberg writes,

> Lehman Brothers feels confident about the future of investment banking in America. The nation is getting more prosperous; consumer industries are expanding with the growing population. The iceman no longer cometh, he is replaced by the refrigerator salesman. The small radio is replaced by the large television set. Automation creates small and big machines which have to be produced — and financed. The capital requirements of America's industries are growing. And the customers keep borrowing more money. Everybody has learned to live on his future earnings. Billions of dollars have to be raised to finance the production of goods, and their consumption.
>
> Lehman Brothers knows where to find the billions and how to channel them from those who have the money to those who use it most profitably. Hand in hand with the new technological developments, Lehman Brothers invents new techniques for raising, buying, and selling the most common merchandise of all — money."

In this quote, we find the whole story. The merchant bankers are described by one of their own as men who create money on the good faith of trade by channeling the means of production and finance into their own coffers. The author is, himself, the son of London merchant bankers. He describes them as "Shrouded in secrecy, steeped in legend, they are the most fascinating and enigmatic of all aristocracy. They are the merchant bankers — the fabulous financiers whose family decisions have shaped the fates of kings and nations."[5]

He is not exaggerating. By simply giving borrowers their promise to pay in bank notes, the merchant bankers discovered that they could create money. It became their chief merchandise. Their dreams, however, extended beyond wealth. Their true quest is that of absolute power and control over the entire earth.

The Woman on the Beast

The merchants of Tarshish have always followed the way of

Baal and Ishtar. These pagan deities have emerged under various titles since the beginning of post-Flood history. Ishtar, the goddess who patterned the lives of Hiram, Ethbaal, and Jezebel, has taken on many identities.

One of the most interesting — and perhaps the latest — of her names is Europa. The Greek historian Herodotus speculated that the name of Europe came from a daughter of the king of Tyre(!) who was kidnapped by Greek sailors and carried to the island of Crete. Thus was born the legend of a pagan goddess whom the Greeks called Aphrodite and the Romans named Venus. In mythology the Tyrian king was named Agenor, and she was carried off to Crete by Zeus, king of the gods.

But no matter what her name — whether the Canaanite Ashtoreth, the Egyptian Isis, or one of her Graeco-Roman titles — she is always the same. She is the pagan goddess of power and fertility.

Where is she today? She is Gaia, Mother Earth, or Sophia, the goddess of wisdom who has recently invaded various mainline church denominations in the name of feminine equality. She is at the heart of the New Age movement.

Thinly veiled, she parades in the proceedings of such varied groups as the worldwide "greenpeace" movement, as well as other assorted peace and ecology activities. Under the New Age rainbow of sorcery, idolatry, Luceferic initiations, Eastern mysticism, divination, crystal therapies, ESP, UFOs, gnosticism, astrology, pyramid power, scientology, spiritism, shamanism, transcendental meditation, and a myriad of similar cultic activities, the goddess is increasingly accepted as a legitimate object of worship.

She is the global goddess who promises peace and the "wisdom of the ages." And her power will ultimately become the basis for a great amalgamation of latter day religions that will worship the man of sin: the Antichrist.

On May 15, 1984, a postage stamp set was published to commemorate the second election of members to the European Parliament. It features two momentous symbols: The first is a woman riding on a beast, and the second, a bridge over waters. Both are biblical symbols.

The woman on the beast is, of course, none other than the harlot of Revelation 17. She is Europa, holding the horn of the beast. Is it the "little horn" of Daniel 7:8? She rides across the waters. In the Bible, they are symbolic of the nations. For example, the beast of Revelation

13 rises out of the sea. It is identical with Daniel's fourth beast, and the seas are the nations.

The sea god (a dolphin) swims beneath her feet. He is Oannes, the ancient fish god and symbol of the pagan resurrection myth. In The Two Babylons, Alexander Hislop writes, "The name Oannes could be known only to the initiated as the name of the Pagan Messiah." In other words, he is the Tammuz of the Babylonian mystery religion of Baal and Ishtar. Initiates of this religion regarded the bull as the ultimate symbol of power. The sacrificial slaying of a bull was the central feature of their worship. This is the beast upon which the woman rides.

Cupid, the son of Venus (or Aphrodite or Ishtar), accompanies her. He completes the symbology of the pagan mother and child, a counterfeit of the virgin Mary and her sinless child, Jesus. Taken together, all of these symbols perfectly depict *"MYSTERY, BABYLON THE GREAT, THE MOTHER OF HARLOTS AND ABOMINATIONS OF THE EARTH"* (Rev. 17:5).

The waters beneath the feet of the beast even feature seven waves or mounds, reminding us of the "seven mountains" of Revelation 17:9.

On the accompanying stamp, a bridge reminds of the Latin, *pontifex maximus*, the ancient title of the caesars, and later, of the pope, himself. It means "chief bridge builder," and speaks of the one who is to unite all humanity under a single religion. The bridge stands upon four columns, reminding us of the four corners of the earth, or the rule of the entire planet. Beneath it are the seas of the nations. This picture symbolizes the global linkage of the nations into a new order; the rebirth of the Holy Roman Empire.

Where is the Great City?

This brings us back to the questions that we asked early in this chapter. Where is the great city, and how could it be so important in the latter days that its destruction could shut down the entire merchant traffic of the world? As we noted before, in Revelation 17:18, the woman in question is, herself, called "that great city."

She is like Tyre, that great ancient city which became a symbol of the merchant traffic of the whole earth. The prince of Tyre, to whom Ezekiel 28 is entirely devoted, is none other than Satan. His earthly emissaries, such as Hiram and Ethbaal, were only the temporary regents of his global enterprise. Down through the centuries there have been hundreds of others.

The merchants of Tarshish centered their activities in Tyre for a while, then moved to Carthage and later to Rome and London. Still later, and in our era, the merchant centers have spread abroad to New York, Los Angeles, Hong Kong, Tokyo, Singapore, and Sydney. But these are all under the control of the merchant bankers. They are still the same merchants of Tarshish, but now they have achieved a global dominance. Even today they unite under the harlot assembly of the New Age. Believing themselves to be above the fray, they bow the knee to no nation.

Her judgment is coming, and so is theirs:

> And he cried mightily with a strong voice, saying, Babylon the great is fallen, is fallen, and is become the habitation of devils, and the hold of every foul spirit, and a cage of every unclean bird.
>
> For all nations have drunk of the wine of the wrath of her fornication, and the kings of the earth have committed fornication with her, and the merchants of the earth are waxed rich through the abundance of her delicacies (Rev. 18:2-3).

The merchants and their false gods will perish in a brief moment of time, as in Rev. 18:10-11: "Alas, Alas that great city Babylon, that mighty city! for in one hour is thy judgment come. And the merchants of the earth shall weep and mourn over her; for no man buyeth their merchandise any more."

Question: What single city on earth is so important that its destruction could halt the merchant traffic of the entire world? The answer is, none. If New York or London or Rome were destroyed, merchant banking would continue as usual. The international electronic system has its redundancies.

Instead, as before noted, we are seeing the description of a global "city." The New Testament Greek term for "great city" is "megalopolis." A recent example of this description can be found in the July 1994 *National Geographic* magazine. Its lead article refers to the Eastern seaboard area from Boston to Washington as "Megalopolis." That is, the region has been combined into one huge city. But even the destruction of this region would not stop world merchant banking.

In our day, we hear the term "global village." The term suggests that the world has become one huge city, or megalopolis. In fact, the destruction of the megalopolis of Revelation 17 and 18 is the simultaneous devastation of every merchant capital on earth. The wailing of the merchant bankers makes this very clear:

> Alas, alas that great city, that was clothed in fine linen, and purple, and scarlet, and decked with gold, and precious stones, and pearls!
>
> For in one hour so great riches is come to nought. And every shipmaster, and all the company in ships, and sailors, and as many as trade by sea, stood afar off.
>
> And cried when they saw the smoke of her burning saying, What city is like unto this great city!
>
> And they cast dust on their heads, and cried, weeping and wailing, saying, Alas, alas that great city, wherein were made rich all that had ships in the sea by reason of her costliness! for in one hour is she made desolate (Rev. 18:17-19).

The language here is practically identical with that of Ezekiel 27:30. The global merchants of Tarshish and their worldwide trade network (the global village or megalopolis) are finally destroyed.

More than that, they have finally been made to see the folly of their false system of worship. In the ancient days, it was the worship of Baal and Ishtar; today the same religion is called the New Age movement.

One final note: The prophecy in James 5, speaks of these merchant bankers in a different light. They "weep and howl." Their "riches are corrupted." They "have heaped treasure together for the last days." Clearly, they have believed that they have at long last arrived at a time when they would control the globe.

But in reality, it has been Satan who has orchestrated their vast program. He is the prince of Tyre, about whom the following is written:

> With thy wisdom and with thine understanding thou has gotten thee riches, and hast gotten gold and silver into thy treasures:
>
> By thy great wisdom and by thy traffic hast thou increased thy riches, and thine heart is lifted up because of thy riches:
>
> Therefore thus saith the Lord God; Because thou hast set thine heart as the heart of God;

Behold, therefore, I will bring strangers upon thee,
the terrible of the nations: and they shall draw their swords
against the beauty of thy wisdom, and they shall defile thy
brightness.

They shall bring thee down to the pit, and thou shalt
die the deaths of them that are slain in the midst of the seas
(Ezek. 28:4-8).

And thus it shall be. Babylon, the global city, and her merchants
of Tarshish will be brought to nothing in a moment of time. And her
true leader, Satan, will fall with the system.

The Sevenfold Death Of Megalopolis

We have examined "MYSTERY, BABYLON THE GREAT"
from the perspective of its commercial history. We seen the ancient
merchants of Tarshish, headquartered first in Tyre, then later in
Carthage, Rome, and other parts of Europe. We have observed that
especially in Ezekiel 27 they provide the prophetic model for the latter
day "merchant bankers" of our era.

Today, these men control the world's commerce, operating
under the ancient premise that their transactions supersede the laws of
the various nations they use to promote their global profiteering. They
have always operated under the so-called "Law Merchant," which
gives them a kind of immunity from the strictures of local practice.
Rather, they are a law unto themselves, and their credo is global
citizenship. It was always so. Even in the days of Tyre, the market was
considered to be worldwide:

The ships of Tarshish did sing of thee in thy market:
and thou wast replenished, and made very glorious in the
midst of the seas (Ezek. 27:25).

Furthermore, their ethics are derived from the pagan religion of
Babylon, and its worship of Baal and Ishtar. This "mystery religion"
has taken many forms over the ages, from the Babylonian mother and
child mythology of Ishtar and Tammuz, through the Egyptian Isis and
Osiris, the Greek Diana and Dionysus, and the Roman Venus and
Adonis.

However, at its heart it relies upon an initiation into a secret
brotherhood. Its members are an exclusive club that worships at the
twin altars of money and the occultic forces — the gods of business
and power. Its banks are its temples. This is the key to understanding

the mystery of Babylon.

Down through time, the names of its deities change from culture to culture, but their goals and ideas remain the same. With the expansion of Christian missions in the nineteenth and early twentieth centuries, their pagan influence dropped into relative obscurity. But now, the religion of the "goddess" is once again quickly emerging, even within mainline Christian denominations, where she is called "Sophia," the goddess of wisdom.

The "Great City"

The Bible predicts that both spiritually and monetarily, Babylon will die a spectacular death. It seems that God has reserved a special measure of His wrath for this system.

In Revelation 17 and 18, the merchants and their occultic system of worship are witnessed as they come to a state of total collapse. However, the angelic announcement of Babylon's destruction is given in Revelation 14:8-10, where she is associated with the beast and his diabolical system of market controls:

> And there followed another angel, saying, Babylon is fallen, is fallen, that great city, because she made all nations drink of the wine of the wrath of her fornication.
>
> And the third angel followed them, saying with a loud voice, If any man worship the beast and his image, and receive his mark in his forehead or in his hand,
>
> The same shall drink of the wine of the wrath of God.

In this passage and seven others which follow it (Rev. 16:19; 17:18; 18:10; 18:16; 18:18; 18:19; 18:21), the Babylonian system is referred to as "that great city." With the pouring of the seventh vial in Revelation 16:19, the city is addressed in a way that suggests that it is an actual geographic location: "And the great city was divided into three parts, and the cities of the nations fell: and great Babylon came in remembrance before God, to give unto her the cup of the wine of the fierceness of his wrath."

But as we have suggested before, this raises a very large question. Namely, what city on earth is so large and important that its destruction can totally halt the merchant traffic, international finance, and false worship of the entire world system? For indeed, that's what "Mystery, Babylon the great" actually is — a well-orchestrated global operation.

The answer — also as we have suggested before — seems to be no answer at all. If New York fell, the system would continue. Or if Tokyo, Rome, London, Sydney, or Babylon in Iraq fell, other parts of the market would quickly take up the slack. So what, and where, is the city?

Megalopolis

Many have attempted to answer this difficult question. But no single answer has thus far seemed satisfactory. Perhaps we can get closer to the solution if we consider the actual designation of the city, as given in the original New Testament Greek language.

Both in the announcement of Babylon's doom in Revelation 14:8, and in the succeeding sevenfold actualization of that doom, the city is referred to as "that great city," from the Greek *he polis he megale* [h poliV h megale]. Literally, this phrase means, "the city, the great [one]." Obviously, it refers to some literal city in a specific geographic location. Or does it?

The terms megale, "great" and polis, "city," have come down to us as the English "megalopolis." It uses the same words as those translated "great city" in Revelation. The *Merriam/Webster New Collegiate Dictionary* defines "megalopolis" as, "1: a very large city, 2: a thickly populated region centering in a metropolis or embracing several metropolises."

There are many cities around the world that would fit this description. More and more, the larger metropolitan areas are being connected with superhighways which, themselves, become lined with rows of smaller cities that eventually merge into one long municipality.

Just this sort of megalopolis is described in a map, published in the previously mentioned *National Geographic* magazine. The map, entitled "Boston to Washington, Megalopolis," covers the area of seven cities. Extending southward, the cities are Boston, Providence, Hartford, New York, Philadelphia, Baltimore, and Washington. Over the years, they have literally grown together into one great city, or megalopolis. Admittedly, it is a "great city." But would its demise spell the end of the international marketplace that the Bible predicts? As tempting as it is to think so, it seems unlikely. Though it would be stunned, there are many other world market headquarters that could take over and share its functions.

In Bonn, London, Rome, Tokyo, and Hong Kong, the computers would continue to hum. Merchant traffic would be redirected, not halted. And there are other megalopolises as well. From Milwaukee, Wisconsin, to Rochester, New York, a chain of cities has, for all practical purposes, merged into one megalopolis. Along with these two cities, Chicago, Gary, South Bend, Toledo, Cleveland, and Buffalo form one huge metropolitan area.

In Europe, the region bounded by Paris, Brussels, Amsterdam, and Bonn is a literal megalopolis. Viewed from the air at night, it appears as a single, huge illuminated area. This also happens to be the location of the European Parliament and the economic directorate of the European business community. But here, too, it seems unlikely that the destruction of this particular area would cause the world system to grind to a halt. And yet, in Revelation 16 through 19, the "great city" is destroyed. The merchants who had invested their very way of life in her, grievously lament her passing. The city is gone, and with it, their business.

Seven Blows from Heaven

Following the angelic announcement of Revelation 14:8, chapter 16, verse 19 features the first of seven judgmental curses upon the woman, the beast, and the merchants. It seems to be some sort of geological catastrophe, in which the "great city" (megalopolis) is "divided into three parts." But this could as well be a global split as a local one.

The beast is the final world empire, prophesied by Daniel as the "fourth beast" (Dan. 7:23). The woman is the false goddess of the ancient Babylonian mystery religion, variously known as Ishtar, Astarte, Diana, Isis, and Venus. She is the goddess of fertility and profit. The merchants are the global moguls of finance and social engineering.

In Revelation 17:18, the woman is, herself, called "that great city." Is she Rome, as many have suggested? If so, her destruction could hardly halt world commerce. She is shown in a position of rulership over the kings of the earth. Her situation is distinctly global.

Revelation 18:10 shows the "great city" as being destroyed in "one hour." Her judgment is catastrophic. Both the kings and the merchants lament her sudden ruin.

The next mention of the city is found in Revelation 18:16. Here, she is described as richly and luxuriously clothed in dazzling garments. These are the very garments that were one of the principle profitmakers for the global merchants. Even at present the international garment trade is a huge and thriving enterprise.

In Revelation 18:18-19, the "great city" is shown burning, with the maritime merchants grieving from afar. These sea traders watch her burning. And just as at their first appearance in Ezekiel 27:30, they "cast up dust upon their heads" in grief. Since they're at sea, where do they get the dust? Is it some kind of fallout from an enormous explosion?

> And every shipmaster, and all the company in ships, and sailors, and as many as trade by sea, stood afar off, And cried when they saw the smoke of her burning, saying, What city is like unto this great city!
>
> And they cast dust on their heads, and cried, weeping and wailing, saying, Alas, alas that great city, wherein were made rich all that had ships in the sea by reason of her costliness! for in one hour is she made desolate.

Babylon's seventh and final stroke of doom is seen in Revelation 18:21. "Thus with violence shall that great city Babylon be thrown down, and shall be found no more at all." These seven blows from heaven end the gentile domination of Planet Earth. Since the days of Nebuchadnezzar and the kings of Tyre, with their international merchant trade, the Gentiles ruled. Seven is the number of completion. The system will be completely destroyed, never to rise again.

Nun, the Symbol of Downfall

On the subject of Babylon's fall, there is a curious symbolism that appears in the Old Testament. In the Hebrew Masoretic text, there is an alphabetic symbol that appears a total of nine times. It is a special form of the Hebrew letter *nun* [ﬨ]. What makes it special is its reversed form, as follows: [ﬨ].

Written in its normal, forward conformation [ﬨ], this letter is said to symbolize faithfulness, soul, and emergence. Symbolically, it is said to represent the man who serves God, bending before Him in humility. But in its final form, used at the termination of a word, it stands straight [ﬨ], in the final day of judgment.

More importantly, this letter is said to symbolize downfall and simultaneous salvation, because it is the initial letter of the word "downfall." We see one of many examples of this event in Amos 5:2: "The virgin of Israel is fallen; she shall no more rise: she is forsaken upon her land; there is none to raise her up."

However, in Amos 9:11, the condition is reversed in the latter days: "In that day will I raise up the tabernacle of David that is fallen, and close up the breaches thereof; and I will raise up his ruins and I will build it as in the days of old."

But in its reversed form, it represents a turning away from faith. Moreover, it is a symbol of God turning His back in judgment upon a reprobate people. The reversed *nun* [נ] is found twice in Numbers 10.

The first time, it appears in boldfaced and enlarged form, just prior to Numbers 10:35-36, as follows:

> נ
>
> And it came to pass, when the ark set forward, that Moses said, Rise up, Lord, and let thine enemies be scattered; and let them that hate thee flee before thee.
>
> And when it rested, he said Return, O Lord, unto the many thousands of Israel.

Here, it can be easily seen that the reversed *nun* [נ] represents the Lord standing in judgment of Israel's enemies. The thirty-sixth verse ends the tenth chapter of Numbers. These first ten chapters are characterized by a sense of order, consecration, and sanctification, as the people are readied for their desert experience. The eleventh chapter, however, displays a tragic turn in the faith of the Israelites. And just as would be expected, with a decline in the people's faith, there follows a judgment from God. Chapter 11, verse 1, begins with the same boldfaced, reversed *nun*.

> נ
>
> And when the people complained, it displeased the Lord: and the Lord heard it; and his anger was kindled; and the fire of the Lord burnt among them, and consumed them that were in the uttermost parts of the camp.

Here, it is the Israelites who are judged, not the enemies outside the camp. The message is perfectly clear in both cases. God has placed an unmistakable mark in Scripture to commemorate His most significant judgments.

The Reversed Nuns of Psalm 107

With that in mind, it is startling to discover that God has reserved the other seven boldface reversed *nuns* for the latter day merchant bankers of Mystery, Babylon.

In Psalm 107, we find the unmistakable mark once again. It

appears just prior to seven very significant verses. It has not been carried over into our English translations, but the unmistakable mark of God's judgment is there, nevertheless. It seems to mark the sevenfold destruction of the Babylonian merchant system. Six of the reversed *nuns* appear before verses 23 through 28, in the following way:

ɩ
They that go down to the sea in ships, that do business in great waters;

ɩ
These see the works of the Lord, and his wonders in the deep.

ɩ
For he commandeth, and raiseth the stormy wind, which lifteth up the waves thereof.

ɩ
They mount up to the heaven, they go down again to the depths: their soul is melted because of trouble.

ɩ
They reel to and fro, and stagger like a drunken man, and are at their wit's end.

ɩ
Then they cry unto the Lord in their trouble, and he bringeth them out of their distresses.

The seventh reversed nun occurs just prior to verse 40:

ɩ
He poureth contempt upon princes, and causeth them to wander in the wilderness, where there is no way.

Truly, God has preordained His judgment upon the world system. Jewish scholars say the reversed *nun* [ɩ] is a sign of exclusion or diminishment. Without a doubt, it has that meaning here. The merchant bankers are to be excluded from God's kingdom, their power totally removed.

It is also quite significant that Psalm 107 was chosen to carry this mark of condemnation. It is the first of the Deuteronomy book of the Psalms. The Deuteronomy Psalms declare the glory of God's kingdom and express the gratitude of those who were rescued from the Tribulation. In them, God is shown to be merciful toward His repentant people.

Most important in this story is God's judgment upon the nations, and especially upon their greedy, apostate leaders. What better way to begin the Deuteronomy Psalms, than with the resounding sevenfold condemnation of Babylon!

As "that great city" — megalopolis — and its enslaving merchant traffic is halted once and for all, we see a picture of global destruction. To live up to its biblical description, this city must be gigantic — a true megalopolis.

But must it be in one geographical location on Planet Earth? Time will tell. Is it the megalopolis of our own east coast? Perhaps it's the megalopolis of Europe? Perhaps.

But for now, it seems much more logical to think of it as a global city. The great city appears to be a global megalopolis, connected by electronic banking and global merchant trade. If any part of it were toppled, it could still survive and function. But if all its major links were destroyed "in one hour," the merchants would truly stay aboard their ships and weep.

Its destruction will be swift and complete. Psalm 107, Ezekiel 27, and Revelation 17 and 18 all agree on that.

Jezebel's Termination

However, just prior to their destruction, they will turn upon the harlot to destroy her completely. In the end, the same global powers who gave their support and allegiance, both to the Antichrist and to his mistress, will demand her blood: "And the ten horns which thou safest upon the beast, these shall hate the whore, and shall make her desolate and naked, and shall eat her flesh, and burn her with fire" (Rev. 17:16).

How curious it is that this was the fate of Jezebel, herself. Even in death, she stands as the perfect model of the latter day harlot who will rise to deceive the nations. During her lifetime, she had ruled with an iron hand. But with the anointing of Jehu as king over Israel, her fate was sealed. Even as the prophet Elisha commanded that Jehu be anointed, he also announced that Jezebel would die with no one to bury her. She would be eaten by dogs.

And so it came to pass, as Jehu came to her palace. She greeted him from a high window, but he commanded that she be thrown down to the pavement.

> And he said, Throw her down. So they threw her down: and some of her blood was sprinkled on the wall, and on the horses: and he trode her under foot.

And when he was come in, he did eat and drink, and said, Go, see now this cursed woman, and bury her: for she is a king's daughter.

And they went to bury her: but they found no more of her than the skull, and the feet, and the palms of her hands (2 Kings 9:33-35).

For a time, it will be earth's darkest hour. Gentile kings, in league with the impostor Antichrist, will dance to the siren song of the harlot's false religion. As Antichrist's mistress, she will complete the power of his evil throne. She represents the illusory authority that is so much a part of the ancient, false goddess religion.

Together, their reign will follow the apostate pattern set by Ahab and Jezebel. In the end, this historical couple came to a dishonorable end. In the same way, *"MYSTERY, BABYLON,"* the harlot, will re-enact Jezebel's public disgrace and spiritual death for the last time.

6

Israel's Contract with the Devil

by William T. James

It is the fuse to Armageddon. (Hal Lindsey, 1995)

Peace is being pursued more vigorously than at any time in human history precisely because Israel, and Jerusalem in particular, has become the greatest potential flashpoint in the arena of global war and peace. Jerusalem is not merely an ancient city that evokes thoughts of religious holy sites. Jerusalem is in and of itself an issue, a hatred-filled detonator that is destined to spark the last world war. Governmental leaders and news-gathering chiefs around the world demonstrate time and time again that they instinctively know that this small speck on the vast region known as the Middle East has become exactly what the prophet Zechariah predicted it would one day be — a burdensome stone weighing heavily upon mankind's humanistic drive to create a world order totally void of influence by the true God of heaven.

> Behold, I will make Jerusalem a cup of trembling unto all the peoples round about, when they shall be in the siege both against Judah and against Jerusalem, And in that day will I make Jerusalem a burdensome stone for all peoples; all that burden themselves with it shall be cut in pieces, though all the nations of the earth be gathered together against it (Zech. 12:2-3).

Regardless of the direction in which major news events of our time channel our attention, all focus is drawn again to Jerusalem, just as if that city is possessed of a magnetic field or gravitational force from which there is no permanent escape. The current peace process seems to be an intensifying effort to sever the invisible elastic cord that holds us captive in order that the utopian dreamers and planners can get on with shaping earth's inhabitants into a single mindset that will produce peace, prosperity, and love for all mankind. "Heaven on earth cannot be established until this matter of Jerusalem is resolved" is the crucial nucleus of thought in the ever-increasing cry for peace. Indeed, before the great social contract is made that will make all people of the world as one, as called for in John Lennon's song, "Imagine," there must be a cessation to the hostilities between the antagonists who carry on the ancient Middle Eastern feud that threatens to break out in a conflagration that will engulf the entire earth. The singular overwhelming factor to remember as we consider the geopoliticians' great plans to prevent such a holocaust from breaking out in the Middle East is this: It is not the size of the state of Israel or its power or its threat or anything else about that tiny nation that makes her enemies determined to go to war against her. It is Israel's very existence they cannot abide.

Israel's present leadership faction is desperately searching for a friend who will stick faithfully by the nation. Wise leadership within the country realizes that the only hope for any semblance of peace for any extended period of time resides in strength through power and might that is contained within its own national character and will to survive. A very few within Israel, as that nation is presently constituted, understand that it is not necessary, it is not wise, to contract with any outside parties to ensure Israel's future security. Strength that can deter the multiplying millions of her Islamic and other enemies, they know, can be found only in a pact — actually, a promise — made thousands of years ago with the God of Abraham, Isaac, and Jacob.

Roots of the Deadly Dispute/ True Source of Israel's Protective Strength

Dr. Richard DeHaan outlined in superb fashion the causes and effects of Israel's misery and turmoil over the past several millennia, and defines with precision the only security arrangement that will ever bring peace and prosperity to that nation.

God made a number of promises to Abraham that

directly related to his descendants, including the guarantee that the land of Palestine would be their inheritance. These pledges, however, were not intended for every person who could claim Abrahamic ancestry. The Edomites, for example, were fathered by Esau, Abraham's oldest grandson, but they were not given any special promises. The same can be said about the Arabs, descendants of Ishmael, and of the six sons of Keturah. All of these peoples were Abraham's progeny, but they were not the "seed" to whom God had given the land of Canaan "for an everlasting possession" (Gen. 17:8).

This gift of the Promised Land and the assurance of universal blessing was bestowed upon the line of Abrahamic descendants who came through Isaac and Jacob. Note Genesis 21:12: "In Isaac shall thy seed be called." Just before Isaac's twin sons were born, the Lord once again identified the one through whom His promises would be fulfilled. He told Isaac's wife, Rebecca: "Two nations are in they womb, and two manner of people shall be born of thee; and the one people shall be stronger than the other people; and the elder shall serve the younger" (Gen. 25:23). The prophet Malachi and the apostle Paul referred to this passage as indicating that the sons of Jacob, not Esau, were the promised seed (Mal. 1:2-3; Rom. 9:10-13).

The line of special blessing therefore went from Abraham through Isaac and Jacob. In turn, the twelve sons of Jacob became the progenitors of the twelve tribes of Israel. Only to this people was given the distinctive place in God's program, and they alone can claim His special promises. They do not apply to the other descendants of Abraham. It is to this line only that the Lord gave the land of Canaan "for an everlasting possession." Of them He said, "I will be their God" (Gen. 17:8).[1]

So bitter is the dispute and so deep is the hatred toward Israel that the antagonism has to be supernaturally inspired and perpetuated. God's Holy Word covers that luciferian engendered hatred from its inception to where it will culminate with an all-out military assault. Revelation 12 portrays the Satan-fostered attack in a swift, panoramic overview of the climax of history through prophecy as recorded by John the apostle.

And when the dragon saw that he was cast unto the earth, he persecuted the woman who brought forth the male child. And to the woman were given two wings of a great eagle, that she might fly into the wilderness, into her place, where she is nourished for a time, and times, and half a time, from the face of the serpent. And the serpent cast out of his mouth water like a flood after the woman, that he might cause her to be carried away by the flood. And the earth helped the woman, and the earth opened her mouth and swallowed up the flood which the dragon cast out of his mouth. And the dragon was angry with the woman, and went to make war with the remnant of her seed, who keep the commandments of God, and have the testimony of Jesus Christ (Rev. 12:13-17).

The woman referred to can be none other than the nation Israel in its remnant form, as it will be comprised while earth's inhabitants endure the reign of the one who will be human history's most vicious tyrant. The Beast's rage stems from Satan's hatred for the Jews, the people through whom the Redeemer, Jesus Christ, came into the world. Peace is an impossible dream, therefore, as long as the spirit of Antichrist stalks the planet.

Peace! Peace! Where's the Peace?

Jesus said, as recorded in Matthew 24, that there will be wars and rumors of wars when the time nears for His second advent. His words strongly imply a marked intensification in the number of what we term today, "hot wars" and "cold wars," while the end of the age approaches. God's prophetic Word is ripe with "that the more men cry peace and safety the more prolific war-making will become." There will develop as the time of the end nears, we are told, a type of peace that destroys, false peace and security arrangements that end in the sudden destruction of those taken in by the deceptions. Dr. J. Vernon McGee made some interesting observations about humanistic efforts at peacemaking and the results thereof. "We are not a peaceful people. War is in our hearts. In recorded history, man has engaged in 15,000 wars and he has signed some 8,000 peace treaties. Yet in all that period, he has only enjoyed 200-300 years of true peace. Man is a warlike creature...." McGee went on to indicate where man's warlike nature, in conjunction with humanism's concept of the peacemaking process, is taking the world.

We are moving today in the direction of a world dictator. . . . Now this is not just the ravings of a preacher here in California. This is something that other men in other walks of life who apparently make no great claim to be a Christian have said. Professor A.J. Toynbee, who is director of studies in the Royal Institute of International Affairs [said], "By forcing on mankind more and more lethal weapons and at the same time making the whole world more and more interdependent economically, technology has brought mankind to such a degree of distress that we are ripe for deifying any new Caesar who might succeed in giving the world unity and peace." . . . That will be the platform that Antichrist is coming in on. Unity of the world, one world, and peace. And believe me, I think if anybody appeared on the scene now and offered the world that, they wouldn't ask whether he came from heaven or hell. I don't think they would care because today there is an obsession. We want peace and we spent billions of dollars for it. G.K. Chesterton observed in his day, "One of the paradoxes of this age is that it is the age of pacifism but not the age of peace."[2]

Hal Lindsey stated: "[Jesus prophesied that] there would be a period of constant warfare, a period where there would be not only actual war, but the constant threat of war. We've seen that develop in spades. The twentieth century will go down . . . as the most destructive period of all human history as far as warfare is concerned. More people have been killed in wars in the twentieth century than in all the other centuries put together. . . ."[3]

The Horrific Nuclear Equation

"Little Boy" and "Fat Man," a couple of inanimate objects affectionately so named, forever altered man's need and drive for peace. Before Little Boy and Fat Man, the cries for peace and safety were made for the sake of provincial interests in a world composed more or less of isolated regions insulated from distant conflicts. Since war and peace ultimately and literally involves, as Shakespeare would have it, the question of whether to be or not to be, the only nuclear weapons ever to be used in warfare — as of this writing and under the staying hand of God — comprise the most persuasive ingredient in the argument in favor of an ongoing peace process.

Despite the lessons of Hiroshima and Nagasaki, however, there seemed to be, until the fiftieth anniversary of the atomic bombings of those cities, and the accompanying media hoopla, a developing amnesia about the horrific consequences such weaponry inflicts. We can only pray and hope, after recently watching the national news networks and others work their revisionist sophistry — for that is what it was, revisionism at its worst — that the tremendous amount of coverage surrounding the anniversary will serve to remind us all of the deadly probabilities if reason does not prevail and if we do not, as Santayana exhorted, remember the failures of the past.

It is frightening to consider that those who should know best the annihilative properties of thermonuclear weaponry have, since the break-up of the Soviet Union, dealt with nuclear stockpiles as if they were merely canned goods on grocery store shelves. Government heads, generals, and top nuclear scientists continue to treat critical nuclear weapons manufacturing materials and information as nothing more or less than benign things with which to upgrade and improve the products and services of the customers for whom they work as consultants.

An analysis by one reporter in 1992 provided some troubling observations about the deteriorating nuclear proliferation state of affairs. Keep in mind that since this early assessment, the problem has become, some believe, hopelessly worse.

> Five years from now (10 at the outside) a dozen or so of the world's nastier nations will find themselves, by conventional military standards, disarmed. This also might be a lot more dangerous, a peril that went unaddressed in the presidential campaign. The problem much simplified is this. Though the military industrial complexes of NATO and the former Warsaw pact are trending down, the planet remains awash in weaponry. Some of it's getting chopped up, blown up, and otherwise deep-sixed. But the rest, especially the former East bloc inventory (minus Germany's) is up for sale. And that's the key word — sale. Gone are the days when relatively small nations — Syria, for example — could maintain massive forces, courtesy of Soviet largesse. The Russians, not to mention the Chinese, North Koreans, and sundry other suppliers, want cash. It may be a buyer's market nowadays, but cash is something many of the more avid purchasers lack, and ironically, the more dependent their forces are, (or become) on bargain-

basement commie and ex-commie stuff, the worse off they'll be down the road. . . ."

The article goes on to give facts about the poor state of maintenance in which former Soviet-bloc military had when the big day came, everything would be up and ready for a brief one-way trip. This means that nations with large inventories of Soviet and similar weapons have forces almost impossible to maintain, especially as spare parts and technical assistance dry up.

The writer continues,

> This inevitable disarmament by breakdown in consumption leads to one hope and to a trinity of dangers. The hope is that the nations possessed of such forces (Syria, again, for example) may finally decide to give peace a chance. But the dangers may turn out to be more real. First, in the short-term, some nasties may succumb to a use-it-before-you-lose-it mentality, i.e., fight while operational confidence is still possible. Or they may decide to de-emphasize increasingly expensive and deteriorated conventional forces and concentrate on two ends of the spectrum of conflict. This gives rise to the second danger that nations formally building large forces may shift to seemingly primitive but imminently usable, low-intensity forces, especially in regional ethnic and religious conflicts. It will look like disarmament; in reality, it will be war by less sophisticated though still terrible means. The third danger is that disarmament by deterioration may beget serious interest in weapons of mass destruction, either in use for local conflicts or as a means of deterring outside intervention. These weapons need not be elegant nor need they be purchased outright as complete systems. All that will matter is that they can be assembled and delivered or in place somewhere. This may have happened already. A few months ago, for example, reports circulated that the Kazakhs had sold a couple of nukes (below dealer's invoice) to their Iranian brethren.

The writer of the article went on to correctly assess that neither the U.S. nor the world community at large had been able to get a handle on controlling the spread of more and more dangerous weaponry.[4] Again, remember that was in 1992. Today the world faces a much more expanded threat and all efforts to put a cap on the flow of weapons from the regions formerly within the Soviet bloc have utterly failed.

Still, the cry for peace grows louder. All the while the world hemorrhages nuclear weapons technology. Weaponry flows into Third World nations with tyrants thirsty for power to expand their dominions. Of those nations siphoning former Soviet bloc weaponry — nuclear weapons that are quickly becoming obsolete because of short shelf life in particular — none are more troubling for the world than are Iran, Iraq, Syria, Libya, and other Islamic entities who themselves are filled with hatred for each other but totally agree on one thing: Israel has to go.

What Peace Dividend?

The evil empire lay in a crumpled heap. The Cold War supposedly had thawed as if microwaved by a sudden, warmly embracing breeze from the very heart of the Kremlin. According to the liberal majority in Congress at the time, the establishment of utopia was surely just around the corner. The billions of dollars formerly necessary to deter the voracious Russian bear must be used to feed the homeless and provide whatever it took for the federal government to begin making the conditions of life for the have-nots of America more resemble the living conditions of the haves. There were, of course, at the same time, throat-clearing and muffled mumblings of doubt about possible relief for taxpayers.

Say! Whatever happened to that peace dividend, anyhow? The following article excerpts provide some thoughts on the matter:

> When the Berlin Wall came tumbling down and the Soviet Union disintegrated, a new era of peace and prosperity seemed on the horizon. There was hope that the billions of dollars fueling the Cold War arms race could be channeled into the civilian economy, the much-anticipated peace dividend. But five years later, there is little talk of peace dividends or defense contractors converting to consumer products. The nuclear arms race between the two superpowers has ended, but regional conflicts from Bosnia to Rwanda to Sri Lanka have sparked races for conventional weapons from missiles, jet fighters, and tanks, to rifles, grenades, and land mines. While defense spending

by industrialized nations has been falling, total military spending in the developing world jumped 12 percent in 1990, and an additional 3 percent in 1991, hitting a new record high of $242 billion. A growing share of world arms sales goes to the Middle East, East Asia, and South Asia."

CQ Researcher goes on to further delineate the post-Cold War weapons proliferation problem.

The dangers posed by the covert sale or theft of U.S.-made arms has been heightened by what Michael T. Klare calls the "deadly convergence" of trends in the post-Cold War era, the rise of Third World military power such as Iraq and North Korea, together with a growing stockpile of sophisticated weapons including chemical and nuclear arms as well as conventional weapons. "With the large supplies of conventional weapons now stockpiled in their military arsenals," he writes, "many of the Third World countries are capable of conducting combat operations over wide areas and at very high levels of violence, levels that one would expect from a major conflict in Europe. Battles fought on such a scale would pose a threat of catastrophic defeat to one side or the other, prompting the loser to resort to chemical or even nuclear weapons to avert disaster. While still a remote possibility, this scenario represents the most plausible set of circumstances we can imagine today for the onset of a global nuclear war"

Shamefully, America seems chief among the hypocritical nations of the world who have continued to sell massive amounts of technology for war-making while calling for peace negotiations between warring factions around the world. The same issue of CQ Researcher points to that hypocrisy.

With defense firms from other nations cutting back on production, the United States has emerged as the undisputed leader in the vast international arms bazaar. The threat of regional conflicts around the globe has brought new buyers for fighter planes, tanks, missiles, and other conventional arms, especially developing countries in the Near East and East Asia. The Clinton administration, meanwhile, is dismaying arms control advocates by promoting exports of weaponry as part of its campaign to enhance U.S. industrial competitiveness.[5]

So the current American president nobly called for all combatants in such places as the former Yugoslavia to come to a settlement that will bring peace. He even used the recent occasion of the fiftieth-year anniversary of the bombings of Hiroshima and Nagasaki to unilaterally discontinue underground nuclear testing and to admonish the rest of the world nuclear powers to do the same. Yet at the same time the president treats arms sales — even to belligerence, in some cases — as merely a means to boost sales for American industry. Meanwhile, any hope of peace moves farther and farther beyond mankind's grasp.

It is painfully obvious that it is war, not peace, that rules the hearts and minds of man, just as God's Word says. Consider the facts about what has taken place during the post-Cold War era that politicians had promised would bring a peace dividend. Again, the CQ Reporter is the source.

> While most of the world's arms purchases have come from wealthier, developing countries in the Middle East and northern Africa, a remarkable $95 billion a year in arms purchases have been made by some of the world's poorest countries. And money spent on weapons is often money denied to important social services. India, for example, ordered 20 MIG-29 fighter aircraft from Russia in 1992 at a cost that would have provided basic education to all 15 million Indian girls without access to schooling. The same year, for the money it spent to buy 80 tanks from the United Kingdom, Nigeria could have immunized all 2 million of its unimmunized children and provided family planning services to 17 million couples. For the cost of 28 U.S. missiles, South Korea could have immunized its 120,000 untreated children and provided safe water for 3.5 million people for three years.[6]

To be fair, it must be said that nations, particularly poor nations, must often have at least a formidable show of force in order to discourage the belligerents who surround them from assaulting them. It is not always simple to separate defensive arms from offensive. Wise leadership in today's world have no choice but to be on the alert for those who would overrun them. While a perfect world would allow that all resources be applied to the needs and the comforts and even the desires of the populace, this fallen planet, if the hand of Almighty God was not upon it — and if not structured under governments backed up by arms — would no doubt devolve to the survival-of-the-fittest jungle long proposed by beasts such as Adolf Hitler.

It is strange but true that God's Word tells us just such a beast will one day come offering to make peace in what will in that day be the most volatile spot on Planet Earth, to be specific, the ancient city of Jerusalem. It will be a peace that will ultimately wreak total destruction upon a world that has rejected all of God's overtures to bring true, lasting peace through His Son, Jesus, who is the Prince of Peace. When the rider on the white horse of Revelation 6:2 makes a covenant with the prophet Daniel's people, the Jews, (Dan. 9:27) promising the beleaguered nation security and peace, God's cup will overflow with wrath. He is a holy, righteously jealous God who has loved His chosen people, yet they choose the beast to be their protector. Israel's contract with the devil will initiate the most horrendous time of trouble in all of humanity's turbulent history.

The Covenant with Death and Hell

Israel signing an agreement with Satan's man, the great political leader who will emerge from the nations that comprise the Roman Empire, will be a false peace which God's prophetic Word says will destroy many. The covenant of Daniel 9:27 is described by Isaiah the prophet as a pact made with death and hell. But it will not seem so at the outset of the peacemaking process when the beguiling man of Satan rides into Palestine on the white horse of promises (figuratively, of course). Evangelist Billy Graham gives some fascinating thoughts about this rider on the white horse of Revelation 6.

> Who is this rider on the white horse? Is this rider on the white horse Christ, as some have suggested? For centuries, biblical scholars and commentators have argued about the identity of this rider. You will note that he is wearing a crown of victory and carrying a bow of great destruction in his hand. In Revelation 19 Christ is pictured on a white horse wearing many crowns, and this has led some to believe that the rider on the white horse here in Revelation 6 is also Christ. However, after careful study I do not believe this to be the case.

The evangelist then gives his analysis.

> In the Greek language the crown worn by the rider of Revelation 6 is called stephanos, which was the crown of victory worn by a conqueror. The crowns Christ wears in Revelation 19, on the other hand, are diadema, or the crowns of royalty. Furthermore, although the rider on the white horse bears a resemblance to Christ, the appearance is actually deceptive because a deeper look reveals his true nature. He is "a conqueror bent on conquest," greedily riding roughshod over all who stand in his way in his lust for power.
>
> Who, therefore, is the rider on the white horse? He is not Christ, but a deceiver who seeks to capture the hearts and souls of men and women. He is one who seeks to have people acknowledge him as Lord instead of the true Christ.

Dr. Graham further portrays this coming man the Scriptures call the Beast.

> This rider's method is that of deception. He promises peace to the world, but it is a false peace. He will be a superman imposing a super system with an iron fist. Jesus said, "I have come in my Father's name, and you do not accept me; but if someone else comes in his own name, you will accept him" (John 5:43).
>
> The world that has rejected God's Christ is ready to receive the Devil's christ.
>
> The Bible teaches that sometime in the future there will be a great superman called the Antichrist. As we read in 1 John 2:18, "the antichrist is coming." On the other hand, previous to the actual Antichrist's coming, John prophesied there will be "the spirit of the antichrist" (1 John 4:3), and there will be "many antichrists" (1 John 2:18).[7]

When the rider on the white horse of Revelation 6 gallops into the spotlight on the world stage, it will be at a time in history that demands drastic action in order to bring a planet boiling with chaos under control. The Bible indicates that that spirit of Antichrist warned about in 1 John 2:18 will by this time be the prevailing spirit. It is my conviction based upon much prayer and study that the Church will no longer be a factor because Jesus Christ will have come to take all living believers home with Him to the Father's house in heaven. The rapture of Christ's Bride will leave the planet, for a time, void of Holy Spirit conviction that God, not humanistic effort, is the only answer to the deadly problems faced by earth's inhabitants.

As stated before, Israel, and Jerusalem in particular, will be the chief bone of contention sticking in the throats of all nations who will demand that Israel bow to the will of the majority. One man will at this point promise resolution that will satisfy the world and even the Israelis. The tiny state, surrounded on all sides by enemies spewing anti-Semitic vehemence, will acquiesce to their enemy's demands and welcome the promises offered by the great man who guarantees that the nation can live in peace and safety. Dr. Richard DeHaan gives an excellent overview of Israel's coming contract with the devil.

> The seven-year period still to come will include the appearance of a false prince and a time of terrible persecution for God's ancient people.
>
> "And he [that is, the false prince introduced in Dan. 9:26] shall confirm the covenant with many for one week; and in the midst of the week he shall cause the sacrifice and the oblation to cease, and for the overspreading of abominations he shall make it desolate, even until the consummation, and that determined shall be poured upon the desolate" (Dan. 9:27).
>
> The "he" in this verse refers to the coming false prince. His people (the Romans) destroyed Jerusalem and the temple in A.D. 70. As the head of the revived Roman Empire, he will make a seven-year pact with Israel. (Remember that these seventy "weeks" are related to Daniel's people and his holy city.) The Jews, or at least a representative group, will be in the land of Palestine. They will feel secure in their treaty with this powerful ruler, not knowing that he is the Antichrist of biblical prophecy. This evil man, who will first appear as a benevolent dictator, will honor the contract, but not for long — about three and one-half years. During that time a temple will be built by the Jews. They will also set up some form of worship. Suddenly, however, this world dictator will turn against them, and on the very wing of their own temple, he will erect an image which he will command them to worship. Daniel pre-

dicted, "And he shall confirm the covenant with many for one week; and in the midst of the week he shall cause the sacrifice and the oblation to cease, and for the overspreading of the abominations he shall make it desolate, even until the consummation, and that determined shall be poured upon the desolate" (Dan. 9:27).

The final words found in this verse, "for the overspreading of the abominations he shall make it desolate," are clearly related to a prophecy the Lord Jesus himself made concerning this abomination of desolation:

"When ye, therefore, shall see the abomination of desolation, spoken of by Daniel the prophet, stand in the holy place (whosoever readeth, let him understand), Then let them who are in Judea flee into the mountains" (Matt. 24:15-16).

Other Scripture passages, including 2 Thessalonians 2:4 and Revelation 13:14-18, indicate that Antichrist will erect an image and have it placed in the Jewish temple. Refusal to worship this idol will trigger a period of dreadful persecution, primarily for the Jews, but also for all inhabitants of the earth.

DeHaan then summarizes the Jewish plight during that future time of unprecedented trouble.

The seven future years of Daniel 9, therefore, will appear to begin favorably. The Jewish people will be assured of protection by the world dictator. But at the midpoint of this time period, they will begin to experience the most bitter and relentless persecution of their long history. This will be the Great Tribulation, spoken of by Jesus in Matthew 24 and described by John in Revelation.[8]

How Near is the Coming of Antichrist?

Again, I am absolutely persuaded through Scripture reading, prayer, and meditation upon God's Word that Christians of the present age will not be on earth at the time Satan's man, the Antichrist, deceives Israel and signs his covenant with that nation. This action will initiate the last seven years of man's rule on earth, ending with man's final war called Armageddon. Christians of the Age of Grace or the Church Age are promised to be kept out of the hour of this period of God's judgment upon a totally rebellious and incorrigible world.

Although this is true, there is much information in God's Word about the Antichrist, who is also called the Beast and the Man of Sin and the Man of Lawlessness. It is proper, I think, to perhaps speculate just a bit further on how near we might be to the coming to power of this, the earth's final fuhrer. Dr. J. Vernon McGee gave us such a fascinating speculation some years ago. When we look about us at all that has transpired since McGee's words were given, it is not far-fetched to conclude that Antichrist's advent is very near. Since we who are Christians are not to be looking for Antichrist but for Jesus Christ in His sudden appearing for us in the Rapture, it is thrilling to know that our Lord's coming is indeed imminent!

About earth's readiness for welcoming Satan's man on the white horse, McGee said:

> The Roman Empire is to be put together again. . . . We are told that [Antichrist] will put it back together again and he will march to world power and will become a world leader. We are told that he will blaspheme the God of heaven. That's found in Revelation 13:6, "He opened his mouth in blasphemy against God to blaspheme His name and His tabernacle and them that dwell in heaven." . . . Now is that a picture of Europe today? It certainly is. It was Dr. Sears of the University of Oklahoma, who after World War II, in fact it was in 1953, that he went through Europe and he said, "It's been less than a decade since the close of World War II with all of its death and destruction. But already," he says, "ample evidence exists that the peoples of Germany and even France are shopping around for the strongman type of leader like Hitler or Napoleon to restore these nations to the grandeur and glory and prosperity they once knew. . . ." Even a man like Fulton J. Sheen made this statement: "The Antichrist will come disguised as the great humanitarian. He'll talk peace, prosperity, and plenty, not as a means to lead us to God, but as ends in themselves. He will explain guilt away psychologically. Make men shrink in shame if their fellow men say they're not broadminded and liberal. He will spread the lie that men will never be better until they make society better. . . ." And the world today is moving in the direction when Europe will come together.

Dr. McGee pointed to the proof that Europe is advancing swiftly toward reunification of the sort that will produce a revived Roman Empire that will be the nucleus of Antichrist's kingdom.

> The young people of these nations like Italy, France, Germany, don't like to be called Germans or Italians or French. They like to be called Europeans today. What a psychological basis for the coming of Antichrist. All he would have to do now is just like ripe fruit hanging on a tree. He could pick it today if he came.[9]

What About the Fact that No Jewish Temple Exists for Antichrist to Desecrate?

Israel's attempt to build a temple on Mount Moriah where the Dome of the Rock now sits would no doubt at this point in time unify all Moslem antagonists into a jihad frenzy that would probably precipitate World War III. Realistic chances for rebuilding the Jewish temple seem to be very slight, yet all other signs tell us that we are most likely very near that moment in history when Antichrist will appear on the scene. God's Word tells us that the man of sin will cause the Jewish sacrifice and oblation rituals to cease and will actually desecrate the temple, much like Antiochus Epiphanes did to the Jewish temple prior to Christ's birth. Not only that, Antichrist will put an image in the temple and demand that all the world worship him as God. Since literally an avalanche of indicators point to the lateness of the hour, it seems appropriate to think about the rebuilding of a Jewish temple, something that must come to pass because God's Word treats the matter just as if it is already an accomplished fact.

Gary Hedrick of the Christian Jew Hour radio program recently said the following.

> This abomination of desolation [the Antichrist] must find its ultimate fulfillment in something that is yet future. You say that's impossible. How can the temple be desecrated when there is no temple? Good question. [Skeptics] used to have a lot to say about that before 1948. But do you know what? They don't have a lot to say about this anymore because now there's the state of Israel and for the first time in more than 2,500 years, the Jewish nation has jurisdiction over the Temple Mount. Even though they've allowed an Arab authority

to administer the area, it's still an Israeli territory.

There are exciting things taking place with regards to plans for rebuilding a temple. Hedrick gives the following report.

And now there are groups like the Temple Institute in Jerusalem and the Temple Mount Faithful who are actively working toward the eventual rebuilding of the Jerusalem temple. We were just there not long ago and had an opportunity to see the Temple Institute where they've reconstructed the temple altars and the lavers and the furnishings and tools and so on. We even saw the brooms and dustpans that will be used when the priests clean up the ashes from the burnt offerings, the burnt sacrifices. They've also woven the special priestly garments made according to the specifications given in the Book of Leviticus. You want to hear something interesting? Every year when we go to the Temple Institute, it seems like they've got something new they're working on. This year when we walked in there was an aquarium we've never seen before. Do you know why it's there? There's a special dye that is used in the priestly garments and the ancient formula from that dye includes an extract of a certain snail and they thought this particular snail had become extinct and they didn't know what they were going to do. But then they found some of them and brought them to Israel and now they're raising these special snails in an aquarium. Remarkable! So how can the Holy of Holies be desecrated during the Tribulation Period? The answer is the temple will be rebuilt! . . . Maybe that will be a part of the peace accord that will be mediated by the Antichrist. . . . Who knows what could happen? There are any number of possible scenarios. But the point is the stage is clearly being set right now for fulfillment of these remarkable end-time prophecies.[10]

Pressuring Israel Through the Peace Process

No nation on earth, including those regions that formerly made up Yugoslavia, receives more pressure to bend to the will of the global governing elite than Israel. Proof that the heat continues to be turned up on the tiny nation is easily found in the manner the state is being made to negotiate with perhaps her most vicious enemy, Hafez Assad of Syria. The dictator is generally acknowledged by truly informed observers of Middle Eastern leadership to be at least the equal to, and many say more beastly than, Iraq's Saddam Hussein in the matter of dealing treacherously with friends and foes alike. It apparently matters not that Assad has been known to, on more than one occasion, declare his intention to someday eradicate the hated state of Israel. World leaders and especially current American leadership demonstrate their absolute determination to force Israel's currently weak leadership to a bargaining table that includes giving back a number of crucial pieces of geography, including the Golan Heights, land they won from their avowed enemies who have attacked them on four occasions.

One newsmagazine article addressed Israel's dilemma when dealing with the Syrian leader while trying to appease the peace-at-any-price factions pressuring the nation.

> No amount of security arrangements can assure that a peace deal will hold up. Assad can't be trusted. Before 1967, Syrian forces on top of the Golan regularly shelled Israeli farms below. Assad has yet to make any public commitment to even seek peace. Just last week, he openly justified the killings of three Israeli soldiers in Lebanon. Syria insists that Israel withdraw to the 1949 armistice line inside Israel's actual international border. Assad still has a potent military, including chemical weapons and missiles to deliver them. And the threat is more than military. Many of Israel's all-important water resources are in easy grasp of Syrian control.

The article continues by giving interesting insight into Assad's true nature.

> Assad has cited the Zionist threat to justify his decades of one-man military rule. So a genuine peace with Israel would undermine a basic tenet of his basest regime and potentially jeopardize Assad's grip on power.

The article went on to state that America could not be trusted to keep the Clinton administration's promise that the United States will minimize Israeli risks with Syria should they give up the Golan Heights as part of a land-for-peace deal. Also, such an arrangement would mean up-rooting 11,000 Jewish settlers who live in the Golan area, most of whom don't want to leave.

American peace monitors would have to remain for years, if not decades, and Israel wants a U.S.-funded, $2 billion plus military package to compensate for loss of the Golan.[11]

The assassination of Prime Minister Yitzhak Rabin on November 4, 1995, has produced fascinating though, for Israel, potentially tragic possibilities. While Syria officially refuses to even join the peace process until Israel agrees to return the Golan Heights, as of this writing, the Hafez Assad-controlled Syrian press lauds Shimon Peres for his willingness to put everything belonging to Israel on the negotiating table, including the Golan Heights.

What is most dramatically illustrated is that Israel is now doing something of great prophetic significance. The Peres government is seriously thinking about permanent peace arrangements that depend upon an outside party or parties guaranteeing Israel's security in exchange for letting down the nation's guard. Popular sympathy for the slain Rabin seems to throw fuel on the emotional fires that burn between those who insist upon peace through strength and those who cry for peace at any price.

Hal Lindsey addressed this formerly almost unthinkable situation.

> If they give up the land they're talking about now, even if they don't give up the Golan Heights, they still are in a position where their airfields are in very easy range of modern, accurate artillery. So they would never get their reserve army mustered together in time to meet an imminent threat. So this means two things. Number one: Israel must find a power strong enough with whom they can make an alliance that guarantees their security. But does that sound familiar? Daniel 9:27 says that's exactly what will happen when the Israelis make a strong covenant guaranteeing their security with this great leader out of Rome, and we know him as the Antichrist. So in other words, Israel, if this present peace accord continues, has set herself up to where she will have to seek out this pact guaranteeing her security.

Lindsey went on to point out the second ramification of letting down Israel's guard by giving up the Golan.

> If this peace accord does hold, it absolutely guarantees a nuclear war in the Middle East. And some of the keenest intelligence sources in the world have said that they believe there will be a nuclear holocaust in the Middle East before the end of the century if this peace accord does hold and Israel does give up the West Bank.[12]

Why do the experts believe that giving up the West Bank and the Golan in particular will automatically mean nuclear conflict in the Middle East? Simply because the loss of those strategic parcels of land will render Israel's conventional defensive military capability inadequate to stave off attacks such as those the nation has endured since 1948. If one discounts the miracles performed by God such as those when 4 million Jews could defeat more than 225 million Arabs in 1948, 1956, 1967, 1973, and 1982, Israel's only chance for survival if they give up the areas in question will be to launch their nuclear arsenal or else be overrun.

Is the present process of attempting to negotiate peace in the Middle East that which will fulfill Daniel 9:27 and thereby initiate the seven years tribulation period? Noted author and prophecy scholar Grant Jeffrey recently addressed that question.

> I believe the Jerusalem covenant cannot be the covenant referred to in Daniel 9:27 because the Jerusalem covenant is an affirmation by Jewish communities around the world that Jerusalem shall remain indivisible. The Antichrist covenant of Daniel 9:27 is clearly a covenant made by a leader of the Gentile kingdoms, although I believe the Antichrist himself will be Jewish . . . and it's a covenant for seven years. The Jerusalem covenant has no date on it at all.

Jeffrey explains further why he believes the current peace accord process cannot be the contract Israel makes with Satan.

> I believe that this covenant has not yet been made. The Palestinian-Israeli agreement in September of '93 is not that agreement. Antichrist must arise, take over the nations of Europe, consolidate rule, then make a seven-

year treaty that has to still be in the future. And I think when it happens, it will be very plain. We could still be here to see that. We could see the beginning stages of that right up to the point . . . that the treaty is signed. [Christians] will be gone, I believe, before the treaty is signed, because that commences the seven-year tribulation period, the time of Jacob's trouble. Though we could see the initial stages, the rise of the kingdoms, we could see even a man come forward [the one who will be Antichrist] before this happens.[13]

God's Final Say in the Matter

The many prophetic events and arrangements gushing into confluence upon today's geopolitical, socioeconomic, religious, and technological world scene cannot but convince the serious observer of biblically predicted end-time matters that the time of Jacob's trouble draws near. Thus, Israel's covenant made with death and hell must be close at hand.

The European Union threatens to swamp even the United States in the wake of its great and growing economic power movement. Russia has made pacts with Islamic belligerents such as Iran and others and continues to, out of necessity, court unstable radical Muslim leaders, all of which begins to look suspiciously like the Ezekiel 38 and 39 Gog/Magog confederation. The Asian and Pacific Rim countries, soon to be dominated in spirit if not through military control by the awakened giant, China, seem to be quickly coming together in a power bloc very closely resembling that described in God's prophetic Word as Kings of the East. Likewise, similar developments in Africa, Egypt, and other places within the region point to a time perhaps not far distant when a power bloc described in biblical terms as being led by the King of the South will become prophecy fulfilled. All these developments point directly at Israel, and specifically at Jerusalem, the apple of God's eye. The tiny state sits almost precisely centered between the behemoths that pressure her from all sides.

Daniel 9:7 tells that when the pressure becomes too great to bear, Israel will call on an outside force for protection. That force will not be the God of Abraham, Isaac, and Jacob, who has overseen Israel's destiny since He first determined to bring that nation into existence. Israel will call on the western kingdom and sign the covenant with its leader, Antichrist. But God Almighty is a righteously jealous God and will not allow this contract made with the devil to stand.

Isaiah 28:18 gives God's final word on the matter. "Your covenant with death shall be annulled and your agreement with Sheoul will not stand."

7

Russia's Fatal Thrust to the South

by Chuck Missler

Oslo II was signed at the White House recently. As we have maintained all along, the entire charade of the "peace process" is doomed to failure since it is built on false premises. It assumes that reducing the size of Israel will appease the Muslim hostility. The underlying issue is not the size of Israel — it is the existence of Israel.

The press called me and asked me to react to Clinton's comment, "We are writing a new chapter in history. . . ."

I pointed out that this is the first time in the history of the current administration that Clinton said anything that I can agree with. The "chapter" they are writing, however, is Ezekiel 38.

The so-called "Peace Accord" guarantees a war in the Middle East. By reducing the borders of Israel it denies them a conventional response to an attack and virtually forces them into a nuclear option.

A Burdensome Stone

Zechariah 12 indicates that the entire world will find itself troubled over the city of Jerusalem. On the face of it, that seems ridiculous. Here is a city with no harbor, no natural resources, no reason to be significant to a secular, materialistic, pragmatic world. Yet today every major capital ponders what to do about the issue of Jerusalem. The pressure of Muslim oil overrules any other value judgments.

Zechariah indicates that the day is coming when the entire world will go to war — a climactic war — over Jerusalem. And the preparations have begun.

Robert Hunter, our ambassador to NATO, in a private meeting at NATO Headquarters in Brussels, confided that "A nuclear war in the Middle East is certain — not just likely. The only question is one of timing."

Rear Admiral Ed Shafer, Director of Naval Intelligence, is quoted as saying, "Somewhere, sometime — but in this decade — someone is going to use a nuclear weapon in earnest."

Russia's "Final March to the South"

Vladimir Zhirinovsky almost seems to have some sense of Russia's place in God's prophetic plan for human history. His book, *Russia's Final March South*, indicates a ravenous desire to mount an invasion into Palestine that very nearly parallels the Ezekiel 38 and 39 scenario. He might just as well have titled such a blueprint *Russia's Fatal Thrust to the South*. Only it will be fatal to the Russian-led Magog force — not to the intended victim Israel.

The more you know about the Ezekiel 38 and 39 passage and the more you know about the current intelligence information involving the Middle East, the more you believe that this battle could happen at any moment. Take the time and energy to get into those chapters seriously. Get whatever helps and resources you have at your disposal. And keep your antenna up as to what's going on in the world.

For many years I was puzzled by the increased strength and power, the tide, the glacier coming that was the Soviet Union. It looked so strong. There was a time that it was so formidable. It had a military substantially larger than ours. But many of us who observe these things were puzzled because prophecy does not speak of a Soviet empire. I presumed that somehow God would stop what was afoot.

I had no idea how quickly things would change. The breakup of the Soviet Union set the stage for Ezekiel 38 in some surprising ways. The Soviet Union consists of 15 republics that embrace over 110 ethnic minorities. Most of these minorities are/were tribal groups. The largest of the 15 republics, of course, is/was the Russian Federation. But it also included/includes a group of republics to the south — five republics of Central Asia that are key to the Ezekiel 38 passage: Kazakhstan, Turkmenistan, Tadzhikistan, Uzbekistan, and Kirgystan, as it's called now.

Kazakhstan is the world's fourth-largest nuclear power, and home of the Baikonur Cosmodrome, the primary space facility of the former Soviet Union. Many of the current space launches have been moved north of their former launch sites because of the harassment of the Kazakhs. The army's trying to protect its supplies and maintain its base, but Kazakhistan, like so many of these republics, is getting very anxious to establish its independence.

The role of these Central Asian countries is little known or understood in regard to their importance in the make-up of the Soviet Union apart from an in-depth study of history. Most of us have grown up knowing the Soviet Union as a whole, but have not understood it in terms of its component parts. The Central Intelligence Agency was badly embarrassed because when the Soviet Union broke up into pieces, the CIA had no databases for the five crucial republics in the southern part — Kazakhstan, Turkmenistan, Uzbekistan, Tadzhikistan, and Kirgystan.

These republics, which I believe will be home to those people who will participate in the Magog invasion, have three things in common: (1) They don't have hard currency to buy food to feed their people. (2) They do have nuclear weapons. (3) They are Muslims. It doesn't take a lot of imagination to realize that they're in a position to trade nuclear material for the things they desperately need to survive. And who are they going to do it with? Their Muslim brethren. So you can see the plot starting to unfold.

Ezekiel's Invasion Prediction

Almost anyone who has had a serious interest in prophecy has had occasion to explore, at least at some level, Ezekiel 38 and 39. God's Word tells us in that account that the people who live in the land called Magog under the leadership of one called Gog, along with a group of allies listed there, are going to embark on an invasion of the nation Israel. This passage is famous among scholars for two reasons. First, it's the occasion that God uses to intervene on behalf of Israel. These invading forces are in for a major surprise. They get, in our vernacular, decimated by the Lord himself. Second, it appears from the language, especially in chapter 39, that the technology may indeed involve the use of nuclear weapons.

Role of Islam

In this regard, we must recognize the role of Islam, which has an openly avowed commitment to attempt to subjugate the Planet Earth by the sword, if necessary. First on its agenda are the Jews. But it doesn't stop there. Second on its agenda are the Christians. Militant Islam is the fastest-growing religion in the world, with more than 1.2 billion followers. The leadership of Islam has announced they believe Islam is replacing Marxism as the ideology of the future because, they say, they have the resources (oil revenues and nuclear weapons) to disconnect the Middle East from its Judeo-Christian world order. We cannot ignore that agenda in view of the resources they now command.

The prophet Ezekiel reports God's words to Gog, the Russian leader, at the time of the Magog invasion: "Be thou prepared, and prepare for thyself, thou, and all thy company that are assembled unto thee, and be thou a guard unto them" (Ezek. 38:7). He gives us a list of which tribes will join in the thrust southward toward Israel. These include most, if not all, hostile Islamic nations of the region. Who will lead them? Magog. Who will supply them with military material? Magog. Russia is desperately dependent upon its export of oil — it is the largest producer of oil in the world — and of military weapons.

So we have portrayed in Ezekiel an invasion led by Russia after Israel has been regathered into the land from many nations. The lead ally is listed as Persia, now Iran (who is joined by the non-Arab Islamic countries of the region). The Arabs are on the sideline, fearful of what they see happening. Sheba and Dedan are portrayed in the Ezekiel account as nervously observing the events. From Isaiah 11:11 we know that the Jews are regathered a second and final time. The first time was after Babylon; the second time is what's been going on for the last 40 or 50 years. So if you look at the battle carefully and enumerate the details as they're provided by Scripture, you know it could not have happened in history. Many scholars superficially say, "Well, that happened way back whenever." But it's not true. It doesn't fit the facts of history or of the text. So this is something yet future.

Timing of the Invasion

Ezekiel 38: 8 says, "After many days thou shalt be visited; in the latter years thou shalt come into the land that is brought back from the sword, and is gathered out of many peoples, against the mountains of Israel, which have been always waste; but it is brought forth out of the nations, and they shall dwell safely, all of them." This is the next issue we're going to address: the timing of this battle. The three major views about the timing of the Gog-Magog engagement are as follows:

1. *After the Millennium* — Gog and Magog happen to be

mentioned in Revelation 20 after the Millennium, so some scholars try to place this battle there. However, it doesn't fit there because it's clearly *before* the Messiah comes back, thousands of years *before* the Millennium.

2. *Part of the Armageddon scenario* — The more classic placement of this by many prophecy experts is as part of the Armageddon scenario. Many scholars link the tribes of the North in Daniel 11 with Magog and place this engagement in the last part of the seventieth week of Daniel. For a number of reasons, I'm among those who believe that this battle *precedes* the seventieth week of Daniel, and maybe by some distance. In fact, I hold the view from my study of the text and from my awareness of current intelligence estimates, that this battle can happen at any moment. The more you know about this passage and the more you're up to date on what's going on in the Middle East, the more you can see all elements getting positioned. I'm not saying it *will* happen soon; I'm saying it *could* happen on the near horizon. And that has some staggering implications for all of us.

Now, when does this happen? Scripture says, "In the latter years [in other words, the end-times] thou shalt come into the land that is brought back from the sword, and is gathered out of many peoples, against the mountains of Israel" (Ezek. 38:8). In other words, "You're going to come against the mountains of Israel." When? When it's been brought back after being desolate so many years. For that and lots of other reasons, you'll see that this is contemporary; it's not something that has happened in the past.

3. *Past history* — Another view that's held by some is that this all happened with some event in past history. But that couldn't possibly be true, because it's associated with the second coming of Jesus Christ, as you'll see. This is an end-time prophecy yet to happen and it will happen.

This invasion will follow Israel's regathering into the land. That's exciting, because what's been going on for the last 40 or 50 years? *The regathering of Israel in the land.* What was desol .e waste is now the fourth-largest exporter of fruit in the world. A country that's a third the size of San Bernardino County in California is now one of the largest exporters of fruit to the world.

"And they shall dwell safely, all of them" (Ezek. 38:8). The word "safely" appears at least three or four times here. Because of the fact that they're apparently dwelling "safely," some experts place this battle at a time when Israel is a beneficiary of the peace treaty with the

Antichrist. That's another reason they place the battle within the seventieth week of Daniel.

Well, first of all, the word "dwelleth safely" is the Hebrew word "batach." It occurs 162 times in the Old Testament. In 130 of those times, it's used "securely," as a state of mind. Translate that "false confidence." Are they dwelling securely? No, they're about to be invaded. So whereas the Hebrew says that they're dwelling "safely," the English would say that means they're "secure." No. They feel secure — and indeed they may feel secure because of some treaties, but not necessarily because of the treaty that is enforced by the coming new world order. That's a technicality that we'll deal with subsequently.

> Thou shalt ascend and come like a storm; thou shalt be like a cloud to cover the land, thou, and all thy hordes, and many peoples with thee. Thus saith the Lord God: It shall also come to pass that at the same time shall things come into thy mind, and thou shalt think an evil thought [this is God speaking to Gog and Magog]; And thou shalt say, I will go up to the land of unwalled villages [bear in mind, Ezekiel probably never saw a village that wasn't walled]; I will go to those who are at rest, who dwell safely, all of them dwelling without walls. and having neither bars nor gates, To take a spoil, and to take a prey; to turn thy hand upon the desolate places that are now inhabited, and upon the people that are gathered out of the nations [notice the plural; this is not the regathering after Babylon, but the regathering out of the diaspora, the whole world], who have gotten cattle and goods, who dwell in the midst of the land. Sheba, and Dedan, and the merchants of Tarshish, with all its young lions, shall say unto thee, Art thou come to take a spoil? Hast thou gathered thy company to take a prey, to carry away silver and gold, to take away cattle and goods, to take a great spoil? (Ezek. 38:9-13).

In other words, Sheba and Dedan and the young lions of Tarshish (whoever they are), are saying, "Naughty, naughty. You shouldn't be doing that." Sheba and Dedan are apparently present-day Saudi Arabia. Today, fitting almost exactly the terrified mindset Ezekiel's prophecy predicts for Sheba and Dedan at the time of the Magog invasion, Saudi's leadership is fearful because we see the

Shi'ites, under the leadership of Rafsanjani of Iran, organizing an "Islamic Crescent" — from the 200 million Muslims in Indonesia, all the way to Muritania and Senegal. Rafsanjani is armed to the teeth with nuclear weapons and a modern air force. As he practices maneuvers, the analysts observing through the reconnaissance satellites are puzzled by the fact that he's practicing amphibious operations under conditions of contamination. That's a tip-off as to what part of his strategy is: his strategy includes the invasion of Saudi Arabia.

Why would he do that? Aren't they're Muslims? Yes. But (1) they're Sunnis, not Shi'ites; and (2) they did the unpardonable sin in Islam: They allowed their real estate to be used by the West against their Muslim brethren during Desert Storm. And more importantly, Rafsanjani, in order to build this Islamic crescent, has to control the holy site, Mecca and Medina. So the House of Saud is on a slippery rock and they know it. That's why for 12 years we've secretly armed them to the teeth to try to establish a balance of power. No wonder Sheba and Dedan are on the sidelines, nervous, as they watch this growing horde. Also, Yeltsin has signed a treaty with Rafsanjani to back Iran in their military intrigues. And that treaty may be the "hook in the jaw" that sucks them into this ill-fated venture.

"Therefore, son of man, prophesy and say unto Gog, Thus saith the Lord God: In that day when my people of Israel dwell safely, shalt thou not know it? And thou shalt come from thy place out of the north parts, thou, and many peoples with thee, all of them riding upon horses, a great company, and a mighty army" (Ezek. 38:14-15). The word, "north parts" in verse 15 actually translates to "the uttermost parts of the north." So even if you don't understand any of this background, all you have to do is take a globe, put your finger on Israel, and go as far north as you can. What do you run into? Russia. Just from the geographical description, you can figure out who Magog is.

A key insight comes out in the following verse: "And thou shalt come up against my people of Israel, like a cloud to cover the land; it shall be in the latter days, and I will bring thee against my land, that the nations may know me, when I shall be sanctified in thee, O Gog, before their eyes" (Ezek. 38:16). "My land," God says. Not the land of the Palestinians. Not the land of the U.N. Who owns this piece of real estate? The God of our universe does. You might be saying, "Well, gee, 'The earth is the Lord's and the fullness thereof.' " Absolutely. And yet, if you study your Bible from Genesis through

Revelation, you discover that the Creator of the universe has carved out a piece of real estate that's His own.

One of the most important concepts for you to recognize as you study your Bible is that God's dealings with Israel and with the Church are, in a sense, mutually exclusive. They have different origins, different missions, different destinies. Don't confuse Israel and the Church. When God says "they will come up against my people Israel," that indicates that this passage is post-Church.

As biblical Christians, our posture with respect to Israel is widely misunderstood. God is intervening in the Magog invasion not for Israel's sake but for His own sake. In Ezekiel 36:19, God's speaking of Israel:

> And I scattered them among the nations, and they were dispersed through the countries [that's, of course, speaking of the diaspora which has lasted a better part of 2,000 years]; according to their way and according to their doings, I judged them. And when they entered unto the nations, to which they went, they profaned my holy name, when they said to them, These are the people of the Lord, and are gone forth out of his land. But I had pity for mine holy name, which the house of Israel had profaned among the nations, to which they went. Therefore, say unto the house of Israel, Thus sayeth the Lord God: I do not this for your sakes, O house of Israel, but for mine holy name's sake, which ye have profaned among the nations, to which ye went. And I will sanctify my great name, which was profaned among the nations, which ye have profaned in the midst of them; and the nations shall know that I am the Lord, saith the Lord God, when I shall be sanctified in you before their eyes (Ezek. 36:19-23).

When Russia and the Muslim allies invade Israel, it is not Israel, but rather the holiness of God that is at issue, so to speak. He said He was going to do something, so it's His reputation that's on the line. They can keep poking their finger in His eye until a point at which He says, "Enough's enough." Boy, it's coming down, and coming down big. Israel is the beneficiary of that intervention, but the reason He's doing it isn't because Israel deserves it — it's because His reputation is on the line. He told the heathen He was going to do it, and He's going to prove that you don't mess around with the God of the universe.

A Close Look

"And it shall come to pass that at the same time when Gog shall come against the land of Israel, saith the Lord God, that my fury shall come up in my face" (Ezek. 38:18). This is the God of the universe talking. What a phrase. "That my fury shall come up in my face." You can almost see Him. "For in my jealousy and in the fire of my wrath have I spoken, Surely in that day there shall be a great shaking in the land of Israel" (Ezek. 38:19).

You want to talk earthquakes? Look at verse 20. I don't know what this is on the Richter scale, but I'll bet it's a record! "So that the fish of the sea, and the fowls of the heavens, and the beasts of the field, and all creeping things that creep upon the earth, and all the men that are upon the face of the earth, shall shake at my presence, and the mountains shall be thrown down, and the steep places shall fall, and every wall shall fall to the ground." Now that's an earthquake!

"And I will call for a sword against him throughout all my mountains, saith the Lord God; every man's sword shall be against his brother. And I will enter into judgment against him with pestilence and with blood; and I will rain upon him, upon his hordes, and upon many people that are with him, an overflowing rain, and great hailstones, fire, and brimstone. Thus will I magnify myself, and sanctify myself; and I will be known in the eyes of many nations, and they shall know that I am the Lord" (Ezek. 38:21-23). That's heavy stuff. Magog is going to get it.

The Battlefield Cleanup

Chapter 39 is a strange chapter. As you study biblical battles in the Bible, one thing you'll notice all the way through is that "A" goes against "B." Somebody wins and somebody loses, and then the story goes on. These battles usually involve Israel. If Israel's in fellowship with the Lord and obedient, she wins against incredible odds. In other cases where she has screwed up, she gets clobbered. No place in the Scripture that I can find describes the Holy Spirit bothering to deal with the cleanup after the battle. However, in this particular case, the Holy Spirit devotes the better part of a whole chapter to detailing the cleanup after the battle.

Since I believe that nothing in the Scripture is trivial or acciden- tal and that it's all there by design, I believe the Holy Spirit is trying make a specific point in chapter 39. I'm going to suggest as my hypothesis that the reason He gives interesting details about the cleanup is to communicate to you twenty-first-century technology in sixth-century B.C. vocabulary.

> Therefore thou son of man, prophesy against Gog, and say, Thus saith the Lord God: Behold, I am against thee, O Gog, the chief prince of Meshech and Tubal, And I will turn thee back, and leave but the sixth part of thee, and will cause thee to come up from the north parts, and will bring thee upon the mountains of Israel (Ezek. 39:1-2).

Some people say, "Five-sixths of them are going to get wiped out." If I say I'm going to decimate you, that technically means reduce you to one-tenth. But we use the term to mean just "wipe out." So He says "I will sixth thee." That might mean that only one-sixth will be left, or it may be idiomatic of saying, "You guys are going to get clobbered. I'm going to decimate you guys."

"And I will smite thy bow out of thy left hand, and cause thine arrows to fall out of thy right hand" (Ezek. 39:3). Under the "Missler translation," this means, "I will smite thy launcher out of thy left hand and cause thy missiles to fall out of thy right."

> Thou shalt fall upon the mountains of Israel, thou, and all thy hordes, and the peoples that are with thee; I will give thee unto the ravenous birds of every sort, and to the beasts of the field to be devoured. Thou shalt fall upon the open field; for I have spoken it, saith the Lord God. And I will send fire on Magog, and among those who dwell securely in the coastlands; and they shall know that I am the Lord. So will I make my holy name known in the midst of my people, Israel, and I will not let them pollute my holy name any more; and the nations shall know that I am the Lord, the Holy One in Israel (Ezek. 39:4-7).

God is declaring, "Enough is enough."

> Behold, it is come, and it is done, saith the Lord God; this is the day of which I have spoken. And they that dwell in the cities of Israel shall go forth, and shall set on fire and burn the weapons, both the shields and the bucklers, the bows and the arrows, and the handspikes, and the spears, and they shall burn them with fire seven years, So that they shall take no wood out of the field, neither cut down any out

of the forests; for they shall burn the weapons with fire; and they shall spoil those that spoiled them, and rob those that robbed them, saith the Lord God (Ezek. 39:8-10).

In other words, the weapons left over after the battle is completed will supply all the energy needs of Israel for seven years. Ancient commentators say, "It's obviously symbolic because nothing can burn for seven years." But today we smile at that quaint myopia. What technology used in weapons today can indeed supply the energy needs of a whole city or nation? Nuclear, of course! Another point you need to understand about a nuclear weapon — as you read the papers and discover there are 43,000 in the Soviet arsenal that are now in the black market — is that a nuclear warhead has a limited shelf life. Most of us think they are permanent. But on the contrary, the effectiveness of a nuclear weapon is dependent upon the very delicate geometry. Depending on its impurities, you have to reprocess the material on some turnover basis. A friend of mine in the Pentagon sent me a copy of the U.S. Naval Institute proceedings in April of 1992, and marked the passage from which you can infer the shelf life of production Soviet warheads. Guess what? It's seven years. (They reprocess the material on a six-year rollover.) One reason the Ukraine has been so gracious in returning the nuclear weapons that were left there is that they've expired. You won't find that in the papers. By the way, there's another implication of the nuclear weapon's limited potency. If you're Rafsanjani of Iran or Assad of Syria, or Daffy Khadafi of Libya, and you acquire a production Soviet warhead, you can either "use it or lose it." These things, in effect, are ticking.

"And it shall come to pass in that day, that I will give unto Gog a place there of graves in Israel, the valley of the travelers on the east of the sea; and it shall stop the noses of the travelers, and there shall they bury Gog and all his multitude; and they shall call it the Valley of Hamon-gog" (Ezek. 39:11). Notice the procedure. Verses 12-14: "And seven months shall the house of Israel be burying, them that they may cleanse the land, Yea, all the people of the land shall bury them; and it shall be to their reknown on the day that I shall be glorified, saith the Lord God. And they shall set apart men for the continual task of passing through the land to bury, with the help of the travelers, those that remain upon the face of the land, to cleanse it; after the end of seven months shall they make their search."

What appears to be the intent of the text is that they wait seven months before entering the area, then they spend seven months clearing the area. Who do they use? They hire professionals, in effect.

The Holy Spirit doesn't stop there. "And the travelers that pass through the land, when any seeth a man's bone, then shall he set up a sign by it, till the buriers have buried it in the Valley of Hamon-gog" (Ezek. 39:15). In other words, if, after the professionals have completed their contract, those who go on a tour of Israel look across a field, and spot a bone that the professionals missed, they don't touch it. They mark its location and let the professionals come and deal with it. And what do they do with all this stuff? They bury it east of the Dead Sea. Read that "downwind."

You can also find this procedure detailed, in effect, in the operator's manual for "Marking Set Contamination Nuclear Biological Chemical," NBC 9905-12-124-5955, a technical manual published by the headquarters, Department of the Army, United States Department of the Defense. Those of you who are in the military who have been briefed on Nuclear, Biological, Chemical Warfare (NBC) know the drill.

I'm in a very strange eschatological position. Because of the numerous contacts around the world which feed our newsletter, and our intelligence operations which try to highlight the biblical relevance of current events, we try to track the latest developments involving preparations for the Magog invasion pretty closely. The more we track these matters, the more it would seem that things are rapidly moving in the direction of Ezekiel 38 happening soon. I don't mean "next Tuesday," I just mean soon. On the horizon. But if I'm correct in my understanding of the passage, then the *Rapture* has to happen first.

Intelligence Update

The future for the Middle East, and for the world, looks nothing short of frightening when considering what is going on in arms dealings throughout the region. Kazakhstan has supplied Iran with a number of nuclear weapons on the black market. Both Russia and China are installing nuclear plants in Iran. These are, of course, for "peaceful use," they say. I'm a little cynical about that.

In that vein, I should also point out that there are 14,000 former Soviet warheads that they can't account for; they can't find them. Some of this is because of sloppy bookkeeping; some have been stolen by various crime syndicates. These are a very marketable commodity in today's black market world. Of course, most try to find their way into the Middle East. So it's getting to be an increasingly tense time.

Let's back up a little bit and talk about Russia's basic strategic dilemma. If you were in Russia, you would have a major problem. Russia has to build a new power base. It is a commodity-oriented economy, heavily dependent on the export of raw materials, primarily oil. In fact, it's the largest oil producer in the world. Russia also depends heavily on the sale of arms. Sales this last year went up 40 percent and they're at about 15 to 20 percent of their capacity.

As you look west, you see a European union heavily dominated by Germany but consisting primarily of former enemies. Despite the rhetoric, despite the political maneuvers, that's the reason NATO was formed: because of the fear of Russia. No one wants to talk in those terms today, but the fear is still there despite the shambles and the problems in Russia. In fact, the instability in Russia today makes it more dangerous than ever.

When I had the opportunity to get an inside briefing at NATO's headquarters in Brussels, our assistant secretary of defense, Robin Beard and our ambassador at NATO, Robert Hunter, both admitted that they regard a nuclear event in the Middle East as inevitable. And they're also concerned about Russia since they have no idea what safeguards are in place to prevent an accident. When the Soviet Union was in place, it was powerful and ruthless, but very organized. We knew the procedures that had to be invoked before an event could take place. Now we don't have any idea even who has the button. In fact, the current information in Russia is that we're not even sure who is running things.

And as Russia looks east, it sees China and Japan, both traditional enemies and both of them getting together. There's nothing to the north.

So economic pressures force Russia to look south to build a new power base. Its strategy for doing so is to embrace the radical Muslims, primarily through Iran. A lot of misinformation is floating around about the nature of Islam. I'm going to suggest to you that most of what you probably have heard is incorrect.

The Rise of Islam

Islam's Beginnings — First, you need to realize that Islam *did not begin with Mohammed.* The main practices of Islam were in place centuries before Mohammed was even born. The chief religion in the Ur of the Chaldeans when Abraham was called out in Genesis 12 was the worship of the moon god, one of 360 idols that they worshiped in the Ka'aba. He was, in Arabic, *Al-Ilah*, the moon god, and his symbol was the crescent moon. *Al-Ilah* becomes Allah ("the god") long before Mohammed; even the name of his father, Abd-allah, attests to the name of Allah.

The keeping of the Ka'aba was entrusted to the Quraysh tribe into which Mohammed was born, so he grew up in that culture. Mohammed's contribution was making this pagan worship *monotheistic*. But it has still remained occultic since its origins.

Islam's Occultic Nature — Secondly, you need to understand its occultic nature. You have to understand that its *jinns* (genies) are demon spirits. You need to realize that most of the practices that characterize Islam were in place long before the sixth-century Arabia of Mohammed's day.

I encourage you to find out what Islam is really all about. As you get into this, you'll discover that Islam is far more than a religion — it's a whole way of life. It's a whole legal system. It's a whole cultural base. It really imposes sixth-century Arabia on its followers. But the point is, Islam divides the world, the entire universe, into only two parts. *Dar Al Islam*: the domain of the faithful to Islam; and *Dar Al Harb*: those with whom they are at war until the judgment day. The militancy of Islam is not directed only at the Jews. They're just first on the agenda.

When Mohammed packaged his religion, he had, for his own reasons, expected the Jews to embrace it and he was really upset when they didn't. So he harbored a deep hostility towards Judaism. He regarded the Christians as just uninformed or ignorant. But his agenda was the Jews first, the *Christians next*.

The goal of Islam is the subjugation of the Planet Earth — by the sword, if necessary. In the past, most of us in the West dismissed all this as incidental history. Most of us regard it as just a cultural tradition of the Middle East. But Islam is the fastest growing religion on earth, and it has a well-financed, aggressive growth movement afoot. There are already 1,100 mosques in the United States. There are more Muslims in the United States than there are Jews. More than 900 churches in Great Britain have been converted to mosques.

The leaders in Islam believe that Islam will replace Marxism as the ideology of the future. They believe they now have the resources (meaning cash flow from their oil sales and possession of nuclear weapons) to disconnect the Middle East from the Judeo-Christian order of the past. They are militantly, aggressively pursuing that.

Two main branches comprise the world of Islam: the Sunnis and the Shi'ites. The Shi'ites are the more radical and aggressive ones. The Shi'ite opposition is starting major protests in Bahrain. They've sparked major riots in a dozen cities. Evidence indicates that Iran has been financing all of these activities. Bahrain is ruled by the Sunnis, but about 60 percent of the population are Shi'ites. From London we hear that about 2,500 people have been detained in special prison camps in the desert and Bahrain's trying to put down the Shi'ite agitation that radicals are starting. Shifting to northern Iraq, the Kurds are starting to fight and Saddam Hussein is sending troops north to deal with them.

Our bases in Turkey that support the "no-fly zone" in Iraq are no longer likely to stay open to us. If you look south from Saudi Arabia, you've got Yemen. There, too, clashes have been going on for 60 years and are intensifying. Yemin appears to be a small country, but the populations are not that different. About 13 million people live in Yemin and about 17 million live in Saudi Arabia. Of course, Saudi Arabia is hoping for a war of attrition, but the net of it is that they're all coming to arms.

So within the Arab world we find these tensions. And again, the radicals, the extremists, are generally of the Shi'ite background. Many of the Muslim nations are run by Sunnis, but they're all on slippery rocks. The radicals are pushing.

Of course, one of the primary leaders in the Muslim world is Iran. Rafsanjani, the president of Iran, is one of the main leaders. He has announced his dream of creating an Islamic Crescent, uniting all the Moslems from Indonesia to Senegal and Muritania. In Indonesia, by the way, there are 200 million Muslims. If you go through the whole crescent, you're talking about approximately 1.2 billion followers.

You'll notice if you watch the news that Muslims are increasingly resorting to suicide attacks. For example, a bus was hit by a suicide bomber. When everybody gathered around to rescue the victims of the bombing, another suicide bomber hit them. If you're a Moslem and die in the cause of Allah, you automatically go to heaven. That's an interesting motivational technique they've developed!

In Ezekiel 38:5-6, which lists Magog's allies, we see Persia, or Iran, mentioned first. In Scripture, lists are usually sorted with the most significant entries near the top. Today, Iran is the leader of the so-called Grand Design, pushing a heavy aviation agenda — they spent more than $14 billion on their air force in the last several years. Remember the 115 aircraft that fled Iraq during the war in the Persian Gulf? Where did they go? To Iran. And of course, Iran is also starting to build up its naval force. That's why the Arabs are so nervous. What do you use submarines for? Laying mines, among other things. In the Persian Gulf, you don't need range.

The Arabs are not in the list of allies in this invasion. As you go through Ezekiel 38:5-6, you'll find Muslims but not Arabs. The Arabs show up in verse 13: Sheba and Dedan. They're on the sidelines, nervous. Why are they nervous? Because Rafsanjani is practicing amphibious operations under conditions of contamination, and the reconnaissance satellite surveillance makes it very clear that that's one of the things he's preparing for, and he doesn't have to do that to invade Israel. It implies that somewhere along the way, he's planning to invade Saudi Arabia. Why? They are Muslims. Well, yes, but with a huge difference. They are Sunni. They are of a different, less fanatical variety of the Islamic faith than Rafsanjani and his followers. Saudi Arabia controls the holy sites of Mecca and Medina. Rafsanjani, if he is to become the real leader of the Islamic world, must wrench control of these holy places from the Sunni sect. So somewhere in the scheme of things, he's planning to invade Saudi Arabia.

Most of us tend to overlook Turkey because it's not really part of Europe and it's not really part of the Middle East, in most people's minds. Meshech was the sixth son of Japheth. He's identified with the ancient Mushki of the Assyrians or the Muskoi of the classical Greek writers. The Assyrian texts, Herodotus, and others, clearly place their residence on the mountains southeast of the Black Sea in a place that was called Anatolia, or ancient eastern Turkey.

With Tubal, we see the same thing. He was the fifth son of Japheth, brother of Meshech. Ninth-century B.C. Assyrian subscriptions again refer to his dwelling just west of Meshech and eastern Anatolia.

Modern Turkey

The Byzantine Empire started to fall apart in the fourteenth and fifteenth centuries. The Turkish tribes in Anatolia established the Ottoman Empire, which lasted until after World War I, when the modern state of Turkey was formed. Kamel Attaturk was committed to converting the theocratic autocracy of Turkey into a western-oriented democracy. In 1922 he abolished the sultanate. In 1924 he abolished Caliphate and the religious courts. In 1925 he made it illegal to wear the fez, which he regarded as a sign of backwardness that was identified with Islam. Once he got rid of the trappings of Islamic repression, he proceeded to aggressively adopt western ways. In 1925 Turkey adopted the western calendar, which marked a deep change for a culture. The next year Turkey adopted the Swiss civil code and later the Italian penal code. In 1928 the country switched to the Latin alphabet. In 1934 all Turks were obliged to take a surname after the western style. And the women were given the vote. Can you imagine the commitments they made to try to be a "western" country?

Following World War II, Turkey joined all the main western institutions: the United Nations in 1945, the International Monetary Fund in 1947, the Organization for Economic Co-operation and Development (OECD) in 1948, the Council of Europe in 1949, and NATO in 1951. In 1963, four years after their application, they became an associate member of the European Community.

They were guaranteed in writing at that time that, by joining as an associate member, they would later receive full membership into the European Community. However, a crisis began about 1987 when Turkey applied for full membership. It turned out that Austria, Sweden, Finland, and Norway, whose applications came after Turkey, were accepted. It became clearer and clearer as time went on that Turkey's application for full membership was being tabled, not approved. It became clearer to Turkey that they were not acceptable as a member of Europe. You can imagine the affront, the rejection, that the Turkish people and the leadership felt from all this after having spent 70 years committing themselves to the West.

The Soviet breakup, which freed up Central Asia, has created a whole new strategic opportunity for Turkey to go back to where it started to embrace Islam and become potential partners with Kazakhstan, Turkmenistan, etc., and Iran and Syria. Iran and Syria have formed an axis already. Four of the five former republics of Central Asia happen to speak Turkish. (Tadzhikistan is the one exception; they speak a Persian dialect.) They are now calling themselves members of Eurasia. I'm fascinated by that map — stretching from the Adriatic Sea all the way to the Wall of China — that's implied by their strategy because that is, of course, the classic map of the people of Magog. The Great Wall of China was called the "Ramparts of Magog" by the ancient writers. In Acts 17 and Deuteronomy 32:8, God appoints the boundaries of these countries.

In fact, currently the main dispute between Turkey and Syria is over the waters of the Euphrates.

The Hooks in Magog's Jaws

As we look at the Middle East and see Iran so well-armed with nuclear weapons, and as we watch Iran start to organize its agenda, we see Central Asia entangled with them. Rafsanjani of Iran has signed a treaty with Yeltsin of Russia that Russia will back Iran in this invasion. I think that treaty will be the "hooks in the jaw" which suck Magog into this ill-fated venture. Then we have Turkey and Armenia and so forth all involved. So much for the players. What happens is described in Ezekiel 38 and 39. God intervenes in the whole thing.

In order to stress its importance, I would like to once again address the timing of the Magog invasion. Some scholars say this happened back in history. No way. They didn't read the passage that describes earthquakes around the world, followed by the second coming of Jesus Christ. I don't think that's happened yet. It also happens in the latter days, after Israel has been regathered in the land. That means it would have to have occurred in the past 40 or 50 years. It hasn't happened yet. Is it about to? Yes, it is.

Another point of identification: "Gog and Magog" are the principal players in the opening part of Ezekiel 38. The names Gog and Magog also show up in Revelation 20. Many scholars try to fit Ezekiel 38 and 39 into the events that transpire in Revelation 20. But you'll discover that doesn't work because of the sequence, aside from other controversies. The sequence is pretty clear. First, there is a Tribulation period that is concluded by the second coming of Jesus Christ. (I'm getting into post-trib, pre-trib issues here.) The Second Coming is obviously after the Tribulation: the Lord comes to earth to set up His kingdom.

Then there's a thousand-year period called the Millennium, in which Satan is bound for a thousand years, after which he is released. Again, there is a rebellion, in which Gog and Magog are involved. And it's not the passage here in Ezekiel 38 and 39. It doesn't fit. None of the details fit. Is Magog wiped out in Ezekiel 38 and 39? It doesn't say that; it says the field forces are wiped out — the people, the country, the land is still there.

When you really want to understand timing, always look at Israel. In Ezekiel 37, you have the famous dry-bones vision, which God interprets for Ezekiel right there in that chapter. It's God's way of describing the return of the Jews back to the nation Israel. This is a strange idiom, but well-traveled ground. The passage is very clear, with little ambiguity. It even states that they'll be brought back initially in *unbelief*, but that an event occurs that startles them to realize that God has His hand on them once again.

From chapter 40 on, we see the millennial temple built. It has its own mysteries, but clearly that's yet future. Between chapters 37 and 40 are two chapters: 38 and 39. It appears to be the event that God uses to startle Israel to realize that God has His hand on them once again.

However, many competent Bible scholars view Ezekiel 38 and 39 as part of the scenario described in Daniel 11, which gives us details of this climactic world battle called Armageddon. We read about a thrust from the kings of the south; the kings of the north come in; a western confederacy comes in; and the kings of the east come in. It's a four-power conflict.

Some prophecy scholars tend to tie Ezekiel 38 to the Daniel 11 sequence, and visualize Ezekiel 38 as occurring as part of the Armageddon scenario. They may be absolutely correct. However, a number of us believe, for a lot of technical reasons, that Ezekiel 38 is not part of the Daniel 11 scenario. Much of that has to do with details in Daniel 11, but let me just focus on Ezekiel 38. The key player is Egypt. Egypt is conspicuous in its *absence of mention*. Also, there is no mention of the role of the Antichrist. All kinds of details are not dealt with in Ezekiel 38.

But there's another aspect to this timing issue that I would like to hit head on. This is perhaps even a more fundamental issue to which we should be sensitive. In Ezekiel 38:16, God says to Gog: "And thou shalt come up against my people of Israel, Like a cloud to cover the land; it shall be in the latter days, and I will bring thee against my land, that the nations may know me, when I shall be sanctified in thee, O Gog, before their eyes." The emphasis is 1) God here refers to Israel as His *people* and 2) this land is God's.

Israel's Uniqueness

Most Christians have not done their homework in terms of the role of Israel and the role of the Church. They're both overlooked; they're both misunderstood. And I strongly alert you, as you get sophisticated in your biblical perspective, to recognize that the Church and Israel are distinct and different. Recognize that they have different origins, different missions and a different destiny. That's very important. About Ezekiel 38:16, a very naive Bible reader would say, "Wait a minute. God always speaks of Israel as His people." No, that's not true. For example, in Hosea 1:9, God has Hosea set them aside. "They're not my people." But He leaves them with the promise that once again they will be His people. God predicted as early as the Torah that there would be a time that Israel would be unfaithful and that they would suffer dispersion as a result. But all the way through the Old Testament, He promises that they will be regathered and that they once again will become His people.

Daniel is given a vision in Daniel 9, the famous 70 weeks of Daniel. The last four verses of chapter 9 are aimed at Israel, the Jews, Judah, Jerusalem, not at the Church. But the passage also highlights the fact that there is an interval between the sixtieth and seventieth weeks, (described in verse 26 of that four-verse set) that will occur after the sixty-ninth but before the seventieth. During that interval, that break in their history, God is going to do something else — something unique.

Others "Securely in the Isles"

A Disturbing Prophecy — There is no question that Magog will be the recipient of God's wrath, according to the Ezekiel account of this invasion. But additional hints in these passages are quite disturbing — a reference to what will befall other land areas at the time of Russia's invasion.

We know there's going to be an earthquake. We know that hailstones of fire will fall on Magog. But in Ezekiel 39:6, God uses a phrase that's a little disturbing. He says, "And I will send a fire on Magog, and among those who dwell securely in the coastlands." The Hebrew word is a word that generally is translated "island or coastlands." The root implies a remote, pleasant place, like a pleasant island somewhere. It is a term that you'd use if you were using ancient Hebrew and were trying to describe a remote continent. Now, by the way, one small point here. The word "securely" can be translated as either "free of care, or carelessly." Again, to repeat, some earlier thought for the sake of importance and emphasis, the word "securely" means a state of mind that engenders the feeling of dwelling without having a care. The term occurs earlier in Ezekiel 38, five or six times. That's one reason some people feel that word "securely" implies that Israel is dwelling under the benefit of some kind of peace treaty. Maybe they are. But it isn't necessarily the treaty that involves the Antichrist. Furthermore, it doesn't really mean they're dwelling securely in the true sense. They're dwelling confidently. They're obviously not secure; they're hated by these people. So be careful about that term.

Now because of this hint, some people conjecture that the fire that will fall upon Magog might be nuclear missiles from Magog's army. This could be Israel; it could be the United States. But because of this phrase, what is suggested in the minds of some is that there may be a nuclear exchange. And it's easy to visualize something like that happening. It almost happened back in the Cuban missile crisis when we almost came to a launch of nuclear weapons against the heartland of the Soviet Union.

The probability of an invasion force against Israel starting to build, causing the United States to saber-rattle with the threat of retaliation, then an escalation of hostilities to the point there is an exchange certainly exists in today's world. That scenario fits absolutely within the framework of God's prophetic Word. Never has the situation in the Middle East been more unstable than today.

Apart from Ezekiel 38, you need to have an informed perspective of the nuclear predicament. I've served on 12 public boards, was chairman and chief executive officer of six of those, four of which happened to be defense contractors. I was, at one time, very deeply into anti-submarine warfare and a deep security supplier to the government. And because of that, I have some background in this area. Let me talk a little bit about anti-submarine warfare.

First of all, you may be surprised to learn that the primary mission of the United States Navy is anti-submarine warfare. By the way, the current technology makes that mission intensely difficult. The primary deterrent in this country is the Ohio class Trident submarine. It's 560 feet long, has a 42-foot beam, and displaces 18,700 tons. It has a single shaft and has about 60,000 horsepower. It has 24 tubes, each equipped with a Trident D-5 or something more recent. Basically, from 5,000 miles away it can put hardened sites at risk. It's a formidable weapon with four torpedo tubes and eight countermeasure launchers. We basically have a plan to keep 18 of them at sea: 9 in the Atlantic, 9 in the Pacific. These things, usually built in pairs, cost about $2 billion per pair.

Now let's talk about the Soviet counterpart to that: the Typhoon class submarine. It's 561 feet long — only one foot longer — but its beam is not 42 feet; it's 78 feet. It has double titanium hulls. It displaces not 18,700 tons, but 25,500 tons — larger than the British World War II cruiser, the HMS *Belfast*. Its speed is in excess of 25 knots. Its depth is unknown. It's designed for depth and speed and combat. It has two shafts, two power plants, and a total of 75,000 shaft horsepower. Specifically designed for under-Arctic operations, it has retractable hydroplanes. Its upper works are uniquely strengthened. It has closed-circuit TV aft of the sail so they can find a spot to break through the polar ice. The idea is to break through, fire, and dive in the Arctic. Why the Arctic? Well, for lots of reasons, not the least of which is that sonar doesn't work there in a normal way.

Each one of these Typhoon submarines has 20 tubes. They are typically loaded with SS-20s. Each one of these has 10 independently targeted warheads that have a 5,000-mile range. That means that each sub can hold 200 cities in hostage.

What makes the Typhoon so formidable isn't just its armament and its construction, it's the technology: They are silent. You can't find them, and with present technology they can operate from home waters and reach the United States with the SS-20s.

Another thing that's disturbing about these is that various aircraft and tanks are *multiple-mission* systems. But a nuclear ballistic missile submarine has only one use. It's for a pre-emptive first strike.

The Typhoon is regarded by some of the experts as the ultimate weapon. You can't fight it. It's independent. And it can hold an entire culture hostage.

We also now discover that the Russian technology can *track our Tridents*. By using advanced sensors on spacecraft or aircraft they can detect them at any depth within a 50-foot accuracy within five minutes. Which means that our Tridents are effectively *compromised*. Yet we don't know where their Typhoons are.

Let's talk about a few numbers. The United States had, a few years ago, about 86 attack subs and about 34 ballistic missile subs. Against our 86 attack subs, the Russians had 131. Against our 34 ballistic missile subs, they had 63. But they've got about 136 other kinds of subs that are in neither of those categories. So against our 120, they've got 342 submarines — *and they've been building since*. When the Soviet Union broke up, they did *not stop* building submarines. Things like these cost a billion dollars each. Why would Gorbachev, when he was running things, keep building Typhoon class submarines when he already had a two-to-one majority over us? What was the strategy?

When I had an opportunity to serve on a board of directors with Dr. Edward Teller, scientific advisor to President Reagan at the time; with General David C. Jones, chairman of the Joint Chiefs of Staff, and former general of the Air Force; and with Admiral Tom Hayward, chief of Naval Operations, we got into some interesting discussions. I discovered, much to my concern, that Gen. Jones, Adm. Hayward, and Dr. Teller all lived in a day-to-day fear of a pre-emptive strike from the Soviet Union. I just thought that must be an occupational hazard for operating in the Pentagon.

They gave me a number of reasons for why they felt that way, the most disturbing of which is their knowledge that all the training materials for the war colleges and for their most senior officers in the Soviet Union are built on the premise that they will have the *advantage of surprise*. Think about that. There were no other training materials that assumed anything other than that they would have the pre-emptive initiative. That's pretty scary stuff.

The Men Who Would Be Gog

Who will command this awesome power that will be used in a lightning-like strike to the south and quite probably against even the United States? Today there seems to be some fascinating candidates for becoming the one who God's Word calls "*Gog.*"

Books have been written about Zhirinovsky, who is called "the man who would be Gog," but let me give you an alternative that intrigues me even more. In December 1993, Yeltsin signed papers to establish the Romanoff Double Eagle as the symbol of Russia. The eagle with two heads is the symbol of the czars. One of the eagle's heads faces east, the other west, connoting the classical posture of Russia straddling Europe and Asia. The version they're using is the one that was used by Peter the Great. The eagle has three crowns, there's an orb in one claw and a scepter in the other. On the breast is a shield with a man riding a white horse, which, of course, biblically considered, is kind of interesting. But you should also understand that St. George the Dragonslayer was the traditional herald of the city of Moscow.

Now the Romanoff eagle actually started being used in Egypt back in the seventh century. It became the emblem of the Byzantine Empire. And when the Byzantine Empire started to fall apart, and when Russia's czar, Ivan III — Ivan "the Great" — married the niece of the last Byzantine emperor, he adopted that symbol to be the symbol of Russia. It was the symbol of the czar from 1472 until July of 1918, when Nicholas II and his family were shot in a cellar by the Bolsheviks under the orders of Vladimir Lenin. It's interesting that the parliament that had repeatedly rejected the acceptance of this symbol in the past, approved it upon Yeltsin's proposal. Yeltsin also renamed the Parliament the Duma, which is what the parliament was called under the Czar.

Yeltsin did another thing which is kind of strange — he gave his permission for a Grand Count Vladimir Kirillovich, a Romanoff and second cousin to Czar Nicholas II, who died in 1992 at the age of 74, to be buried in St. Isaac's Cathedral in St. Petersburg. That's an imperial honor that had never been bestowed upon anyone else during the 70 years of Communist rule because it was so anti-aristocracy.

Not many people realize that Grand Count Kirillovich had a great grandson, 14-year-old Count Georgii Romanoff, who lived with his mother, Grand Duchess Maria Romanoff, who lives in Madrid. Georgii Romanoff is now enlisted in St. Petersburg's Nachimov Naval Academy, which is the traditional path of training for the Czar.

When Yeltsin visited Spain last year, he secretly visited young Count Georgii Romanoff. Referendums are being circulated in Russia to establish a constitutional monarchy, with young Georgii Romanoff taking the throne, and Yeltsin presumably serving as his regent. This is an interesting strategy because some experts feel that if he can pull this off, he'd immediately get the support of the Russian Orthodox church, major chunks of the army, possibly even the KGB and the GRU, and what everybody is desperate for — the hardliners and everybody — is stability, a return to order. They feel a thousand-year-old monarchy has more legitimacy than a three-year-old democracy which is failing.

There are numerous other potential candidates, including, surprisingly, Mikhail Gorbachev. Numerous candidates are being encouraged from the military to run for the Duma; and the number of potential contenders to challenge Yeltsin is increasing.

So the truth of the matter is that the experts who are watching this are not sure of what really is going on. We, just like everyone else, watch. And as I've often repeated, my friends in Russia say that in Russia, "even the past is uncertain!"

Gog, the Demon-King

One of the problems with "Gog" is that, while he is obviously the leader of Magog, he shows up in Ezekiel 38 from nowhere. This is very unusual in the Scripture for a key player not have a link somewhere.

A couple of years ago, I stumbled into an insight in Amos 7:1. In our English Bible it reads, "Thus hath the Lord God shewn unto me;

and, behold, he formed grasshoppers in the beginning of the shooting up of the latter growth; and, lo, it was the latter growth after the kings mowings."

What does that mean? It doesn't seem to make sense.

The Septuagint Translation reads quite differently. It is an ancient translation of the Hebrew Scriptures into Greek completed in the third century before Christ and about 1,000 years older than the common Masoretic text upon which our English Bible is based. The Septuagint reads, "The Lord hath shewn them, behold, a swarm of locusts were coming, and behold, one of the young devastating locusts was Gog the king."

If you studied the Book of Revelation, you may recall that in chapter 9 one encounters some strange creatures portrayed as locusts. And Revelation 9:11 mentions that these locusts have a king whose name is Abaddon in the Greek or Apollyon in the Hebrew. If you do your homework you discover that in Proverbs 30: 27, the Holy Spirit tells us "the locusts have no king." This tells us that these "locusts" are idiomatic for demons. That suggests that the Amos 7:1 passage reveals that Gog may be a demon king. Gog, whoever he turns out to be, will be a demon leader.

This also would explain why, 1,000 years after the second coming of Jesus Christ, Gog (a title) can show up again.

When I first ran into this, I was stunned. How could a verse like this (Amos 7:1) have been overlooked all these years? I scooped up my notes and spent until 3:00 a.m. with Hal Lindsey in his library and it all checked out. Hal wasn't surprised. He pointed out that this discovery was just a fulfillment of Daniel 12: that "many shall run to and fro and knowledge shall be increased." Now some people apply that very broadly. But scripturally speaking, it means that scriptural insight will increase during the latter days. He said we should not be surprised at being given knowledge that eluded scholars of the past because we are getting close to the end time. So don't be surprised when, during your own study, you receive insight that has escaped scholars of the past. Be cautious in this, of course, but recognize that the Holy Spirit — not Chuck Missler or anybody else — is your primary teacher as you seek to understand God's Word.

In Summary

To repeat, I do not believe you have any chance of understanding the news broadcasts of our time unless you know your Bible. And there has never been a more exciting time to do your homework and to find out what the Bible is saying, not just with the subject of Magog, but in the broad range of global issues and events. For example, the rebuilding of Babylon by Saddam Hussein is fulfilling prophecies in some fascinating ways. Find out more about Israel, about Jerusalem, about the rebuilding of the temple, and the stunning discoveries taking place.

The point is, it's all taking place so rapidly. The more we track issues and events, the more it would seem that things are rapidly moving in the direction of Ezekiel 38 happening soon. But if I'm correct in my understanding of the passage, then the Rapture has to happen first. As I'm fond of pointing out, the analogy that as you're driving down Main Street and you notice all the stores are decorating for Christmas, you know that Thanksgiving's not far away. What does that mean? I think one of the things it means is it's time for you and me to start taking our Christianity seriously. I think it's time for all of us to start doing our homework. It's time for all of us to seriously explore our position in Jesus Christ.[1]

If you are reading this and you don't know Jesus, I encourage you, in the privacy of your own will, to hand your life over to Him. He will take it from there. You will then be on the winning side, God's side, when Russia makes her fatal thrust to the south.

If you make that commitment, then share it with someone you trust spiritually.

8

The Beast in the Temple

By J. R. Church

For the Antichrist to commit the "abomination of desolation," there must be an existing and functioning Jewish sanctuary on the Temple Mount. For this man to "cause the sacrifice and oblation to cease" (Dan. 9:27), there must be a return to sacrifice worship by religious Jews in Jerusalem. Yet over the past two millennia, the Temple Mount has remained void of a Jewish presence. Islam controls the area. Two mosques stand defiant as "abominations" to the rabbis.

Over the centuries, the deepest desire of Judaism has revolved around hopes that someday the chosen people would return to Jerusalem and rebuild their temple. This dream stems from an ancient biblical teaching that "almost all things are by the law purged with blood; and without shedding of blood is no remission" (Heb. 9:22). The practice of blood sacrifices lies at the heart of the Jewish desire for a temple. The concept of sacrificing animals for the atonement of sin is as old as history itself. The earliest biblical account shows God's plan for redemption: "Unto Adam also and to his wife did the Lord God make coats of skins, and clothed them" (Gen. 3:21).

Where did God get those coats of skins? From sacrificial animals, of course. The lesson is repeated in the very next chapter as Abel brings a sacrifice from his flock: "And Abel, he also brought of the firstlings of his flock and of the fat thereof. And the Lord had respect unto Abel and to his offering" (Gen. 4:4).

Temple worship is distinctly and intricately associated with animal sacrifices. This is far different from the function of a synagogue. Rather than simply nurturing a congregation, temple liturgy is primarily concerned with a priesthood, whose main function is the sacrificing of animals. Synagogues can be built anywhere but God had a special location for His temple — Mount Moriah.

In the process of time, Abraham was called to leave Ur of Chaldees and head west toward a "Promised Land" — a territory whose western border lay alongside the Mediterranean Sea. In its heartland stood Mount Moriah. There, God proposed to have a place for sacrifices. Melchizedek lived there — the high priest of a religion that worshipped the true Creator. Abraham was a member of his congregation. The story of Isaac and his substitute ram also marked the very place where God wanted His temple built.

The tabernacle built at Sinai was not intended to be a permanent sanctuary. It was to serve Israel only until a temple could be constructed. This system of worship was so dear to the heart and soul of Judaism that no expense was spared. God deserved the best from His people.

The Wealth of the Sanctuaries

The materials assembled for the Mosaic tabernacle contained one ton of gold, three and three-fourth tons of silver, and two and one-half tons of bronze. At today's prices the tabernacle would be worth over $16 million. The golden lampstand weighed about 75 pounds. It would be worth a half million dollars for its gold alone. Solomon's Temple contained 3,750 tons of gold and 37,500 tons of silver — value: $56 billion. The most holy place of Solomon's Temple was lined with cedar from Lebanon and covered with 600 talents of gold — worth $270 million. Solomon's income was 666 talents of gold per year — $300 million. According to 1 Kings 10:27, during the reign of Solomon, the "king made silver to be in Jerusalem as stones." The Queen of Sheba brought Solomon 120 talents of gold worth $54 million. Solomon made 200 massive shields, each 300 shekels in weight, to hang on the walls of his palace. His ivory throne was overlaid with gold: "So King Solomon exceeded all the kings of the earth in riches and wisdom" (2 Kings 10:23).

In the days of Herod the Great, the size of the temple compound was increased from 17 to 34 acres and a magnificent temple was built, the top of which was crowned with gold. Cicero wrote of great influxes of gold to Jerusalem. The total sum of gold and silver contributed annually at the time of Jesus has been estimated to be in the order of $500 million per year. Evidence suggests that the bulk of the income was stored up year after year. Thus, the Roman plunder could have netted a treasure worth tens of millions of dollars. When the temple was burned in A.D. 70, the golden crown that skirted its roof melted and ran down between the stones. The Romans totally dismantled the temple and broke the stones apart to extract the gold.

Of all the treasures of the temple throughout history, it is believed that at least some were buried in the subterranean passages under the Temple Mount. The dream of archaeologists, digging around the Temple Mount today, is to recover the lost treasures of the temple.

In 1953 a copper scroll was found in a cave near the Dead Sea which listed 64 locations of buried treasure — gold and silver, along with vessels, from the temple treasury, hidden by the priesthood shortly before the Romans destroyed the temple in A.D. 70. According-ing to the copper scroll the treasure totaled an estimated 138 tons of gold and silver. So far, none of it has turned up, but archaeologists continue to dig.

The wealth of Solomon's Temple could hardly be reproduced today. All of the religious Jews in the world would be hard-pressed to collect enough gold to gild such an edifice in the style of Solomon's Temple. Yet a sanctuary is being planned for Jerusalem. Beginning in 1984, some 90 implements for temple liturgy have been recon-structed. However, they do not have the money to build with the grandeur of Solomon. It will take the coming of the Messiah to match the wealth of Solomon.

In 1974 I interviewed one of Israel's leading archaeologists and asked him why his crew was excavating along the western wall area. He replied that they were preparing for the rebuilding of the temple. I asked him when the actual construction would commence and his reply was that the Messiah would build the temple when He comes. He was expecting the Messiah soon.

Zechariah's View of the Future Temple

The Old Testament prophet Zechariah predicted exactly that. He said that Messiah would build the millennial temple. He was in-structed to direct the attention of his people toward their high priest, Joshua. Zechariah likened him to the future Messiah and gave a prophecy that this future Messiah, Joshua (the Old Testament name for Jesus), would build the final temple:

Then take silver and gold, and make crowns, and set them upon the head of Joshua the son of Josedech, the high priest;

And speak unto him, saying, Thus speaketh the Lord of hosts, saying, Behold the man whose name is The Branch; and he shall grow up out of his place, and he shall build the temple of the Lord:

Even he shall build the temple of the Lord; and he shall bear the glory, and shall sit and rule upon his throne; and he shall be a priest upon his throne: and the counsel of peace shall be between them both (Zech. 6:11-13).

Note that Zechariah was not calling Joshua, "The Branch." He was only using the high priest as an object lesson. The Joshua who stood before Zechariah was a grown man, but Zechariah was referring to the Messiah who would "grow up out of his place." It is this future Messiah who will build the final temple.

Haggai's View of the Future Temple

Haggai, a contemporary of Zechariah, also spoke of the final temple. He too, directed his prophecy to Joshua. He wrote that the future Messiah, who owns all the gold and silver in the world, would build a sanctuary that would exceed the glory of Zerubbabel's Temple and Solomon's as well:

Who is left among you that saw this house in her first glory? and how do ye see it now? is it not in your eyes in comparison of it as nothing?

Yet now be strong, O Zerubbabel, saith the Lord; and be strong, O Joshua, son of Josedech, the high priest; and be strong, all ye people of the land, saith the Lord, and work: for I am with you, saith the Lord of hosts:

According to the word that I covenanted with you when ye came out of Egypt, so my spirit remaineth among you: fear ye not.

For thus saith the Lord of hosts; Yet once, it is a little while, and I will shake the heavens, and the earth, and the sea, and the dry land;

And I will shake all nations, and the desire of all nations shall come: and I will fill this house with glory, saith the Lord of hosts.

The silver is mine, and the gold is mine, saith the Lord of hosts.

The glory of this latter house shall be greater than of the former, saith the Lord of hosts: and in this place will I give peace, saith the Lord of hosts (Hag. 2:3-9).

Note that it is the Lord of hosts who has enough gold and silver to endow the future temple with a greater glory. Only the Messiah's temple can rival the wealth and grandeur of Solomon's. Until He comes, however, some kind of temporary sanctuary will be erected. I hardly think the Antichrist would commit the abomination of desolation in a temple constructed by King Messiah. It is likely therefore, that a temporary sanctuary will be erected on the Temple Mount just prior to the onset of the Tribulation period.

Ezekiel's View of the Future Sanctuary

This also appears to be the consensus of Ezekiel. He foresaw a different kind of Temple than Solomon's. Ezekiel's vision seems to be that of a working museum — a building that houses an old tent.

After God carried Ezekiel to Jerusalem to see the ruins of Solomon's Temple and the bones of the slain who filled the Tyropean and Kidron valleys, the prophet turned his faith toward the future and predicted a time when the bones would live again. He recorded the promise that a "sanctuary" and a "tabernacle" would be set up just prior to the battle of Gog and Magog:

And say unto them, Thus saith the Lord God; Behold, I will take the children of Israel from among the heathen, whither they be gone, and will gather them on every side, and bring them into their own land. . . .

And they shall dwell in the land that I have given unto Jacob my servant, wherein your fathers have dwelt; and they shall dwell therein, even they, and their children, and their children's children for ever: and my servant David shall be their prince for ever.

Moreover I will make a covenant of peace with them; it shall be an everlasting covenant with them: and I will place them, and multiply them, and will set my sanctuary [Kodesh] in the midst of them for evermore.

My tabernacle [Mishkon] also shall be with them: yea, I will be their God, and they shall be my people.

And the heathen shall know that I the Lord do sanctify Israel, when my sanctuary [Kodesh] shall be in the midst of them for evermore (Ezek. 37:21,25-28).

Since Ezekiel mentions both a "sanctuary" (Kodesh) and a "tabernacle" (Mishkon), it may be that the sanctuary will be both a place of worship and a working museum to house the tabernacle of David. My opinion is that David's tabernacle is the one referred to by the Kodesh and Mishkon. The Hebrew word Kodesh refers to a "very holy place." Mishkon means "with Shekinah" and refers to the presence of God's glory.

Following the battle of Gog and Magog, Ezekiel is taken once again to Jerusalem. This time, he travels into the future to observe Jerusalem's Temple Mount as it actually appears today:

"In the visions of God brought he me into the land of Israel, and set me upon a very high mountain, by which was as the frame of a city on the south" (Ezek. 40:2).

Ezekiel said that he was transported in a vision to the temple site, and saw the *"frame of a city on the south."* He did not see complete roofed houses, only the remains of what were once the dwellings of Jerusalem. This description speaks to me of the archaeological diggings along the southern wall. Since 1967 archaeologists have uncovered the ruins of the old city. Therefore, we conclude that Ezekiel was transported into the future to this present generation and was allowed to describe the Temple Mount as it appears today. Note Ezekiel's description of today's eastern gate:

"Then came he unto the gate which looketh toward the east, and went up the stairs thereof, and measured the threshold of the gate, which was one reed broad; and the other threshold of the gate, which was one reed broad" (Ezek. 40:6).

According to Ezekiel, there are stairs just inside the eastern gate. I've been there. I have walked down those stairs to the lower level inside of the double-gate area. Ezekiel could not have known about those stairs except by the divine revelation of his vision. Also, I stepped off each of the two gates. Each are approximately ten feet across, conforming to the measurement of Ezekiel's gates.

Furthermore, Ezekiel describes the wall of the Temple fortress as it appears today: "And there were narrow windows to the little chambers, and to their posts within the gate round about, and likewise to the arches: and windows were round about inward." (Ezek. 40:16).

Exactly! Ezekiel's description perfectly fits the long narrow windows located along the eastern wall. Just inside each narrow window is an arched, rounded area where soldiers could stand protected.

Ezekiel also noted that the eastern gate was closed: "Then said the Lord unto me; This gate shall be shut, it shall not be opened, and no man shall enter in by it; because the Lord, the God of Israel, hath entered in by it, therefore it shall be shut" (Ezek. 44:2).

Indeed, the eastern gate is closed. In 1967, Jordan's King Hussein decided to open the eastern gate. He had a crane set up just outside the gate. Air hammers were laid inside with plans to open the gate the next day. That night the Six Day War broke out — June 6, 1967. Needless to say, the gate remains closed. This is an amazing description! I feel confident that Ezekiel's description was indicative of the temple grounds during this modern age.

According to Ezekiel 42:15-20, the prophet describes the measuring of the temple site. He comes to the eastern gate and describes the measurements: "He measured it by the four sides: it had a wall round about, five hundred reeds long, and five hundred broad, to make a separation between the sanctuary [Kodesh] and the profane place" (Ezek. 42:20).

The Scripture records that a wall will be built to make a separation between the sanctuary and the *"profane place."* Could this profane place be the Mosque of Omar? Could a Jewish sanctuary be erected just north of the Dome of the Rock?

In the book of Revelation, the Apostle John is told to take a reed and "measure the temple of God, and the altar, and them that worship therein. But the court which is without the temple leave out, and measure it not; for it given unto the Gentiles: and the holy city shall they tread under foot forty and two months" (Rev. 11:1-2).

According to John's description, the court which is *"without the temple"* is not measured. It is given over to Gentiles. John was familiar with the layout of Herod's Temple, in which the court of the Gentiles lay to the south in the area from today's Mosque of Omar to the El Aksa Mosque. Perhaps the sanctuary will be built just north of the Mosque of Omar at the site of a small cupola which Moslems call the Dome of the Tablets.

Measuring the Temple

Ezekiel described the measurements of the future temple, which appear somewhat small. It is more likely the width of the tabernacle of David. Ezekiel explains that it is, in fact, the *"breadth of the tabernacle:"* "Afterward he brought me to the temple [Hechel], and measured the posts, six cubits broad on the one side, and six cubits broad on the other side, which was the breadth of the tabernacle [Ouhel]" (Ezek. 41:1).

It is my opinion that temple liturgy will be restored in the tabernacle of David. According to Ezekiel, the temple or *Hechel* was 12 cubits wide, which was the breadth of the tabernacle or *Ouhel*. That's only about 18 feet — rather modest in size.

Amos' View of the Latter-Day Tabernacle

At least 150 years prior to Ezekiel, Amos made a distinct reference to the tabernacle of David as the one being erected in "that day:"

> For, lo, I will command, and I will sift the house of Israel among all nations, like as corn is sifted in a sieve, yet shall not the least grain fall upon the earth.
>
> All the sinners of my people shall die by the sword, which say, The evil shall not overtake nor prevent us.
>
> In that day will I raise up the tabernacle [Sukkah] of David that is fallen, and close up the breaches thereof; and I will raise up his ruins, and I will build it as in the days of old:
>
> That they may possess the remnant of Edom, and of all the heathen, which are called by my name, saith the Lord that doeth this (Amos 9:9-12).

About 760 B.C., some 40 years before the northern ten tribes were taken into Assyrian captivity, and at least 150 years before the Babylonian captivity, Amos predicted a dispersion among all nations. His prophecy concerned God's judgment upon the "sinners of my people" until the time that the Tabernacle of David would be erected. He was referring to "that day" when descendants of dispersed Israel and Judah would return to their homeland.

Amos also refers to a host of Gentiles upon whom the Lord's name is called. We must note that when Amos delivered that prophecy, there were absolutely no Gentiles that met that description. However, some 800 years later, such a phenomenon commenced. It was the introduction of New Testament Gentile Christianity.

Following the death and resurrection of Christ, two apostles were allowed to introduce the gospel to Gentiles. Peter opened the door with the conversion of Cornelius, and later Paul was called to be an apostle to the Gentiles. Such a thing was difficult for Jewish believers to accept. Some Judaizers followed Paul, attempting to force his Gentile converts to keep the Mosaic law. The controversy finally reached Jerusalem where a council met to settle the question. After much discussion, the conclusion was reached to allow fellowship with Gentile believers without forcing the Mosaic covenant upon them. James, the moderator of the meeting, cited the conversion of Cornelius as evidence that God was saving Gentiles without requiring adherence to the 613 laws of Moses:

> But there rose up certain of the sect of the Pharisees which believed, saying, That it was needful to circumcise them, and to command them to keep the law of Moses.
>
> And the apostles and elders came together for to consider of this matter.
>
> And when there had been much disputing, Peter rose up, and said unto them, Men and brethren, ye know how that a good while ago God made choice among us, that the Gentiles by my mouth should hear the word of the gospel, and believe.
>
> And God, which knoweth the hearts, bare them witness, giving them the Holy Ghost, even as he did unto us;
>
> And put no difference between us and them, purifying their hearts by faith.
>
> Now therefore why tempt ye God, to put a yoke upon the neck of the disciples, which neither our fathers nor we were able to bear?
>
> But we believe that through the grace of the Lord Jesus Christ we shall be saved, even as they.
>
> Then all the multitude kept silence, and gave audience to Barnabas and Paul, declaring what miracles and wonders God had wrought among the Gentiles by them.
>
> And after they had held their peace, James answered, saying, Men and brethren, hearken unto me:
>
> Simeon hath declared how God at the first did visit the Gentiles, to take out of them a people for his name.
>
> And to this agree the words of the prophets; as it is written,
>
> After this I will return, and will build again the

tabernacle of David, which is fallen down; and I will build again the ruins thereof, and I will set it up:

That the residue of men might seek after the Lord, and all the Gentiles, upon whom my name is called, saith the Lord, who doeth all these things.

Known unto God are all his works from the beginning of the world.

Wherefore my sentence is, that we trouble not them, which from among the Gentiles are turned to God:

But that we write unto them, that they abstain from pollutions of idols, and from fornication, and from things strangled, and from blood" (Acts 15:5-20).

James said Cornelius, the Roman centurion, was the first convert among Gentiles — the first of millions to come. He proclaimed that God was calling out of the Gentiles a people who would be called by His name. Then he quoted the Amos passage, which predicted the raising up of the tabernacle of David, at which time a remnant of Jews would seek after the Lord, along with all the Gentiles who are called by His name. There is only one group of Gentiles who are called by God's name. We are called Christians.

According to the prophecy, the re-establishment of temple worship is one of the major events we are to look for. James appears to be saying that the setting up of the tabernacle of David will come at or near the conclusion of the dispensation of Gentile Christianity.

What Was the Tabernacle of David?

The tabernacle of David was different from the Mosaic tabernacle. It was a separate tent designed and built to house the ark of the Covenant. In order to establish the difference, let's take a brief review of the history of each.

After leaving Egypt, the children of Israel camped at the foot of Mt. Sinai. Moses went up to establish their covenant with God and was given plans for building the Mosaic tabernacle.

When construction was complete, Moses gathered the tribes to dedicate the tabernacle. We are told in the last chapter of Exodus that the glory of the Lord descended upon the place as a pillar of fire. It was an historic occasion when God himself came to dwell among His people. For the next 40 years — through their wilderness journey — the tabernacle stood as a symbol of God's presence and power.

Though it is called a tabernacle in our Bible, there are two

Hebrew words used to describe it. The most important was *Mishkon*, (meaning "with Shekinah") a word describing the detailed structure of the acacia wood boards, overlaid with gold, comprising two rooms — the Holy Place and the Holy of Holies.

The second Hebrew word used to describe the tabernacle was *Ouhel*. It simple means "a tent." There was nothing special about the word *Ouhel*, for it is used in many places throughout the Old Testament to describe a tent. Actually, the *Mishkon* stood under the *Ouhel* or tent.

After Israel conquered the Promised Land, the *Mishkon* was set up at Shiloh, a small community about 20 miles north of Jerusalem. For the next 400 years the Levitical priesthood served at Shiloh — until the days of Eli when Hophni and Phinehas, his wicked sons, took the ark of the Covenant into battle against the Philistines. The army suffered defeat that day — the Philistines captured the sacred ark.

When news of the tragedy reached the aging Eli, he fell backward off his stool, broke his neck, and died. When the wife of Phinehas heard that her husband had been killed and that the ark of God was taken, she also died — giving premature birth to their expected child. She named him Ichabod, meaning "the glory hath departed." Tears flowed in Israel that day because the ark of the covenant and the Shekinah glory was gone.

The interesting thing is that the ark was never returned to the Mosaic Mishkon. From that day forward the Holy of Holies remained empty. But the story does not end there. The captured ark was taken to the temple of Dagon — fish god of the Philistines. According to the story, a plague fell upon them, for they had desecrated the ark.

Eventually, they loaded the golden chest onto a wagon, hitched two milk cows to it, and pointed them in the direction of Israel. According to Scripture, they turned neither to the right nor to the left until they had brought the ark of the covenant up the Sorek valley and stopped at a large rock near the city of Beth-Shemesh.

When the Israelis saw the ark, they gathered around the wagon and rejoiced. Out of curiosity someone opened the ark. God's judgment fell upon them, killing 50,070 men. The Levites of Kirjeth-Jearim were called upon to fetch the sacred ark and take it to the home of Abinadab, where it remained for at least the next 20 years.

Meanwhile, the Mishkon, or tabernacle of Moses, was dismantled at Shiloh and moved to the city of Nob — believed to have been located on Mount Scopus which lays along the northern ridge of the Mount of Olives where the Hadassah hospital is located today. You may recall, David came there one day, while running from Saul, and was given the shewbread to eat. When Saul heard about the kindness to David, he had the 85 priests of Nob slaughtered.

The tabernacle was then taken from Nob and set up at the high place of Gibeon. All this time the ark of the covenant remained in the house of Abinadab at Kirjath-Jearim, another Gibeonite city. It was not returned to the Mosaic Mishkon.

Then came the day when David wanted to bring the ark to Jerusalem. He made the mistake of putting it on a new cart pulled by oxen. He failed to understand that God had insisted the ark be carried upon the shoulders of the sons of Korah — Kohathites. The wagon had not gone far until Uzzah reached up to steady the ark. Well, it happened again. The same fate befell him that had brought death to 50,070 Israelis some years before.

David was frightened and would take the ark no further. Instead it was left at the home of Obed-Edom — until they could decide what went wrong. After three months David heard that the Lord had blessed the house of Obed-Edom and was encouraged to fetch the ark. By this time he had learned that the ark should be carried upon the shoulders of the Kohathites.

It is important to note that David left the *Mishkon* at Gibeon. He did not return the ark to the Holy of Holies. Instead, he built another tent and placed it in the City of David at Jerusalem. It was called the tabernacle of David. The story is found in the Chronicles: "So they brought the ark of God, and set it in the midst of the tent [Ouhel] that David had pitched for it: and they offered burnt-sacrifices and peace-offerings before God" (1 Chron. 16:1).

Leaving the Mosaic *Mishkon* at Gibeon, the king brought the ark of the covenant to Jerusalem and placed it in a special tent. David divided the priesthood, appointing some to attend the ark and others to serve before the *Mishkon* at Gibeon, which was about six miles northwest of Mt. Moriah:

> So he left there before the ark of the covenant of the Lord Asaph and his brethren, to minister before the ark continually, as every day's work required:
> And Obed-Edom with their brethren, threescore and eight; Obed-edom also the son of Jeduthun and Hosah to be porters:
> And Zadok the priest, and his brethren the priests,

before the tabernacle of the Lord in the high place that was
at Gibeon,

> To offer burnt-offerings unto the Lord upon the altar
> of the burnt-offering continually morning and evening,
> and to do according to all that is written in the law of the
> Lord, which he commanded Israel" (1 Chron. 16:37-40).

David divided the priesthood, appointing Zadok, the high priest,
in charge of religious worship at the *Mishkon*, while he chose Asaph,
along with others, to attend the ark of the covenant at the tabernacle
of David in Jerusalem.

Not long after, David desired to build a permanent temple for
housing the ark of the covenant. When he mentioned it to Nathan, the
prophet encouraged him to proceed. But that night the Lord appeared
to Nathan in a dream and told him that Solomon, not David, would
build the temple. Among the things Nathan was instructed to tell
David was that God had dwelt in both a tent and a tabernacle:

> Go and tell my servant David, Thus saith the Lord,
> Shalt thou build me an house for me to dwell in?
> Whereas I have not dwelt in any house since the time
> that I brought up the children of Israel out of Egypt, even
> to this day, but have walked in a tent [Ouhel] and in a
> tabernacle [Mishkon] (2 Sam. 7:5-6).

Please note the terminology used by the Lord when He spoke to
Nathan that night in the dream. God said, "I have walked in a tent and
in a tabernacle." It appears that He was saying, "I have walked in a
tent," meaning the Ouhel of David and "I have walked in a tabernacle," meaning the Mishkon of Moses.

David did not normally offer burnt sacrifices at his tabernacle.
Usually, when he wanted to sacrifice before the Lord, he went to
Gibeon — to the *Mishkon*. However, there came the day when David
found it necessary to offer sacrifices on Mount Moriah. He had
disobeyed the Lord and a great plague was brought upon the people.
The story is given in the Chronicles:

> God sent an angel unto Jerusalem to destroy it: and as
> he was destroying, the Lord beheld, and he repented him
> of the evil, and said to the angel that destroyed, It is enough,
> stay now thine hand. And the angel of the Lord stood by the
> threshing-floor of Ornan the Jebusite. . . .

> Then the angel of the Lord commanded Gad to say to
> David, that David should go up, and set up an altar unto the
> Lord in the threshingfloor of Ornan the Jebusite (1 Chron.
> 21:15, 18).

According to the story, David bought the threshing-floor of
Ornan for a place of sacrifice. That threshing-floor was to become the
site for Solomon's Temple.

Strangely enough, though the Mosaic *Mishkon* was described in
the book of Exodus, we have nowhere in the Scripture a detailed
description of the *Ouhel* of David. If discovered today, the only way
it could be identified is if it was accompanied by the ark of the
covenant. Now, why is this important? Because the prophet Isaiah
declared that in the last days the *Ouhel* of David would be set up: "And
in mercy shall the throne be established: and he shall sit upon it in truth
in the tabernacle of David" (Isa. 16:5).

Isaiah referred to that future day when the *Ouhel* of David would
be set up — not the *Mishkon* of Moses. Furthermore, as we have noted,
Amos also referred to the tabernacle of David. But, in his prophecy,
he used neither the word *Mishkon* nor *Ouhel*. He used an altogether
different word — *Sukkoh*:

> In that day will I raise up the tabernacle of David that
> is fallen and close up the breaches thereof, and I will raise
> up his ruins, and I will build it as in the days of old (Amos
> 9:11).

The tabernacle of David, along with the ark of the covenant,
could be set up on the temple site just north of the Mosque of Omar.
Since the ark was never returned to the *Mishkon* after the Philistines
captured it, it is safe to assume that the ark of the Covenant could be
set up on the Temple Mount under the tabernacle of David, and that
the tabernacle of Moses could be placed in a museum.

Where Was the Temple Built?

There are at least two suggested locations on the Temple Mount
where Solomon's Temple could have been built. In the March 1983
issue of *Biblical Archaeology Review* magazine, an article was
published by the Jewish archeologist, Asher S. Kaufman, identifying
his proposed spot where the Jewish Temple once stood. According to
Dr. Kaufman, a professor of physics at the Hebrew University in
Jerusalem, the Foundation Stone upon which the ark of the covenant

rested in both Solomon's and Herod's Temples, still stands today on the Temple Mount in Jerusalem.

According to Kaufman, there is a small unimposing cupola situated on the wide flagstone area just north of the Mosque of Omar. Under the cupola lies the exposed bedrock of the top of the mountain. Dr. Kaufman believes the ark of the covenant once stood on the bedrock beneath the cupola. It is called the Dome of the Tablets and is thought to mark the spot where the two tablets of stone containing the Ten Commandments were kept in the ark of the covenant.

The Dome of the Tablets lies directly west of the eastern gate and, according to Dr. Kaufman, marks the spot for the Holy of Holies in both Solomon's Temple and Herod's Temple.

Leen Ritmeir's Square

Other equally eminent scholars disagree with Kaufman. Dr. Leen Ritmeir worked for several years with Dr. Benjamin Mazar on the excavations along the southern wall and is convinced that the temple was situated directly on the rock where the Mosque of Omar stands. His measurements are equally impressive, leaving one to wonder who is correct. Ritmeir found a square area measuring 500 cubits by 500 cubits. If his measurements are correct, then the temple is more likely to have been placed over the rock. His measurement started on the north side of the eastern gate where Phoenician stones abruptly end. Measuring 500 cubits to the south, the eastern wall makes an unexplained turn. Ritmeir claims that Herod's workmen simply continued what Solomon had previously built so as not to disturb the square platform that once marked the site for Solomon's Temple.

Measuring 500 cubits to the west, Ritmeir came upon an outcropping of stone work that ran parallel to the eastern wall. Reading from ancient descriptions of the temple, he became convinced that the building itself was placed at the same spot where the Mosque of Omar now sits.

For several years, Jewish scholars have claimed that the mosque must go. Religious Jews do not wish to share the site with a pagan shrine. They have offered to dismantle and move it at their own expense to Mecca or any other location that would be acceptable to Islam.

Others simply await a miracle. They expect God to destroy it. In Hal Lindsey's book, *The Late Great Planet Earth*, he quoted a noted Jewish historian who suggested that one day the Dome of the Rock would have to be removed before the Jewish temple could be rebuilt. When asked by a reporter how he thought that might be accomplished, Israel Eldad replied, "It is, of course, an open question. Who knows, maybe an earthquake."[1] There are others, however, who are not willing to wait upon the Lord. They are determined to rid the sacred hill of Islam's influence altogether.

Attacks on the Temple Mount

In the early 1970s, Israeli courts ruled in favor of religious freedom. Laws were passed to allow freedom of worship, but because of Islamic protests they were never enacted. During the decade of the 1980s several attempts were made to destroy the Moslem mosques. Groups such as the *Kach Movement*, the *Gush Immunim*, the *Temple Mount Faithful*, and the *Temple Institute* have been pressing the Israeli government to allow a Jewish presence on the temple site.

In 1982 an American immigrant, Alan Goodman, charged into the Mosque of Omar firing an automatic rifle, killing a Moslem guard and wounding nine others. He was sentenced to life imprisonment. In 1983 police disrupted a plot by another Jewish group to seize the area, but a court acquitted 29 suspects due to insufficient evidence. There were no convictions. The El Aksa mosque still shows the scars of a 1969 fire set by an Australian, Dennis Rohan, who claimed he was acting on divine instructions. He was deported after a brief term in a mental institution.

The late Rabbi Meir Kahane, then leader of the nationalist Kach movement once said that the Moslem shrines should be dismantled and the holy site returned to Jewish control. He said that he would not condemn attempts to blow up the Moslem shrines because he believed the presence of Moslems in the most holy Jewish site was a sin.

On March 10, 1983, 38 young Jewish men organized an effort to enter through an underground tunnel into the "Solomon's Stables" area below the El Aksa mosque. A Moslem guard heard the commotion just before daybreak and summoned police. Four of the Yeshiva students were arrested at the tunnel. Others were arrested a few hours later. The young men were determined to bring world attention to the fact that Jews are not allowed religious freedom to worship on the temple site in Jerusalem.

On January 27, 1984, two men with guns and grenades were seen attempting to scale the Temple Mount wall. They were trying to break into the El Aksa mosque — with enough explosives to cause many casualties and heavy damage. Moslem guards alerted Israeli police.

Both men fled, leaving behind their explosives.

Police picked up four men but released them after questioning failed to produce a solid lead on who was behind the attack. These incidents are examples of several that occurred during the 1980s. They demonstrate the importance of allowing Jewish worship on the Temple Mount. Most attempts for access to the temple site have been non-violent, but some groups are not quite so patient. So far, the Israeli government has resisted demands and ignored demonstrations seeking Jewish access to their sacred site.

A Jewish presence on the Temple Mount would represent an affirmation of Jewish sovereignty over Jerusalem. For the religious community, ascension to the Temple Mount for prayer is a way of hastening the coming of the Messiah, Who must arrive before a rebuilding of the final temple can commence. And for the Christians, at least for those who take prophecy literally, a Jewish presence on the Temple Mount would be regarded as a fulfillment of prophecy.

The Official Rabbinical View

For many years, Jews have been banned by the rabbis from setting foot on the mountain. According to rabbinical law, all human beings — Gentiles as well as Jews — are regarded as "unclean" and thus unfit to walk on Mount Moriah. Orthodox Jews have been forced to admire the Temple Mount from afar or from photographs. One is even forbidden to fly in a plane over the Temple Mount, as its holiness extends into the heavens.

Sephardi Chief Rabbi Mordechai Eliahu said that as far as he is concerned, everyone — Jew and non-Jew alike — is forbidden to tread on the Temple Mount. His Ashkenazi counterpart, Chief Rabbi Abraham Shapiro, concurs that until the coming of Messiah, ascent to the holy mount should be forbidden.

In 1977, then-Chief Rabbi Ovadia Yosef ruled that no one was authorized to decide where the temple stood or to allow Jews to tread anywhere on the mountain. This statement came a week after his colleague, the late Ashkenazi Chief Rabbi Shlomo Goren, told reporters in a radio interview that he was completing a book mapping out areas on the mount that were "not holy" and on which the Jewish people could walk.

Shlomo Goren was one of the few to make this statement, and he did so as far back as the early 1960s, when he was chief rabbi of the Israeli Defense Forces. He maintained that on the basis of his studies, he had succeeded in identifying an area south of the Temple Mount that was definitely outside the area forbidden to the unclean.

According to Jewish law, a person becomes unclean through contact with the dead. One can only be cleansed with a ritual ceremony involving the ancient ashes of the red heifer — which have been missing for 2,000 years. While the Vendyl Jones group has been exploring caves near the Dead Sea in search of the ashes, others are breeding a red heifer for the purpose of producing a new batch. Until all questions of ritual cleansing are solved, Jews are considered unclean and cannot enter the Temple Mount. Rabbi Goren, however, believed that it was permitted to enter a specified southern area after cleansing oneself from other forms of uncleanness, and observing those regulations applying to reverence for the temple site.

Since 1967 some religious groups have proposed that animal sacrifices be permitted again, based on an ancient Jewish law which declares that they may offer sacrifices although there is no temple. But this has been firmly rejected by the majority of modern Jewish scholars. Meanwhile, a study of the art of temple sacrifice worship is underway at a special school called the Yeshiva Torat Hacohanim meaning, "School on the Law of the Priesthood."

There were varying degrees of holiness on the Temple Mount. The Holy of Holies where the ark of the covenant was kept, was the most sanctified area. The high priest was the only person allowed to enter — and then only once each year on Yom Kippur, for the Day of Atonement service. Jews who were ritually unclean were forbidden to enter the temple area. Today, that includes everyone. All are unclean. Two missing ingredients are needed to cleanse them. In addition to needing the ashes of the red heifer for ritual cleansing, religious Jews also needed to find the source of the *tekhelet*, an ancient blue/purple dye used for the curtain that covered the Holy of Holies, the ribbons of their prayer shawls, etc. For centuries, their tallits have been adorned with black ribbons — a violation of the Mosaic law. But in 1984, that problem was solved.

Sacred Blue/Purple Dye Discovered

A centuries-old Jewish writing in the Talmud (Menahot 44a) says that once every 70 years the shores of the land of Israel are visited by the segulit snail from which the *tekhelet* (blue/purple dye) used to mark certain religious items was made. The *Jerusalem Post* (November 10, 1990) reported that these snails were found in abundance along the Mediterranean coast. Some Orthodox Jews believe the reappearance of these snails is a sign of the approaching Messianic age.

In the seventh century A.D. the manufacturing of the "tekhelet" was confined to the Phoenician coast near the ancient city of Tyre. The "Tyrian purple," a reddish shade derived from a sea snail, brought wealth to its Phoenician manufacturers who supplied sovereigns, as well as synagogues, with beautiful purple woolens.

It has been thought by the rabbis that the shellfish was extinct. Evidently, the seventh-century Arab invasion brought an end to the industry by killing off the key people who knew the secret formula. Furthermore, no sample of the dyed cloth had been known to survive the centuries. If it had, a chemical analysis would have led to the discovery of the dye long before now. Without an actual sample of the dyed cloth to use as a reference, subsequent Scripture translators identified the prescribed color as anything from purple to green to indigo or even yellow.

While most English Bibles render the translation as blue, Martin Luther thought the Greek term "hyakinthos" suggested the color of a local flower by that name, and he translated the word as "gelb," which means yellow. (Boy, did he really miss it!) By comparing the descriptions of early forgeries to some lesser-known Hebrew references to *tekhelet*, Jewish scholars identified the desired color as blue-purple. But which animal produced it?

That was the problem which faced the Jewish people for the past 1,300 years. Since then, they have dyed their ribbons black. It seemed that God had turned their day into night. Jewish tallits used in religious worship have carried the black ribbons — some say because they mourn the destruction of their temple. To be sure, they have had their share of heartaches. Solomon's Temple was destroyed in 587 B.C. and the Babylonian captivity enslaved their families. With the destruction of Herod's Temple in A.D. 70, the great Diaspora drove the Jew from his land to spend the next 1,800 years wandering among the nations of the world. They have had plenty of heartaches. But the fact of the matter is, the borders of their tallits are black instead of blue because they lost the formula for making the blue dye.

However, by piecing together chemical, historical, and archaeological evidence, Irving Ziderman of the Israel Fiber Institute, discovered the ancient blue/purple dye. The discovery was announced in the September 8, 1984, issue of *Science News*, a weekly publication, which told the story of the discovery announced at a meeting of the American Chemical Society in Philadelphia, Pennsylvania. This incredible achievement has led to the renewal of an ancient Jewish practice and the birth of a new industry in Israel. The rediscovery of their ancient blue dye marks an important step toward the renewal of temple worship.

More and more these days, one who travels to Jerusalem sees Orthodox Jews wearing new and colorful prayer shawls as they go to the western wall to pray. Some tallits are sporting blue ribbons and some are showing pink, mauve, and purple ribbons. Only a few years ago all prayer shawls displayed black ribbons. But all that has changed since the discovery of the source of Israel's ancient blue/purple dye.

Irving Ziderman identified a shellfish still found along the shores of the Mediterranean as the source of the key ingredient. The shellfish is called a banded dye-murex. Ziderman indicated that before the dye can be commercially produced, methods must be developed to breed the snails on a larger scale — a big undertaking. One can hardly imagine the enormous size of the industry that will be needed to service the Jewish religion around the world. Marine biologists in Haifa have already begun to explore methods by which they can breed the banded dye-murex shellfish on a large scale. The rediscovery of this ancient dye formula is thought to represent a major step toward the restoration of temple worship.

Just as the prophets foretold, the chosen people have returned to their beloved Jerusalem and are preparing to restore temple liturgy. But what the Jews do not yet understand is that Satan has a plan to steal their dream. Lucifer is preparing for his own son to become the object of worship in a restored Jewish sanctuary. When the son of Satan makes his move, he will commit the ultimate abomination.

What is the Abomination of Desolation?

The prophet Daniel introduced us to the "abomination of desolation:" "And he shall confirm the covenant with many for one week: and in the midst of the week he shall cause the sacrifice and the oblation to cease, and for the overspreading of abominations he shall make it desolate, even until the consummation, and that determined shall be poured upon the desolate" (Dan. 9:27).

This abomination was referred to again by Jesus Christ, during His Olivet Discourse in Matthew 24. Both looked forward into the far future when the Antichrist, that final, ultimate man of sin, commits the predicted abomination on the Temple Mount in Jerusalem. The expression *"abomination of desolation"* is cited twice in the New Testament — Matthew 24:15 and Mark 13:4.

An abomination in the Old Testament was an inward spiritual

and moral revulsion, a great wrong in religious matters. All images and visible representations of God used for worship are abhorrent to Him, as well as all forms, ceremonies, rituals, and objects connected with idolatry. An abomination in the context of religion is a revulsion or a repulsive object of an idolatrous or sacrilegious nature. Such an event is recorded in 2 Kings 3:26-27. It is there that the story of a public human sacrifice to a pagan god by King Mesha of Moab is recorded. The king sacrificed his own son.

In Daniel 9, the reference is given to a distinctly sacrilegious abomination — one which utterly desolates a highly significant religious object or place — namely the temple site.

Antiochus IV Epiphanes

It was thought by early Jewish historians that Antiochus IV Epiphanes fulfilled Daniel's prophecy. The Syrian general sacrificed a sow at the temple in 168 B.C. However, when Jesus spoke of the "abomination of desolation" in Matthew 24:15 and Mark 13:4, He clearly placed the event in the future. Though Antiochus committed an abomination of desolation, the ultimate abomination awaits the Antichrist.

There are some who believe that the prediction was fulfilled by the Romans in A.D. 70. They feel that Titus and his Roman army destroyed Herod's Temple and thus fulfilled the prophecy concerning the abomination that made the place desolate of Jewish worship.

However, the apostle Paul wrote of a time when the Antichrist would desecrate the temple rather than destroy it:

> Let no man deceive you by any means: for that day shall not come, except there come a falling away first, and that man of sin be revealed, the son of perdition;
> Who opposeth and exalteth himself above all that is called God, or that is worshipped; so that he as God sitteth in the temple of God, showing himself that he is God (2 Thess. 2:3-4).

Though he did not use the precise terminology "abomination of desolation," he did speak of a time (yet in the future) when that final man of sin would desecrate the temple. He would sit in the temple of God claiming to be God! Obviously, that final "abomination of desolation" has not yet come to pass. It will be perpetrated by the Antichrist and, according to Daniel 9:27, it will be at the mid-way point of a seven-year covenant. In my opinion, this places it in the middle of the Tribulation period.

It is believed that the Antichrist will come to the Temple Mount where the Jews will have erected their Tribulation sanctuary. The antichrist will cause the sacrifices to stop. He will then enter the Holy of Holies, a place where only the high priest is allowed to enter — and then only once a year. He will desecrate that sacred site by entering it himself. It is possible, then, that he will remove the ark of the covenant and establish his own throne, claiming to be, not only messiah, but God as well.

A Golem?

In the Book of Revelation, we are given a further description of what the Antichrist will do when he commits the "abomination of desolation." We are told that the he will set up some sort of image in the Temple and make it appear to be alive:

> And deceiveth them that dwell on the earth by the means of those miracles which he had power to do in the sight of the beast; saying to them that dwell on the earth, that they should make an image to the beast, which had the wound by a sword, and did live.
>
> And he had power to give life unto the image of the beast, that the image of the beast should both speak, and cause that as many as would not worship the image of the beast should be killed.
>
> And he causeth all, both small and great, rich and poor, free and bond, to receive a mark in their right hand, or in their foreheads:
>
> And that no man might buy or sell, save he that had the mark, or the name of the beast, or the number of his name.
>
> Here is wisdom. Let him that hath understanding count the number of the beast: for it is the number of a man; and his number is Six hundred threescore and six (Rev. 13:14-18).

There are stories from ancient Jewish legends that certain members of a secret Jewish sect — the *Lamed Hay* — have the ability to bring a statue or Golem to life. The *Lamed Hay* consists of 35 men who were chosen centuries ago as keepers of the ineffable name of

God. When a new member of the *Lamed Hay* was initiated into the secret order, he would make a Golem — a clay statute — and engrave Hebrew letters *emet* meaning "truth" on its forehead. When he had memorized the incantations involved in pronouncing the ineffable name, he would call the thing to life. According to legend, the Golem should be put to death within 24 hours. The member of the *Lamed Hay* could do this by erasing the *aleph* one of the three letters on the forehead of the Golem. By erasing the first letter of the three it would change the Hebrew word to meht meaning death, which would kill the Golem.

On the first day, the Golem would call its creator "Master." The second day, the Golem would call its creator, "Friend." However, if allowed to live until the third day, the Golem would call his maker, "Servant." At this point, the Golem would become uncontrollable. There are stories dating from medieval Europe about the making of Golems. For example, I am told that the early story of Frankenstein was said to be of a Golem who got away.

There is a sixteenth century legend about a Golem built during the Spanish inquisition. Soldiers were about to invade a Jewish village and destroy the people. The local rabbi happened to be a member of the *Lamed Hay*. Along with the citizens who helped him, he built a giant Golem. He called the thing to life, and drove away the Spanish inquisitors. That is a part of Spanish history. It is said that the inquisitors never came back to that village again. That's one theory on what the image of the beast could be.

A Computer?

A more modern concept of the "image" might be that of a computer. For the first time in history, a machine can store memory — and it never forgets! Up until this century, only the human brain could store and calculate facts. Since Revelation 13 also refers to the image as having the ability to cause "all . . . to receive a mark in their right hand, or in their foreheads," one may assume that the image also has the ability to identify and track all commerce. That is exactly the function of a computer. Society is moving quickly toward a New World Order and a single world economic system where all transactions can be monitored. The possibility of a central computer, in the hands of a dictator, controlling the marketplace is entirely feasible.

The Coming Antichrist

A specific reference to the term "Antichrist" is found four times in Scripture, all in the epistles of John (1 John 2:18, 22; 4:3; and 2 John 7)." Aside from those specific terms, however, there are many other places in the Bible which refer to the Antichrist. He is called the "beast," "the man of sin," "the son of perdition," "the little horn," etc.

The *Zondervan Pictorial Encyclopedia of the Bible* suggests that there have been an almost unlimited number of identifications of Antichrist in history.[1] Some of the early Roman emperors were considered candidates for Antichrist. The most prominent was Nero, the Roman emperor who gave the orders for the execution of the apostle Paul. During the rise of Islam, Mohammed was thought to be Antichrist. In more recent years, there have been such modern characters as Napoleon, Mussolini, and Hitler. We are reminded that Jesus said there would be many. However, that final man of sin is yet to be revealed.

As I have written in my book, *Guardians of the Grail,* it is my feeling that this "seed of the serpent" will have a genealogy traceable back to the tribe of Dan. He will claim to be the long-looked-for Jewish Messiah.[2]

Daniel's Little Horn

In Daniel 7, four world empires were predicted. The fourth is described as a dreadful beast with ten horns representing a ten-kingdom confederation — a loosely-knit world government. Daniel saw a "little horn" rise up among the ten. This is Daniel's prophetic view of the future Antichrist. Verse 25 predicts that he will "wear out the saints of the Most High." Once he commits the abomination of desolation he will set out to persecute religious Jews who vigorously protest his abominable act. His intense persecution will cause them to flee into the mountains for safety.

It is my feeling that this designates the time in which the "Mark of the Beast" will be introduced. He will tighten his control on all nations by requiring a personal identification for every citizen. No one will be able to participate in the marketplace without complete government control. Over the next three and a half years, however, his empire will deteriorate. It will fall apart under his reign of terror. Eastern nations will reject his "mark" and launch an invasion by 200 million soldiers. They will converge upon Israel for the express purpose of killing every Jew on the planet.

By this time, world opinion will blame the Jewish Antichrist and the entire nation of Israel for the catastrophic predicament facing all nations. During these crucial three and a half years, God will pour out

His wrath upon the nations. Earthquakes will be commonplace. Drought and famine will be widespread. Disease will be rampant. All nations will face seeming certain destruction — and the world dictator will be powerless to stop it. Jesus said:

> For then shall be great tribulation, such as was not since the beginning of the world to this time, no, nor ever shall be. And except those days should be shortened, there should no flesh be saved: but for the elect's sake those days shall be shortened (Matt. 24:21-22).

As Armageddon rages, astronomical events will turn all eyes toward the sky. The sun will be darkened and the moon dimmed as Christ returns in power and great glory. Only the second coming of Jesus Christ will save the human race from self-destruction.

9

Cyberspace Storm Troopers Rampage

by David Webber

Peace is not just over the horizon and man is not done with war. In fact, the twentieth century will doubtless be remembered as the bloodiest and most brutal period in all of man's history.

The Bible shows the ugly root and reason for war in James 4:1-4. "From where come wars and fightings among you? Come they not here, even of your lusts that war in your members? Ye lust, and have not; ye kill, and desire to have, and cannot obtain; ye fight and war, yet ye have not, because ye ask not. Ye ask, and receive not, because ye ask amiss, that ye may consume it upon your lusts. Ye adulterers and adulteresses, know ye not that the friendship of the world is enmity with God? Whosoever, therefore, will be a friend of the world is the enemy of God."

This passage demonstrates the spiritual warfare that continuously rages between God and this world. Even Christians are caught up in this deadly conflict when they conform to this world and lose their first love for our Lord Jesus Christ.

Because of exploding population (Gen. 6:1); increase of knowledge and travel (Dan. 12:4); and the ability to wage war in the heavens, (Joel 2:30, 32), global war and cyberwar may break out before the end of this century!

Governments commit genocide as this century readily confirms; and only God—not people—can control and put down governments.

I refer to Walter E. Williams' column in the *Sunday Oklahoman*, August 20, 1995, which gives the national statistics. Quoting from his article entitled, "People Must Control Mankind's Most Brutal Institutions":

> Generically, what's the most brutal institution on the face of the Earth? If you said governments, go to the head of the class. If anyone is in doubt of that fact, he need only read *Death by Government*, recently published by professor R.J. Rummel of the University of Hawaii's political science department. . .
>
> So far this century, international wars and civil wars have taken about 39 million lives. But that's small in comparison to deliberate government murder. Since the beginning of this century — and keep in mind there are four years left — governments have murdered 170 million people, mostly their own citizens.
>
> The top government murderers are those most adored by America's campus leftists and their counterparts in the media and political arena: the former Soviet Union and the People's Republic of China. Between 1917 and 1987, the Soviet Union, where even President Clinton traveled to protest against our involvement in Vietnam, murdered 62 million of its own citizens. Between 1949 and 1987, mostly under that leftist favorite Mao Tse–tung's rule, 35 million Chinese citizens were murdered by their own government.
>
> Hitler's Nazis were pikers by comparison to the Communists. They managed to exterminate about 21 million Jews, Slavs, Serbs, Czechs Poles, Ukrainians, and people they deemed misfits, such as homosexuals and the mentally ill.
>
> Trailing badly behind the U.S.S.R., China, and the Nazis, Japan murdered 6 million unarmed citizens in Asian countries they conquered during World War II.

Rummel estimates that pre–twentieth century government murder, from the Christian Crusades and slavery of Africans to witch hunts and other episodes, totals about 133 million. Therefore, our century is clearly mankind's most brutal, and we might ask why. Rummel gives the answer in his book's very first sentence:

Power kills; absolute power kills absolutely. . . . The more power a government has, the more it can act arbitrarily according to the whims and desires of the elite, and the more it will make war on others and murder its foreign and domestic subjects. That's the long, tragic, ugly story of government: the elite's use of government to forcibly impose its will on the masses.

Our government has massive power to do evil. Murderers like Josef Stalin, Adolf Hitler, Mao Tse–tung, and Pol Pot would have loved to have the kind of information about its citizens that agencies like the Internal Revenue Service and the Bureau of Alcohol, Tobacco and Firearms have.[1]

We might also add the C.I.A. and the F.B.I.

Since the whole world watched news coverage of "Operation Desert Storm" in January and February of 1991, waging war will never be the same. This marked the beginning of hi–tech war fought by computers, satellites and radar. World War III will be global and inter–spatial and the spiritual nature of combat will begin to overshadow the physical role as the complexities of warfare are enlarged.

Throughout the three chapters of Joel, the Day of the Lord is the predominant theme; and the strange army in Joel 2 appears to be alien or humanoid — and unlike any army ever seen on this planet.

Blow the trumpet in Zion, and sound an alarm in my holy mountain. Let all the inhabitants of the land tremble; for the day of the day of the Lord cometh, for it is near at hand; a day of darkness and of gloominess, a day of clouds and of thick darkness, like the morning spread upon the mountains; a great people and strong; there hath not been ever the like, neither shall be any more after it; even to the years of many generations. A fire devoureth before them; and behind them a flame burneth; the land is like the garden of Eden before them, and behind them a desolate wilderness; yea, and nothing shall escape them. The appearance of them is like the appearance of horses; and like horsemen, so shall they run. Like the noise of chariots on the tops of mountains shall they leap, like the noise of a flame of fire that devoureth the stubble, like a strong people set in battle array. Before their face the peoples shall be much pained;

all faces shall gather blackness. They shall run like mighty men; they shall climb the wall like men of war, and they shall march every one on his ways, and they shall not break their ranks. Neither shall one thrust another; they shall walk every one in his path, and when they fall upon the sword, they shall not be wounded. They shall run to and fro in the city; they shall run upon the wall; they shall climb up upon the houses; they shall enter in at the windows like a thief. The earth shall quake before them; the heavens shall tremble; the sun and the moon shall be dark, and the stars shall withdraw their shining (Joel 2:1–10).

Verses 2, 3, and 4 of Joel 2 could indicate that this is a demonic army unleashed from the pit of hell, as described in Revelation 9. Or verses 5–10 might denote an alien invasion from outer space by fallen angels who give their allegiance to Satan, the fallen angelic prince (Luke 10:18).

Regardless, this weird army is unlike any force that has ever fought upon the battlefields of this earth or ever will wage war upon the continents of this planet again (Joel 2:2). The wars of the tribulation will polarize in the final battle of this age — Armageddon. For a description of this earth–shaking, heaven–rending apocalyptic event we go logically to Joel 3.

> Proclaim this among the nations, Prepare war, wake up the mighty men; let all the men of war draw near; let them come up; beat your plowshares into swords, and your pruning hooks into spears; let the weak say, I am strong. Assemble yourselves, and come, all ye nations, and gather yourselves together round about; there cause thy mighty ones to come down, O Lord. Let the nations be wakened, and come up to the Valley of Jehoshaphat; for there will I sit to judge all the nations round about. Put in the sickle; for the harvest is ripe; come, get down; for the press is full, the vats overflow; for their wickedness is great. Multitudes, multitudes in the valley of decision; for the day of the Lord is near in the valley of decision. The sun and the moon shall be darkened, and the stars shall withdraw their shining. The Lord also shall roar out of Zion, and utter his voice from Jerusalem, and the heavens and the earth shall shake; but the Lord will be the hope of his people, and the strength

of the children of Israel (Joel 3:9–16).

All-out war of physical and spiritual dimensions are indicated in this cryptic passage. The millennial edict of Isaiah 2:4 is reversed as God awakens and beckons the mighty warriors of heaven and earth to join the battle of all the ages. The language of this stern directive is apocalyptic (verse 13), and involves the Valley of Megiddo (verse 14); the universal effects of Armageddon are signified in earth and in heaven as God brings men and angels to the brink of destruction (verses 15 and 16); but God's personal intervention assures victory for the righteous and salvation for Israel.

Other Scripture passages that appear to address man's final battle are Isaiah 13:9–13, Jeremiah 4:23–28, Ezekiel 32:7–10, and Revelation 6:12–17.

One of the battles of the seven-year Tribulation will result in the deaths of one–third of the world's population.

> And the fifth angel sounded, and I saw a star fall from heaven unto the earth; and to him was given the key of the bottomless pit. And he opened the bottomless pit, and there arose a smoke out of the pit, like the smoke of a great furnace; and the sun and the air were darkened by reason of the smoke of the pit. And there came out of the smoke locusts upon the earth, and unto them was given power, as the scorpions of the earth have power. And it was commanded them that they should not hurt the grass of the earth, neither any green thing, neither any tree, but only those men who have not the seal of God in their foreheads. And to them it was given that they should not kill them, but that they should be tormented five months; and their torment was like the torment of a scorpion, when he striketh a man. And in those days shall men seek death, and shall not find it; and shall desire to die, and death shall flee from them (Rev. 9:1-6).

This eerie invasion is from the inner core or bowels of the earth and brings forth a great army of demonic creatures from the bottomless pit. The center of the earth is believed to be extremely hot, and hence the great clouds of smoke darken the sun and our atmosphere.

This catastrophic appearance of creatures described as locusts is reminiscent of the Egyptian plagues, but much more frightening and terrible. The five-month period of May through September is the time for locusts. These demonic creatures are commanded to not hurt or devour the grass or trees or any green things; and they are only permitted to torment those men who do not have the seal of God in their foreheads as do the 144,000 servants of God in Revelation 7:1–5.

All the people who are not under God's divine protection will be so tormented and afflicted during this time period of five months; that they will want to die: but death takes a holiday. "And in those days shall men seek death, and shall not find it; and shall desire to die, and death shall flee from them" (Rev. 9:6).

Now continuing to quote Revelation 9:7–16:

> And the shapes of the locusts were like horses prepared unto battle; and on their heads were, as it were, crowns like gold, and their faces were like the faces of men. And they had hair like the hair of women, and their teeth were like the teeth of lions. And they had breastplates, as it were breastplates of iron; and the sound of their wings was like the sound of chariots of many horses running to battle. And they had tails like scorpions, and there were stings in their tails; and their power was to hurt men five months. And they had a king over them, who is the angel of the bottomless pit, whose name in the Hebrew tongue is Abaddon, but in the Greek tongue hath his name Apollyon. One woe is past and, behold, there come two woes more, hereafter. And the sixth angel sounded, and I heard a voice from the four horns of the golden altar which is before God, saying to the sixth angel who had the trumpet, Loose the four angels who are bound in the great river, Euphrates. And the four angels were loosed, who were prepared for an hour, and a day, and a month, and a year, to slay the third part of men. And the number of the army of the horsemen were two hundred thousand thousand; and I heard the number of them.

These strange androgynous creatures that come forth out of the bottomless pit make up a huge army numbered at 200,000,000 demons (verse 16) Apparently, the four fallen angelic princes are also loosed from their captivity to lead this incredible army of demons into battle according to God's appointed timetable.

In completing our brief study of Revelation 9 and this unearthly demonic army, we quote the last five verses of the chapter.

> And thus I saw the horses in the vision and them that sat on them, having breastplates of fire, and of jacinth, and brimstone; and the heads of the horses were like the heads of lions, and out of their mouths issued fire and smoke and brimstone. By these three was the third part of men killed, by the fire, and by the smoke, and by the brimstone, which issued out of their mouths. For their power is in their mouth, and in their tails; for their tails were like serpents, and had heads, and with them they do hurt. And the rest of the men who were not killed by these plagues yet repented not of the works of their hands, that they should not worship demons, and idols of gold, and silver, and bronze, and stone, and wood, which neither can see, nor hear, nor walk. Neither repented they of their murders, nor of their sorceries, nor of their fornication, nor of their thefts (Rev. 9:17–21).

The fire, the smoke, the brimstone that issues from these bizarre beings results in the death of one–third of the population of this earth. The activities of this legendary army are detailed in verses 17, 18, and 19.

In spite of the number of deaths and terrible carnage, the people of this tribulation time do not cease from their murderous ways, their drugs, their illicit sex, and their stealing! What demon power will be unleashed upon the whole world! This will signify the mystery of iniquity coming to the entire earth; and this time frame shows the madness of earth's rebellion. Even the world senses that such a time is coming, because the technology is already being prepared.

As an example, "Onward Cyber Soldiers" is a nine-page report on cyberwar. This extensive report is quoted from *Time*'s August 21, 1995 issue. Quoting the first six paragraphs:

> In a secure vault in the U.S. Army's super–secret Intelligence and Security Command in northern Virginia, Colonel Mike Tanksley sketches the barest outlines of the new Armageddon. These are only "What ifs?" he insists, so there cannot really be details. Yet his war scenario resounds with almost biblical force. The next time a tyrant

out of some modern Babylon (Baghdad, Tehran, or Tripoli, for example) threatens an American ally (Riyadh, Cairo, Jerusalem) the U.S. doesn't immediately send legions of soldiers or fleets of warships. Instead Washington visits upon the offending tyranny a series of thoroughly modern plagues born of mice, video screens, and keyboards.

First, a computer virus is inserted into the aggressor's telephone–switching stations, causing widespread failure of the phone system. Next, computer logic bombs, set to activate at predetermined times, destroy the electronic routers that control rail lines and military convoys, thus misrouting boxcars and causing traffic jams. Meanwhile, enemy field officers obey the orders they receive over their radios, unaware the commands are phony. Their troops are rendered ineffective as they scatter through the desert. U.S. planes, specially outfitted for psychological operations, then jam the enemy's TV broadcasts with propaganda messages that turn the populace against its ruler. When the despot boots up his PC, he finds that the millions of dollars he has hoarded in his Swiss bank account have been zeroed out. Zapped. All without firing a shot. A glow comes over Colonel Tanksley as he talks about this bloodless retribution. "We may be able to stop a war before it starts," he says. Or, more likely, wage war in a whole new way.

The vision from the vault in Virginia is of "information warfare" — now the hottest concept in the halls of the Pentagon. Info warriors hope to transform the way soldiers fight. Their goal: to exploit the technological wonders of the late twentieth century to launch rapid, stealthy, widespread, and devastating attacks on the military and civilian infrastructure of an enemy. In interviews with scores of military, intelligence and Administration officials, *Time* discovered that the Pentagon has wide–ranging plans to revolutionize the battlefield with information technology much as tanks did in World War I and the atom bomb in World War II. Says Admiral William Owens, vice chairman of the Joint Chiefs of Staff: "This is America's gift to warfare."

The cyberwar revolution, however, poses serious problems for the U.S. Some are ethical: Is it a war crime to crash another country's stock market? More perilous are the security concerns for the U.S., where a tyrant with inexpensive technology could unplug NASDAQ or terrorist hackers could disrupt an airport tower. Giddy excitement over infowar may be shaken by an electronic Pearl Harbor. Last year the government's Joint Security Commission called U.S. vulnerability to info-war "the major security challenge of this decade and possibly the next century."

Info-war evolved with every recent U.S. military foray. In the first day of the Persian Gulf War, Air Force stealth planes armed with precision–guided munitions blinded Saddam by knocking out his communications network and electrical power in Baghdad. The Pentagon launched a sophisticated psy–ops campaign against Haiti's military regime to restore deposed President Jean–Bertrand Aristide. Using market research surveys, the Army's 4th Psychological Operations Group divided Haiti's population into 20 target groups and bombarded them with hundreds of thousands of pro–Aristide leaflets appealing to their particular affinities. Before U.S. intervention, the CIA made anonymous phone calls to Haitian soldiers, urging them to surrender, and sent ominous E–mail messages to some members of Haiti's oligarchy who had personal computers.

This was just the beginning. The promise of info-war has grown exponentially with the increasing power and pervasiveness of computer microprocessors, high–speed communications and sophisticated sensors — all with tremendous battle potential for those who know how to manipulate them.

Biblical expressions come forward to describe such hi–tech warfare; Armageddon comes into ever–sharper focus.

The byline of this incredible article immediately gets our attention! "The U.S. may soon wage war by mouse, keyboard, and computer virus. But it is vulnerable to the same attacks." It further tells us that info-war offices are being set up in the Army, Navy, and Air Force.

The first info-war officers were graduated in June 1995, trained in computer defense and virtual reality.

Battle gear for Cyberwar is shown in a picture of a modern day soldier:

1. Integrated headgear is the soldier's helmet and it collects information and the latest intelligence for the soldier right on the field. The lightweight helmet provides greater protection against enemy fire; and also night–vision sensors, a miniature video, and voice-activated computer built into the soldier's body armor.

2. The body armor also protects the soldier against chemical and nuclear attacks.

3. The computer in the body armor operates the soldier's technology, gives him friend or foe identification, detects mines and chemicals, and pinpoints his location on the battlefield.

4. A wireless connection links his weapon to his helmet monitor so he can aim at targets without exposing himself to the enemy.

Information warfare will be the order of the day. Under the world's final ruler — Antichrist — our world will be drastically changed. Activities by F.E.M.A. police will plunge the people into an Orwellian world. Cyberspace activities will dominate the information super highway; and life will no longer be tranquil and unhurried.

People will function in a gray area called virtual reality, and tele–communications plus computers linked together by satellite will emerge before the dawning of the twenty-first century.

If we did not have the prophecies of the Old Testament and Revelation, we could not begin to understand the world of tomorrow. Joel 2:30-31 describes Star Wars and the results of interstellar activities.

> And I will show wonders in the heavens and in the earth: blood, and fire, and pillars of smoke. The sun shall be turned into darkness, and the moon into blood, before the great and the terrible day of the Lord come.

Zechariah 14 describes Armageddon, and the nuclear plagues that befall the enemies of Israel; and Christ's second coming with His armies from heaven.

> For I will gather all nations against Jerusalem to battle; and the city shall be taken, and the houses rifled, and the women ravished; and half of the city shall go forth into

captivity, and the residue of the people shall not be cut off from the city. Then shall the Lord go forth, and fight against those nations, as when he fought in the day of battle. And the Lord shall be king over all the earth; in that day shall there be one Lord, and his name one. And men shall dwell in it, and there shall be no more utter destruction; but Jerusalem shall be safely inhabited. And this shall be the plague with which the Lord will smite all the peoples that have fought against Jerusalem: their flesh shall consume away while they stand upon their feet, and their eyes shall consume away in their holes, and their tongue shall consume away in their mouth.

If it were not because of God's supernatural intervention, Planet Earth would surely become a desolation and nuclear winter would spread over the earth like a curse and a global blanket of judgment. "The earth also is defiled under the inhabitants thereof; because they have transgressed the laws, changed the ordinance, broken the everlasting covenant. Therefore hath the curse devoured the earth, and they that dwell therein are desolate; therefore, the inhabitants of the earth are burned, and few men left (Isa. 24:5–6). "And he will destroy in this mountain the face of the covering cast over all people, and the veil that is spread over all nations. He will swallow up death in victory; and the Lord God will wipe away tears from all faces; and the rebuke of his people, shall he take away from all the earth; for the Lord hath spoken it" (Isa. 25:7–8). I suggest that this veil and covering are the result of nuclear war and a literal radioactive covering over the face of the whole earth.

The pentagon is surely working on the initial phases of such fourth-dimensional warfare.

Consider five such areas pinpointed by *Time* in their August 21, 1995, article on Cyberwar.

1. Electromagnetic Pulse: Delta force commandos infiltrate the enemy's capitol and detonate a non–nuclear electromagnetic pulse device the size of a suitcase. The bomb, near a central bank, fries the electronics of the bank's computer and communications systems, shutting down most of the financial operations.

2. Computer Viruses: The C.I.A. inserts computer viruses into the switching network for the country's phone system, causing massive failure of telecommunications.

3. Info Attack: Air Force electronic jam–planes break into the communications equipment of the enemy and overwhelm its leaders with false information.

4. Commando Solo Plane: The Air Force's commando solo psy–ops plane jams signals for the government television station and releases unfavorable propaganda to depose the nation's leader.

5. Logic Bomb: Logic bombs shut down the computers that run the country's air–traffic control systems and route its railroads. Consequently, planes and trains are misdirected; and military supplies end up at wrong destinations.

To sum it all up: "Future warfare may look like today's science–fiction thrillers." Perhaps someday national leaders will fight virtual wars before they decide to go to war at all!

Before the final battle of Armageddon, God's wrath will be supernaturally poured out upon the earth, the seas, and the sun in the seven vials of judgments.

> And I heard a great voice out of the temple saying to the seven angels, Go your ways, and pour out the bowls of the wrath of God upon the earth. and the first went, and poured out his bowl upon the earth, and there fell a foul and painful sore upon the men who had the mark of the beast, and upon them who worshiped his image. And the second angel poured out his bowl upon the sea, and it became like the blood of a dead man; and every living soul died in the sea. And the third angel poured out his bowl upon the rivers and fountains of waters, and they became blood. And I heard the angel of the waters say, Thou art righteous, O Lord, who art, and wast, and shalt be, because thou hast judged thus. For they have shed the blood of saints and prophets, and thou has given them blood to drink; for they are worthy. And I heard another out of the altar say, Even so, Lord God Almighty, true and righteous are thy judgments. (Rev. 16:1–7).

These judgments are primarily focused upon this solar system. The sun is drastically affected (verses 8-9). The judgments have to do with earth, air, and water (verses 2, 3–6, 17) God's supernatural judgments also are specifically intended for the kingdom of the beast, the men with the mark of the beast, and the deception of the un–holy trinity. (verses 2, 10-11, and 13–14).

> And the seventh angel poured out his bowl into the air, and there came a great voice out of the temple of heaven, from the throne, saying, It is done. And there were voices, and thunders, and lightnings; there was a great earthquake, such as was not since men were upon the earth, so mighty an earthquake, and so great. And the great city was divided into three parts, and the cities of the nations fell; and great Babylon came in remembrance before God, to give unto her the cup of the wine of the fierceness of his wrath. And every island fled away, and the mountains were not found. And there fell upon men a great hail out of heaven, every stone about the weight of a talent; and men blasphemed God because of the plague of the hail; for the plague was exceedingly great (Rev. 16:17–21).

The seventh vial signals the change of administration, the plague of huge hail, greater than the time of Joshua's long day, and the greatest earthquake of all time. In spite of all these catastrophic events, the men of the kingdom of the beast do not repent.

Daniel's 70 weeks prophecies reveal that "Unto the end of the war desolations are determined" (Dan. 9:26).

God grant us courage and faith to be strong in the Lord and in the power of His might; until He comes and fulfills this heavenly edict!

> And the seventh angel sounded; and there were great voices in heaven, saying, The kingdom of this world is become the kingdom of our Lord, and of his Christ, and he shall reign forever and ever. And the four and twenty elders, who sat before God on their thrones, fell upon their faces, and worshiped God, saying, We give thee thanks, O Lord God Almighty, who art, and wast, and art to come, because thou hast taken to thee thy great power, and hast reigned (Rev. 11:15–17).

10

The Ultimate Hiding Place

by David Webber

Noah's ark was a refuge and a hiding place from God's pristine judgment of the great Flood. Eight souls were preserved from this universal judgment. Eight is the number of Christ and the number of new beginnings.

Since Jesus Christ died on the cross to redeem Adam's race, He became our ark of safety. May God speak to many hearts to enter in right now, believe the gospel, and be saved by faith in Him (1 Cor. 15:1-4).

Israel looked upon their God Jehovah as a Rock of refuge and the Cornerstone of their salvation. "The Lord is my Rock, and my fortress, and my deliverer; my God, my strength, in whom I will trust; my buckler, and the horn of my salvation, and my high tower" (Ps. 18:2). In the New Testament, the symbolism is the same.

Moreover, brethren, I would not that ye should be ignorant, how that all our fathers were under the cloud, and all passed through the sea (1 Cor. 10:1).

And were all baptized unto Moses in the cloud and in the sea (1 Cor. 10:2).

And did all eat the same spiritual meat (1 Cor. 10:3).

And did all drink the same spiritual drink: for they drank of that spiritual Rock that followed them: and that

Rock was Christ (1 Cor. 10:4).

In Isaiah 26:4 we see the mighty rock of God's deliverance for the remnant of Israel: "Trust ye in the Lord for ever: for in the Lord Jehovah is everlasting strength."

The footnote in my Pilgrim Bible is, "Everlasting strength in the Hebrew is Rock of Ages."

So it is altogether fitting that the rock city of Petra (Petra means rock) should become a hiding place for the one-third of Israel — the Remnant of Israel — during the time of Israel's greatest affliction, "the time of Jacob's trouble" (Jer. 30:7).

Petra was possibly the land of the biblical Horites about the time of Abraham (2000 B.C.) Apparently, this was the area called Edom and the dwelling place of Esau after he lost his birthright to Jacob.

About 800 B.C., the Nabateans, possibly from North Africa, settled in Petra. With the wealth they amassed from robbing passing caravans they built up Petra with temples, houses, and tombs, and it became a thriving, busy city.

The Romans later conquered Petra in A.D. 106 and also built temples, marketplaces, and an amphitheater that seated about 6,000 people.

The interesting feature about this mysterious city (20 square miles) was that the rose-red city was lost to the world for hundreds of years until it was re-discovered by John Burckhardt in 1812.

It has been told that a well-known minister of the last century named Blackstone hid thousands of New Testaments in the numerous caves that abound in this natural fortress. It is as though God has prepared this remote area for a remnant of the covenant people in the last days as a rocky sanctuary.

Daniel 11:41 could indicate such a hiding place for the Jews. "He shall enter also into the glorious land, and many countries shall be overthrown; but these shall escape out of his hand, even Edom, and Moab, and the chief of the children of Ammon."

The end of the prophetic picture seems to center around the remnant of Israel that flees from the face of Antichrist when he stands in the Temple and declares to the world that he is god and takes away the daily sacrifice.

I am convinced that the Lord has a prepared place to preserve His covenant people, at least a remnant who call upon His Name; and that He will in some manner lead them to the place of safety. When He returns at the Second Coming, He will personally return to Petra and lead them on the King's Highway back to the Promised Land. The Scriptures also indicate that they will not be safe unless they stay in their hiding place until the Lord returns.

The Lord says to Israel: "I will go and return to My place till they acknowledge their offense and seek my face; in their affliction they will seek me early" (Hos. 5:15).

As the believing remnant begin to cry out unto God in Psalm 60:1: "O God thou has cast us off, thou hast scattered us, thou hast been displeased; Oh turn Thyself to us again," we find God's answer and His salvation:

> Thou hast given a banner to them that fear thee, that it may be displayed because of the truth. Selah (Ps. 60:4).
>
> That thy beloved may be delivered; save with thy right hand, and hear me (Ps. 60:5).
>
> Who will bring me into the strong city? who will lead me into Edom? (Ps. 60:9).
>
> Wilt not thou, O God, which hadst cast us off? and thou, O God, which didst not go out with our armies? (Ps. 60:10).
>
> Give us help from trouble: for vain is the help of man (Ps. 60:11).
>
> Through God we shall do valiantly: for he it is that shall tread down our enemies (Ps. 60:12).

God further establishes the fact of His personal deliverance of the chosen of Israel in Isaiah 63:1-4 and 8-9:

> Who is this that cometh from Edom, with dyed garments from Bozrah? this that is glorious in his apparel, traveling in the greatness of his strength? I that speak in righteousness, mighty to save (Isa. 63:1).
>
> Wherefore art thou red in thine apparel, and thy garments like him that treadeth in the winefat? (Isa. 63:2).
>
> I have trodden the winepress alone; and of the people there was none with me: for I will tread them in mine anger, and trample them in my fury; and their blood shall be sprinkled upon my garments, and I will stain all my raiment (Isa. 63:3).
>
> For the day of vengeance is in mine heart, and the year of my redeemed is come (Isa. 63:4).

For he said, Surely they are my people, children that will not lie: so he was their Saviour (Isa. 63:8).

In all their affliction he was afflicted, and the angel of his presence saved them: in his love and in his pity he redeemed them; and he bare them, and carried them all the days of old (Isa. 63:9).

Perhaps God reveals in a different way His sanctuary and His salvation for His ancient people in Isaiah 26:20-21:

Come, my people, enter thou into thy chambers, and shut thy doors about thee: hide thyself as it were for a little moment, until the indignation be overpast (Isa. 26:20).

For, behold, the Lord cometh out of his place to punish the inhabitants of the earth for their iniquity: the earth also shall disclose her blood, and shall no more cover her slain (Isa. 26:21).

Surely God's supernatural intervention is portrayed in Isaiah 16:1-5, as the ancient name for Petra — Sela — is used:

Send ye the lamb to the ruler of the land from Sela to the wilderness, unto the mount of the daughter of Zion (Isa. 16:1).

For it shall be, that, as a wandering bird cast out of the nest, so the daughters of Moab shall be at the fords of Arnon (Isa. 16:2).

Take counsel, execute judgment; make thy shadow as the night in the midst of the noonday; hide the outcasts; bewray not him that wandereth (Isa. 16:3).

Let mine outcasts dwell with thee, Moab; be thou a covert to them from the face of the spoiler: for the extortioner is at an end, the spoiler ceaseth, the oppressors are consumed out of the land (Isa. 16:4).

And in mercy shall the throne be established: and he shall sit upon it in truth in the tabernacle of David, judging, and seeking judgment, and hasting righteousness (Isa. 16:5).

These distinctive verses also show that these events are in the context of the Day of the Lord, and the fulfillment of the angel's message to Mary concerning Christ sitting upon the throne of David.

He shall be great, and shall be called the Son of the Highest: and the Lord God shall give unto him the throne of his father David (Luke 1:32).

And he shall reign over the house of Jacob for ever; and of his kingdom there shall be no end (Luke 1:33).

These verses in Isaiah 16 could also indicate that the sequence of events will be the same as in ancient days. The tabernacle of David will be restored as promised in Amos 9:11: "On that day I will raise up the tabernacle of David, which has fallen down, and repair its damages; I will raise up its ruins and rebuild it as in the days of old." (Also see Acts 15:16.) Christ, returning in great power and glory, will build the third Temple.

And speak unto him, saying, Thus speaketh the Lord of hosts, saying, Behold the man whose name is the Branch; and he shall grow up out of his place, and he shall build the temple of the Lord (Zech. 6:12).

Even he shall build the temple of the Lord; and he shall bear the glory, and shall sit and rule upon his throne; and he shall be a priest upon his throne: and the counsel of peace shall be between them both (Zech. 6:13).

My footnote in the Pilgrim edition of the KJV has this to say concerning "My Servant the Branch": "Here is a definite prophecy more than five hundred years before the coming of the Messiah. My Servant is often used in the Book of Isaiah for our Lord Jesus Christ as Messiah. So in Zechariah; the Branch is also His name, as we read in 6:12: "Whose name is the branch." He is spoken of six times in the Scriptures as the branch (Isa. 4:2; 11:1; Zech. 3:8; 6:12; Jer 23:5; 33:15), under four headings, and these four headings are set forth in the four Gospels as they picture the Lord Jesus Christ:

1. "A righteous branch . . . a King" (Jer. 23:5; 33:15) — the Gospel of Matthew: "Behold, a King."
2. "My Servant the branch" (Zech. 3:8) — the Gospel of Mark: "Behold, My Servant."
3. "The man whose name is the branch" (Zech. 6:12) — the Gospel of Luke: "Behold, the man."
4. "The branch of Jehovah" (Isa. 4:2) — the Gospel of John: "Behold your God."

Today, there are more than five million inhabitants in contemporary Israel — about four million are Jews who have returned to the land. Ancient prophecies tell us that two-thirds of the Jews in the land will die during the seven years of terrible tribulation. But one-third will be divinely protected and delivered from the fiery trials of this time period.

> And it shall come to pass, that in all the land, saith the Lord, two parts therein shall be cut off and die; but the third shall be left therein (Zech. 13:8).

> And I will bring the third part through the fire, and will refine them as silver is refined, and will try them as gold is tried: they shall call on my name, and I will hear them: I will say, It is my people: and they shall say, The Lord is my God (Zech. 13:9).

We interpret the one-third as believing Israel of Romans 11:26; and the godly remnant that God supernaturally protects in a specially prepared hiding place (Isa. 26:20-21). We have a symbolic picture of Israel, the sun-clad woman, who brings forth the man child — Jesus Christ — who according to His humanity is of the seed of David and destined to rule all nations with a rod of iron.

> And there appeared a great wonder in heaven; a woman clothed with the sun, and the moon under her feet, and upon her head a crown of twelve stars (Rev. 12:1).

> And she being with child cried, travailing in birth, and pained to be delivered (Rev. 12:2).

> And there appeared another wonder in heaven; and behold a great red dragon, having seven heads and ten horns, and seven crowns upon his heads (Rev. 12:3).

> And his tail drew the third part of the stars of heaven, and did cast them to the earth: and the dragon stood before the woman which was ready to be delivered, for to devour her child as soon as it was born (Rev. 12:4).

> And she brought forth a man child, who was to rule all nations with a rod of iron: and her child was caught up unto God, and to his throne (Rev. 12:5).

> And the woman fled into the wilderness, where she hath a place prepared of God, that they should feed her there a thousand two hundred and threescore days (Rev. 12:6).

Notice the devil in his pristine setting as the great red dragon is in deadly opposition to Israel — the woman — and to her child, the incarnate Son of God.

Between verses 5 and 6, we span many centuries going right from the birth of the promised seed into the seventieth week of Daniel, when the woman — Israel — flees for her life into the wilderness.

God's chosen remnant — the believing Jews of Romans 11:25-26 have a specially prepared place for the last half of the Tribulation, three and one-half years.

> And when the dragon saw that he was cast unto the earth, he persecuted the woman which brought forth the man child (Rev. 12:13).
>
> And to the woman were given two wings of a great eagle, that she might fly into the wilderness, into her place, where she is nourished for a time, and times, and half a time, from the face of the serpent (Rev. 12:14).
>
> And the serpent cast out of his mouth water as a flood after the woman, that he might cause her to be carried away of the flood (Rev. 12:15).
>
> And the earth helped the woman, and the earth opened her mouth, and swallowed up the flood which the dragon cast out of his mouth (Rev. 12:16).
>
> And the dragon was wroth with the woman, and went to make war with the remnant of her seed, which keep the commandments of God, and have the testimony of Jesus Christ (Rev. 12:17).

Apparently, her escape will be by airplane (Rev. 12:14 and Isa. 40:31). Today at Mount Sinai, there is a landing field right out in the desert. When the believing remnant arrives at the rock city of Petra, the devil tries to drown them in a flood; but the earthquake prone area opens up and receives the avalanche of waters.

> And after threescore and two weeks shall Messiah be cut off, but not for himself: and the people of the prince that shall come shall destroy the city and the sanctuary; and the end thereof shall be with a flood, and unto the end of the war desolations are determined (Dan. 9:26).

Since the signing of a peace treaty between Jordan and Israel, Jews with a foreign passport have been able to visit Petra. Some of the impressions of Haim Shapiro who writes for the *Jerusalem Post* are recorded in a recent article, "Don't Sing the Petra Song in Petra."

"Don't sing the Petra song in Petra" — that was one of several guidelines for Israelis visiting Jordan.

I probably would not have thought of the song were it not for the rule, but as my horse plodded along the canyon leading to the famed city, I could barely restrain myself from breaking out into song.

The most amazing thing about the visit to Jordan was that I was there at all. Perhaps this feeling of wonder made every sight even better than I had imagined. The red rocks of Petra were more striking than the photographs, and the detailed carving in the rock more impressive, the colors of the mosaic map at Madaba were clearer than in any picture, and the Roman theater at Jarash was more impressive than on Jordan television.

The Jordanians were admitting Israelis only if they had foreign passports, but former restrictions which had decreed that no sign of Israel besmirch these passports have been forgotten. Israel's restrictions on its citizens traveling directly into Jordan have also been lifted.

Galilee Tours, which organized the tour, reports that thus far, "the demand has been brisk. With the signing of a peace treaty, it can only be a matter of weeks before Israelis will be able to enter Jordan on Israeli passports."

Perhaps this is a preview of Jews fleeing for their lives from the face and fury of the Antichrist in their final holocaust. This time, they will sing the Petra song as they sang praises to God after the exodus from Egypt.

Israel is God's earthly people and He has been pleased to make a covenant with them. According to the prophecies, God will make a new covenant with Israel in the last days when He re-gathers them into the Holy Land.

> Behold, the days come, saith the Lord, that I will make a new covenant with the house of Israel, and with the house of Judah (Jer. 31:31).
>
> Not according to the covenant that I made with their fathers in the day that I took them by the hand to bring them out of the land of Egypt; which my covenant they brake, although I was an husband unto them, saith the Lord (Jer. 31:32).
>
> But this shall be the covenant that I will make with

the house of Israel; After those days, saith the Lord, I will put my law in their inward parts, and write it in their hearts; and will be their God, and they shall be my people (Jer. 31:33).

Also God reveals His divine providence over Israel against curses and in the day of battle. Balaam's four prophecies reveal many wonderful things about God's watch care over Israel.

> And he took up his parable, and said, Balak the king of Moab hath brought me from Aram, out of the mountains of the east, saying, Come, curse me Jacob, and come, defy Israel (Num. 23:7).
> How shall I curse, whom God hath not cursed? or how shall I defy, whom the Lord hath not defied? (Num. 23:8).
> For from the top of the rocks I see him, and from the hills I behold him: lo, the people shall dwell alone, and shall not be reckoned among the nations (Num. 23:9).
> Who can count the dust of Jacob, and the number of the fourth part of Israel? Let me die the death of the righteous, and let my last end be like his! (Num. 23:10).

This passage shows Israel dwelling alone and possibly indicates that one–fourth of Israel will be the remnant that God miraculously protects.

The second prophecy reveals that ultimately Israel would have a king; and that no enchantment can touch God's covenant people; and the blessing that God gave to Abraham has never been nullified (Num. 23:18-24).

> Now the Lord had said unto Abram, Get thee out of thy country, and from thy kindred, and from thy father's house, unto a land that I will shew thee (Gen. 12:1).
> And I will make of thee a great nation, and I will bless thee, and make thy name great; and thou shalt be a blessing (Gen. 12:2).
> And I will bless them that bless thee, and curse him that curseth thee: and in thee shall all families of the earth be blessed (Gen. 12:3).

The third prophecy of Balaam is a beautiful picture of Israel back in their own land in the last days and how God's prosperity will rest upon them as He prepares to pour out His Spirit like water out of many buckets.

> And he took up his parable, and said, Balaam the son of Beor hath said, and the man whose eyes are open hath said (Num. 24:3).
>
> He hath said, which heard the words of God, which saw the vision of the Almighty, falling into a trance, but having his eyes open (Num. 24:4).
>
> How goodly are thy tents, O Jacob, and thy tabernacles, O Israel! (Num. 24:5).
>
> As the valleys are they spread forth, as gardens by the river's side, as the trees of lign aloes which the Lord hath planted, and as cedar trees beside the waters (Num. 24:6).
>
> He shall pour the water out of his buckets, and his seed shall be in many waters, and his king shall be higher than Agag, and his kingdom shall be exalted (Num. 24:7).
>
> God brought him forth out of Egypt; he hath as it were the strength of an unicorn: he shall eat up the nations his enemies, and shall break their bones, and pierce them through with his arrows (Num. 24:8).
>
> He couched, he lay down as a lion, and as a great lion: who shall stir him up? Blessed is he that blesseth thee, and cursed is he that curseth thee (Num. 24:9).

This is doubtless the same prophecy of Joel 2:28-29:

> And it shall come to pass afterward, that I will pour out my spirit upon all flesh; and your sons and your daughters shall prophesy, your old men shall dream dreams, your young men shall see visions (Joel 2:28).
>
> And also upon the servants and upon the handmaids in those days will I pour out my spirit (Joel 2:29).

This is pre-determined by two parallel prophecies.

> Until the spirit be poured upon us from on high, and the wilderness be a fruitful field, and the fruitful field be counted for a forest (Isa. 32:15).
>
> Neither will I hide my face any more from them: for I have poured out my spirit upon the house of Israel, saith

the Lord God (Ezek. 39:29).

God also reaffirms His covenant blessing to Abraham in Numbers 24:9.

The fourth prophecy has to do with both the first and second comings of Christ.

> I shall see him, but not now: I shall behold him, but not nigh: there shall come a Star out of Jacob, and a Scepter shall rise out of Israel, and shall smite the corners of Moab, and destroy all the children of Sheth (Num. 24:17).
>
> And Edom shall be a possession, Seir also shall be a possession for his enemies; and Israel shall do valiantly (Num. 24:18).
>
> Out of Jacob shall come he that shall have dominion, and shall destroy him that remaineth of the city (Num. 24:19).

This is a complete prophecy for the last days. The Star out of Jacob is the sign of Christ's birth. The scepter that shall rise out of Israel signifies the coming kingdom or God from heaven (Dan. 2:44). Verse 18 demonstrates that God has not forgotten the believing remnant that He will hide in Edom or Petra.

> And Edom shall be a possession, Seir also shall be a possession for his enemies; and Israel shall do valiantly (Num. 24:18).

11

All the King's Men Storm to Armageddon

by Dave Breese

What is that distant thunder?

Why, of course, it is the sound of war. It is the booming of the cannon and the rattle of machine gun fire, the roar of airplanes and the rumble of engines. It is the making of mechanisms which are dedicated to operate in the killing fields and to turning the terrain into a vast cemetery, reaching as far as the eye can see. That distant thunder is the echo of the plague of our day and of all time. It is the sound of war.

There is, in fact, no good way to analyze the meaning of history without recognizing that history is the story of interminable warfare. With the exception of a few short years, the history of the twentieth century has been that of wars, large and small, conducted in one place or another.

First there came World War I. Here massive armies dug trenches a few hundred feet from one another. After four years of intense battle day and night, the war subsided, with millions dead and the front lines not having moved but a few yards forward and backward. The world looked at the awful carnage of World War I and said with high purpose and deep sadness, "Never again!" "Never again!"

But, of course, World War I was followed by 20 years of troubled peace. During those 20 years, the world of science aligned itself with the world of the military. Between them they incorporated the lessons of World War I and built armaments that were stronger, larger, faster, and more efficient as killing machines. These soon found themselves in deadly use once again as World War II broke upon the world. Beginning with the again provocative city of Sarajevo, World War I became the staging area, the trigger mechanism for World War II. World War II gave us armies more massive that ever before, high speed aircraft, tanks that had been developed and perfected, and especially the atomic bomb. The world still remembers with a fair degree of remaining astonishment the awful carnage of World War II.

Nevertheless, the world allowed itself to be divided since those days and continued its practice of war. This time around, the excuse for war was ideological, but the bloody results were the same. There came, first of all, the carnage of the Korean War. Here the troops from east and west grappled with one another in the bloody plains, the frozen heights, and the muddy valleys of this hitherto unimportant land. Korea ended in a stalemate, but the call for war continued.

That call brought additional millions of men to South Vietnam, where the rice fields ran red with blood and the soldiers of both sides died by the tens of thousands. It was in the Vietnam War that, for the first time in history, the American armies were vanquished from the battlefield. Never before had the flag of the States been dragged through the mud by a conquering army. Now, however, the world has seen this.

With an understandably more feeble response, the United States then joined the political/economic conflict in Haiti. This was followed by her involvement in Somalia. Here Americans died, but no one explained the nature of the conflict.

There now boils up a new and confusing confrontation in the Balkans, where the nations of Serbia, Croatia, and Bosnia lock themselves in a bloody embrace.

This continuing series of bloody conflicts causes the world anew to ask, "When will it end?" "What can we do to bring peace and the end of bloodletting to this troubled and foolish world of ours?"

The Coming King

Of interest to all of us is the fact that the world refuses to listen to the proper answer to that question because the answer is never. Never will the world come to the end of wars and begin to live in peace. Never, that is, until the King of the universe returns to impose His program of peace upon the reluctant belligerence of the world. Until then, we have the Word of Christ as to the nature of things. He says, "And you shall hear of wars and rumors of wars; see that you be not troubled; for all these things must come to pass, but the end is not yet" (Matt. 24:6).

Christ expanded on that statement just a bit by saying, "For nation shall rise against nation, and kingdom against kingdom; and there shall be famines, and pestilences, and earthquakes, in various places. All these are the beginning of sorrows" (Matt. 24:7-8). So it is that the Scripture tells us that the world has moved and will move progressively further into an era that will be literally characterized by "wars and rumors of wars." In fact, one could easily argue that the twentieth century has been a perfect fulfillment of that prophetic promise. It takes not a great deal of imagination to see ourselves as being involved in that awful carnage of war which our Lord said will continue until the end of this age.

In fact, the Bible specifically foresees a series of wars at the culmination of history and the ultimate war that is still before the world, that is, in the world's future. Yes, there will be what we might call the "Ultimate Battle" for the conquest of earth. It will finally rage across the valley called Armageddon and culminate at the walls of the city of the great king — Jerusalem. This battle will involve the nations of the world and will result in one of the most spectacular events in all of history. Even now, the situation may well be being prepared for the kings of the earth to involve themselves in that great confrontation. Before that great confrontation, in fact, leading up to it, will be, therefore, wars and rumors of wars from all across the world. This anticipation of Jesus Christ is being, in part, fulfilled in our very time. We may, however, expect that the frequency and intensity of warfare will increase as we move toward that awful consummation of history. In fact, it has already become a truism that no one really understands history without recognizing warfare as one of its major components.

Allowing War

In fact, so obvious will this be the case, that people already are asking anew, as they've asked many times before, the question, "Why does God allow war?"

This question is very understandable as we see again the story of multiplied murder, rape, pillage, arson, and destruction that grow out of southeastern Europe at this very time. Millions really ask, "Could not God have prevented this carnage?" "Where is God when these devastations come upon the world?" "Why does God allow such terrible things to take place anyway?" Despairing of the answers to these questions, many have doubted the reality of God to the place where they have moved into incipient despair. But the question remains — Why, really, does God allow war? There are certainly a number of reasons which readily come to mind.

1. God allows war to prevent us from becoming too comfortable in this world. One of the concomitants of war is the destruction of the social order. This then turns many an area into anarchy and suffering. The roads are filled with refugees and the ditches are populated with those who can hobble no further. Those who are refugees and survive will never again believe that the world is their final dwelling place. Indeed, it is not. This world is the place of testing, suffering, and probation for heaven. We are supposed to despair of the dependability and solidity of this world and never settle down to the place where we foolishly think that any cottage on earth is our eternal dwelling.

2. God allows war to teach us the non-value of human and material things. Each of us is tempted to hold something in our hand, a gold coin, a diamond ring, a treasured friendship, a beautiful home, a lively automobile, or the like. The list is endless of the things to which we may become attached. The lesson of warfare is that no human thing has within itself, intrinsic value. The loot that the armies of Napoleon took from Moscow became fatal impediments before their final escape from the snows of Russia and the armies of Marshall Kudichev. All values are relative in this world, but alas, this lesson has been learned by but a few. Too many people die clutching worthless diamonds. Because of those diamonds, they have neglected to place their ultimate trust in Jesus Christ as the Son of God.

3. God allows war to prove the futility of human solutions. We are certainly moving into the day of "autonomous man." Presumptuous humanity is saying, "Evolution has brought us to the place where now we can control our own evolution. We, therefore, are smart enough, strong enough, insightful enough to master the future. Destiny is in our hands and we will bring to pass a better than ever society. This boast of humanity will certainly mature into the fulfillment of the truism of Scripture, "There is a way that seemeth right unto man, but the end thereof are the ways of death" (Prov. 14:12).

Adolf Hitler preached to the world about the master race and how he would produce of the Germanic people a One-Thousand-Year Reich that would rule the world into the future. That plan expired when Hitler put a bullet through his head. It went up in the smoke of burning corpses in the collapsing city of Berlin.

In our time it is totally incredible the way the doctrine of human confidence is preached to the exclusion of any confidence toward God. The utter futility of human solutions is proved with great clarity in the ashes of warfare.

4. God allows warfare to show the results of human sin. The Scripture says, "Wherefore, as by one man sin entered into the world, and death by sin, and so death passed upon all men, for all have sinned" (Rom. 5:12). The entrance of sin into the world through the disobedience of Adam produced immediate spiritual death and ultimate physical death. It is, therefore, true that every human thing in the world is infected by this dreadful disease called "sin." Every plan is warped, every conversation is tainted, every hope is subverted because of sin. Therefore, every person has become a conspirator against God. Apart from faith in Jesus Christ, the entire human race has been so reprobated by sin that nothing of good consequence can be produced by it.

Many times, however, the despair of war has produced a revival of spiritual interest, and many turning — having despaired of all of the things — to Jesus Christ.

5. God allows war to force us to trust in Him alone. Few pieces of advice are more valid in life — and should be given to everyone — than the words of Solomon, "Trust in the Lord with all thine heart, and lean not unto thine own understanding. In all thy ways acknowledge him, and he shall direct thy paths" (Prov. 3:5-6). Both the Bible and life teaches with sparkling clarity the absolute wisdom of this heavenly admonishment. Trusting in men is always a mistake and trusting in the Lord is never done in vain. The world, of course, does not believe this and constantly turns to its own solutions, its own weapons, its own plans to work out its problems. Up until now the world has produced zero good results from this course. Nor will that change until faith in man is turned into faith into God. Faith in man is shown to be hollow mockery by the devastations of war. Until that faith changes, those devastations will continue. God has promised us this.

For want of learning these lessons, the Bible teaches that a most turbulent scenario will come upon the world. As we look into the Word of God, we can learn a number of lessons in the sequence of bloody events that come under the heading of "Armageddon." That set of events should be soberly contemplated by every person who lives in this era of grace. They will come to pass during that period of time called the "Tribulation," which will be that set of events taking place in these seven years immediately after the rapture of the Church.

First of all, the world will come to the point of a violent rebellion against God.

The Raging Nations

Some of the most astonishing words in the entire Bible are found in the words of the Psalmist, "Why do the nations rage, and the peoples imagine a vain thing? The kings of the earth set themselves, and the rulers take counsel together, against the Lord, and against his anointed, saying, Let us break their bands asunder, and cast away their cords from us" (Ps. 2:1-3).

Here the Lord himself is speaking and He is doing so with a degree of astonishment. The picture, which would be humorous if it weren't so very tragic, is before us. The nations of the world, all of them, imagine a vain thing. That vain thing is that the nations, in their rage, believe that they can win a war against God himself. It is as if a few tiny ants on the ground were to pick a fight with the intention of winning against a grown human being. It is like a tiny chicken coming up against a great lion and swearing that he will do away with that lion. The picture is quite inconceivable and, therefore, we have this statement, "He who sits in the heavens shall laugh; and the Lord shall have them in derision" (Ps. 2:4).

The ridiculousness of this picture is enhanced by the Scripture statement, "The rulers take counsel together, against the Lord, and against his anointed" (Ps. 2:2). So, here we have not a frivolous decision or the emotion of a moment. Here we have the best thoughts of rulers, sinful man, imagining the impossible. We are thereby reminded of the complete corruption, to the point of irrationality, that will have taken over in the minds of the rulers of earth.

In their counsels together, the rulers say, "Let us break their bands asunder, and cast away their cords from us" (Ps. 2:3). So the leadership of the world decides to disconnect itself with reality, with sanity, yes, with God himself.

So the nations of the world march against Israel and against the city of Jerusalem, with the intent of doing battle not merely with the Jews, but with God.

Why does this take place? Yes, why do the nations rage? What strange insanity is taking over in the minds of men so that they aspire to accomplish the preposterous?

Could it be that their gods have failed them? From across the world we have the pitiful picture of millions of people bowing before pagan idols of wood and stone. Dropping into progressive insanity, they believe that those gods will help. Can we imagine that there will come a time of disillusionment when a world realizes that it has worshiped gods that are false and failing? Most of us would be angry if we suddenly realized we had put all of our time and money into a thankless situation. We would certainly rage against someone.

Could it be that the world's philosophies have proved false? The world today pretends at sophistication and announces that it believes in existentialism, humanism, secular optimism, or a dozen of the other empty philosophies going in our time. Never realizing that it has been ruled from the grave of false philosophers who are dead, the world has suddenly realized that it has been tricked into believing in these men. Philosophy generally is interesting talk that produces a bad outcome. For these and many other reasons, the world could, by this time, become disillusioned. Then God says, "Then will I speak unto them in my wrath and vex them in my great displeasure" (Ps. 2:5).

What possibly could deceive the kings of the earth into moving against God in this hopeless battle? The only answer is satanic deception.

Indeed, this is what the Scripture teaches concerning the prelude to Armageddon.

> And I saw three unclean spirits, like frogs, come out of the mouth of the dragon, and out of the mouth of the beast, and out of the mouth of the false prophet. For they are the spirits of demons, working miracles, that go forth unto the kings of the earth, and of the whole world, to gather them to the battle of that great day of God Almighty. Behold, I come as a thief. Blessed is he that watcheth and keepeth his garments, lest he walk naked, and they see his shame. And he gathered them together into a place called in the Hebrew tongue Armageddon (Rev. 16:13-16).

Yes, demonic miracles will be a part of the delusion that will come upon the world in that day.

Reading this, we dare to ask the question, "Are we living in a time in which too much traffic is being made of so-called miracles? We are not told in the Word of God that miracles are always a divine thing. The Antichrist and the false prophet will be able to work miracles and, indeed, they will do this. Miracles are intended to certify the truth of an apostolic speaker. They are never given for the simple purpose of amazing people or beguiling them out of their good sense.

Let us also note that when the armies of earth move into World War, finishing in Armageddon, they will have fantastic weapons at their disposal. In giving us one of the pictures of the last days, the Bible presents the horsemen of the Apocalypse. The fourth horseman should be especially noted, "And when he had opened the fourth seal, I heard the voice of the fourth living creature say, Come. And I looked and, behold, a pale horse, and his name that sat on him was Death, and Hell followed with him. And power was given unto them over the fourth part of the earth, to kill with sword, and with hunger, and with death, and with the beasts of the earth" (Rev. 6:7-8).

There was a time when this prediction sounded fantastic, impossible to any who read. How could a fourth part of the earth be killed by any known methodology of those days? That question is now no longer a mystery. This, because the age of nuclear power has come upon us. In our time, despite efforts at nuclear non-proliferation, perhaps a dozen nations of the world have a degree of nuclear capability. Russia has still 30,000 nuclear warheads — with 10,000 of them pointed at the United States. America has a powerful nuclear arsenal which, foolishly, is being reduced. Britain and France are nuclear powers, along with India, Pakistan, North Korea, and other nations, some of which may be unknown.

Russia, despite its pretensions toward disarmament, is even now buying nuclear weapons from the Ukraine and aircraft delivery systems as well. This seems like a strange behavior for a nation that is now calling for peace and nuclear reduction.

By the time the scenario of the Revelation matures, it speaks in a most interesting fashion.

> And thus I saw the horses in the vision, and them that sat on them, having breastplates of fire, and of jacinth, and brimstone; and the heads of the horses were like the heads of lions, and out of their mouths issued fire and smoke and brimstone. By these three was the third part of men killed, by the fire, and by the smoke, and by the brimstone, which issued out of their mouths (Rev. 9:17-18).

Here again we have an astonishing prophecy which could not be interpreted years ago but now is predicting military equipment unprecedented in history. Along this very line, a recent *Jerusalem Post* article reported:

The Armored Corps last week unveiled the Baz-2 fire-control system, which revolutionizes tank gunnery, especially mobile firing and target detection.

The Baz-2, developed mainly by El-Op, is installed on Merkava-3 tanks, considered the world's best main battle-tank.

The all-weather day and night system enables the commander and gunner to lock on a fixed or moving target while the Merkava itself is moving. The acquired target remains locked in the gun sight regardless of its own or the Merkava's movement.

The system links the tank's hydraulic turret controls to the main computer system, which follows the target until it is destroyed. The hydraulic stabilizing system nullifies the tank's vibrations on rugged terrain.

"This represents a tremendous qualitative leap forward," OC Armored Corps Brig.-Gen. Dovik Tal said at the Armored Corps memorial in Latrun, where the system was displayed.

So we see that high-tech, combined with military development, is producing weapons that render obsolete those being used in warfare up until now. We cannot doubt that "progress" in armament will continue.

Are we really speaking about great numbers of men participating in the battles of Armageddon? We receive part of the answer by looking further into the Book of the Revelation.

And the sixth angel sounded, and I heard a voice from the four horns of the golden altar which is before God, saying to the sixth angel who had the trumpet, Loose the four angels who are bound in the great river, Euphrates. And the four angels were loosed, who were prepared for an hour, and a day, and a month, and a year, to slay the third part of men. And the number of the army of the horsemen were two hundred thousand thousand; and I heard the number of them (Rev. 9:13-16).

In parallel fashion, the Scripture says, "And the sixth angel poured out his bowl upon the great river, Euphrates, and its water was dried up, that the way of the kings of the East might be prepared" (Rev. 16:12).

An awesome picture is before us! The kings of the earth move to that great battle with an army of *two hundred million*. This will be the largest number of men ever to have been assembled in an army group. Two hundred million men exceeds the population of most entire countries in the world. Is there a nation, however, that could produce such an army? The answer, of course, is China.

The Kings of the East

With this in mind, we recall that the founder of Communist China, Mao Tse Tung, during the awful days of his reign, promised that China would participate in the battle of the world. He said that when it happens, China would bring to the field an army of 50 million. However, before he slipped away to his eternal non-reward, Mao Tse Tung changed his prediction. He said that in the battle for the world, China will field an army of two hundred million men. It is surely no coincidence that the leader of the largest nation in the world predicted a figure, a number of an army group that exactly corresponds with the statement in Scripture. This is not to be discounted.

We also note in the Scripture that the Euphrates would be dried up to make way for the kings of the east moving to the Battle of Armageddon. This was thought very unlikely, but it is no more. The fact is that Turkey has placed a dam across the Euphrates and, with the press of a button, can dry up the river completely. It has already done this on two occasions and, we can be sure, is ready to do it again. By drying up the River Euphrates, the armies of the kings of the east would have a perfect pathway opened for them to move down to the plains of Jezreel. We also remember with interest that the Chinese occupation of the land of Tibet produced an interesting consequence. It became necessary for China to build a highway, stretching from central China, across Tibet, and down to the River Euphrates. Can anyone doubt that the way of the kings of the east have been in fact prepared before our very eyes?

It is interesting also to note that, during the days of the Carter administration, America promised to assist in the re-arming of China. Is it, therefore, possible that weapons forged in the United States, via the re-arming of China, could be useful in the Battle of Armageddon? Indeed, it may be that many Americans have already labored to produce the devices that will lend their strength of the final holocaust of the world? A fascinating scenario is before us.

So we see that awesome numbers of men and colossal arma-ments will be concentrated in the battle of those days. By this time, the world will be under of the leadership of that dreadful ruler, the Antichrist. He will stake his life and fortune on obliterating the very memory of God by destroying the land of Israel and the city of Jerusalem. Noting this, how we wonder at the question, "What will be the outcome of the great Battle of Armageddon?" Concerning this, the Scripture says:

> And I saw an angel standing in the sun; and he cried with a loud voice, saying to all the fowls that fly in the midst of heaven, come and gather yourselves together unto the supper of the great God, that you may eat the flesh of kings, and the flesh of captains, and the flesh of mighty men, and the flesh of horses and of them that sit on them, and the flesh of all men, both free and enslaved, both small and great. And I saw the beast, and the kings of the earth, and their armies, gathered together to make war against him that sat on the horse, and against his army. And the beast was taken, and with him the false prophet that wrought miracles before him, with which he deceived them that had received the mark of the beast, and them that worshiped his image. These both were cast alive into a lake of fire burning with brimstone. And the remnant were slain with the sword of him that sat upon the horse, which sword proceeded out of his mouth; and all the fowls were filled with their flesh (Rev. 19:17-21).

In all of the accounts written of warfare in history, it would be difficult to find a more stirring account of the outcome of a great battle. To walk any battlefield is to see the smoking ruins of lives, equipment and the reputation of nations. To walk the battlefield that will have seen the Battle of Armageddon must and will be an overwhelming experience indeed. I personally expect to walk on that battlefield. The Battle of Armageddon will turn into the supper of the great God. Meaning, of course, that the triumph of Jesus Christ, the King of all kings, will be universal and unassailable that day.

The Battle's Finale

What will be the actual event that precisely brings an end to the Battle of Armageddon? That event is also beautifully described for us in Scripture:

> And I saw heaven opened and, behold, a white horse;

and he that sat upon him was called Faithful and True, and in righteousness he doth judge and make war. His eyes were like a flame of fire, and on his head were many crowns; and he had a name written, that no man knew, but he himself. And he was clothed with a vesture dipped in blood; and his name is called The Word of God. And the armies that were in heaven followed him upon white horses, clothes in fine linen, white and clean. And out of his mouth goeth a sharp sword, that with it he should smite the nations, and he shall rule them with a rod of iron; and he treadeth the winepress of the fierceness and wrath of Almighty God. And he hath on his vesture and on his thigh a name written, "KING OF KINGS, AND LORD OF LORDS" (Rev. 19:11-16).

What have we here? It is the picture of the second coming of Jesus Christ. It is the gripping presentation of His glorious return. He comes back from heaven with power and great glory and we note that His first item of business is to win the Battle of Armageddon. Does He win that battle? Yes, indeed. He does it with a sharp sword that precedes out of His mouth. The carnage is so great that it is described as "the flesh of captains, and the flesh of mighty men, and the flesh of horses and of them that sit on them, and the flesh of all men, both free and enslaved, both small and great" (Rev. 19:18). The conclusion of the Battle of Armageddon will be a confrontation so devastating that the army opposing God is obliterated. The armies accompanying Jesus Christ in that re-invasion of earth are totally victorious.

A vital truth is expressed in this account that needs to be noted by every true believer. The armies that come from heaven with Christ — who are they? Jude answers this question by quoting Enoch's prophecy, "Behold, the Lord cometh with ten thousands of his saints, to execute judgment upon all and to convict all that are ungodly among them" (Jude 14-15). So we have it, the army that returns with Jesus Christ is composed of the saints of God.

Who is a saint? A saint is *"hagios."* That word in the New Testament Scripture applies to every person who is a believer in the Lord Jesus Christ. Therefore, the army of the saints is composed of believers, Christians who have become holy by imputed righteousness.

Who then will deliver the world from the dreadful clutch of Satan and bring liberation from sin along with Jesus Christ? It is the saints, Christians, the Church, the Body of Christ. Yes, the physical, the actual triumph of good over evil will be produced by that army from heaven, under the leadership of the Lord Jesus and composed of sergeants, lieutenants, captains, colonels, and generals who are believers in the Son of God. Yes, some faithful saints seen in church on Sunday may in that day be wearing the armor of light, be a deliverer of the world from the captivity of Satan.

The Kingdom Comes

What will the Battle of Armageddon bring to pass? It will bring the end of that period of time called the great Tribulation and it will usher in the reign of Jesus Christ. Satan will be deposed and the Day of the Kingdom will come to pass in the world.

> And I saw an angel come down from heaven, having the key of the bottomless pit and a great chain in his hand. And he laid hold on the dragon, that old serpent, who is the Devil and Satan, and bound him a thousand years, and cast him into the bottomless pit, and shut him up, and set a seal upon him, that he should deceive the nations no more, till the thousand years should be fulfilled; and after that he must be loosed a little season (Rev. 20:1-3).

It's at this point that the kingdom of God comes to earth under the reign of Jesus Christ.

> And I saw thrones, and they sat upon them, and judgment was given unto them; and I saw the souls of them that were beheaded for the witness of Jesus, and for the word of God, and who had not worshiped the beast, neither his image, neither had received his mark upon their foreheads, or in their hands; and they lived and reigned with Christ a thousand years (Rev. 20:4).

What a difference that will make! Satan is bound and the Antichrist is deposed into the lake of fire. No more will they deceive the nations and no more will they subvert the lives of people. There will then begin an era that will be wonderful beyond description. The reign of Jesus Christ over all the world will now come to pass.

There are many great lessons to be learned in the account of these marvelous things in the Word of God. One of the greatest is that God will triumph in history. Yes, there will be many variations in the nature of the lives of people on earth. They will move between sunshine and shadow, between persecution and plenty, between darkness and light. Over it all, however, Christ presides now and will preside in great detail. We can, therefore, be confident, because God will triumph in history, that serving Him today is not a mistake. Far, far better it is to die for a cause that will ultimately triumph than it is to live for a cause that will ultimately fail. The cause of Jesus Christ is exactly that cause. Let no one, therefore, ask "What is God doing and why does He apparently pay so little attention to us?" The premise behind the question is false. God is working with the total of His divine power every moment of every day to bring to pass those things which will result for our good and for His glory. There are no exceptions because "All things work together for good to them that love God, to them who are the called according to His purpose" (Rom. 8:28).

We must also remember that God has special privileges in eternity and in His kingdom for those who have served Him well. Paul promised Timothy that "If we suffer, we shall also reign with him" (2 Tim. 2:12). The promise of reigning with Christ is so marvelous that it ought to be the object of some degree of our attention each day. The fact is that this world, which seems so important to many, is soon to pass. In the meantime, our sojourn in this world in the Scripture is called "our light affliction, which is but for a moment, worketh for us a far more exceeding and eternal weight of glory, while we look not at the things which are seen, but at the things which are not seen; for the things which are seen are temporal, but the things which are not seen are eternal" (2 Cor. 4:17-18).

Yes, God has told us these things so that we may lift our eyes of anticipation toward the future, toward the kingdom, toward heaven itself. The experiences which come to us in this quickly passing world may be many kinds. None, however, be they the greatest joys or the deepest sorrows, should cause us to misinterpret the nature of this present moment. It is passing, it is transient, it is soon gone. This world is not final reality, it is the prelude to reality. It is a quickly passing moment before the dawn of eternity bursts upon us all. God has given us the account of Armageddon because it destroys every secular proposition and fulfills every Christian anticipation. Let us, therefore, reach forth into the things which are to come and press toward the mark of the high calling of God in Christ Jesus.

SECTION III:

Approaching A.D. 2000

Rush Limbaugh, the talk show host, is in the ongoing process of formulating what he calls the "Kook Test." The designation "kook" is given anyone who entertains globalist conspiracy theories much in the same way current redneck jokes poke fun at those exhibiting certain characteristics that make them prone to, shall we say, less-than-sophisticated attitudes and actions. The Kook Test was born in large measure out of Limbaugh's opinion of those who believe that earth is being moved toward world government. If you believe in such conspiracies, according to the Kook Test, you are most likely just that, a kook.

God, then, must be a *kook* because if He says what He means and means what He says, He believes world government is coming. Revelation 13 of His Holy Word says that that government will be an absolute dictatorship ruled by history's most vicious despot who has ascended through the ranks of his fellow political world leaders by his power of persuasion and sheer force of his will. (Rev. 17:11-14.) He will ultimately be possessed by Satan himself.

Mr. Limbaugh, who is a man of brilliant analytical mind and wit in my opinion, obviously has a blind spot in the matter of what is taking place in the top echelons of world power brokerage. This is not surprising, based upon a recent disclosure he made in response to a caller who said he looked at the state of the nation and world from a somewhat fatalistic perspective. Rush told the caller — a man who had opened his comment with *"Christian dittos"* — that in effect, such an outlook is wrong, counterproductive, and totally frustrating to the talk show host. Rush said near the end of his lecture to the man and to his radio audience that his own father believed that the Book of Revelation doesn't belong in the Bible. He then asked, just as the time for a station break arrived, "Now what do you think about that?"

This is not to attack Rush Limbaugh. I have been and continue to be in agreement with the majority of his viewpoints on most topics. However, it is apparent that his blind spot in matters concerning movement toward world government comes from ideas gathered early in life while sitting at the feet of the man he has said on numerous occasions was the most influential in his life. While it is true that if the Book of Revelation is nothing more than symbolism or the ravings of a hallucinating old man marooned on an Aegean island almost 2,000 years ago, it does not belong in the canon of Scripture. It is also true that if God intended for Revelation to be taken literally, it is a deadly serious matter to trivialize the apostle John's prophecies.

Revelation 22:18-19 warns, "For I testify unto every man that heareth the words of the prophecy of this book, If any man shall add unto these things, God shall add unto him the plagues that are written in this book; And if any man shall take away from the words of the book of this prophecy, God shall take away his part from the tree of life, and out of the holy city, and from the things which are written in this book."

God cannot tell a lie. He is Truth. Everything within His Word points toward the Revelation of Jesus Christ and His return to Planet Earth to put an end to man's disastrous attempts to govern himself. Lucifer is the actual conspirator who fuels and generates and directs the anti-God, anti-Christ rage within this world system. But be assured that any success he might have will be short-lived. He was defeated at Calvary nearly two millennia ago.

— William T. James

12

Rabin's Assassination: The Aftermath

by David A. Lewis

In the twilight, in the evening, in the black and dark night (Prov. 7:9).

Night had fallen over the Holy Land. Tel Aviv was alive with the sound of music and hopes for peace were in the air. Not known to join frequently in public singing, the prime minister surprised those around him by unfolding the song sheet and lifting his voice singing a "Song of Peace." The words swelled and crescendoed from the lips of the assembled crowd. Yitzhak Rabin was overjoyed with the enthusiastic throng of more than 100,000 Israelis who had shown up for the peace rally. But now the song sheet, which he folded and put in his shirt pocket, is covered with his blood.

Yigal Amir, a fiery young zealot, a political extremist, lurked near the path Rabin would walk to his automobile. Amir, posing as a driver for the prime minister's entourage, walked directly behind the leader of Israel. He pulled a gun and fired into Mr. Rabin's body two times. One of the leaden slugs dealt a fatal wound. The police said Amir came out of the crowd in Tel Aviv's Kings of Israel Square and fired three shots with a Beretta pistol. Rabin, hit in the back and stomach, died 90 minutes later. The third bullet wounded a bodyguard. All people of good will and conscience must strongly renounce and resist this type of behavior.

Israel is a democracy. Never had this small nation experienced the murder of one of its leaders at the hand of one of his own fellow Jews. Likud leaders were quick to denounce this new Jewish terrorism. Benjamin Netanyahu, leader of the conservative Likud party, made it clear that Amir's behavior was unacceptable. He declared that while strong disagreement exists between Labor and Likud, issues should be settled by ballots, not bullets. Israel has always taken pride in its democracy which, while often verbally violent, allows peaceful transition of power.

Yigal Amir, Assassin

TEL AVIV, Israel (Nov. 6, 1995) Reuters — A Jewish yeshiva student Yigal Amir confessed in a Tel Aviv court Monday to killing Israeli Prime Minister Yitzhak Rabin, saying: "I acted alone but maybe with God." Police said his brother Hagai Amir was an accomplice who prepared at least one of the dumdum bullets that smashed into Rabin at a peace rally in Tel Aviv Saturday.

Amir said he shot the Israeli leader because he was handing over land to Palestinians. He called Rabin a groveler who was "not my prime minister."

Police told a magistrate they were investigating if the 25-year-old law student belonged to an illegal group, the shadowy extremist organization known as Eyal. "I did not commit the act to stop the peace process because there is no such concept as the peace process, it is a process of war," Amir said, using his court appearance to air views.

The court ordered Amir held for 15 days while police prepare possible charges, including premeditated murder, the attempted murder of Rabin's bodyguard and participation in an illegal organization. At a later hearing in Tel Aviv, a magistrate ordered the killer's brother, also arrested Saturday, held for seven days. "He [Hagai Amir] took a bullet, drilled a hole in it and turned it into a lethal bullet which causes far more damage than a regular one," a police officer told the court in a transcript carried by Israel's domestic news agency Itim. A dumdum bullet has a cut in its point that causes it to expand on impact. Police said one of the bullets the brother prepared was taken from Rabin's body.

Hagai Amir "was a willing accomplice in this assassination, even if he only failed to prevent the crime," the officer said. "On the day of the incident they both sat and watched television and Hagai saw him (Yigal) leave. We believe he knew where he was going and didn't try to stop him."

The Itim report quoted the assassin's brother as telling the judge: "I added an iron pellet to the tip of the bullet. This created a hollowness which enabled the bullet to be more accurate, and nothing else."

The man who admitted to Israel's first assassination of a prime minister sat calmly during his court appearance, hands clasped and flanked by two policemen. — Reuters.

Dignitaries, heads of state, diplomats, and friends came from all over the world to Mount Herzl in Jerusalem. They came to attend the funeral of Prime Minister Yitzhak Rabin, to pay their respects, to speak words of condolence to his surviving wife and children. Perhaps the most poignant words of eulogy were spoken by Rabin's granddaughter.

Rabin's Granddaughter

The lovely granddaughter of Prime Minister Yitzhak Rabin, Noa Ben-Artzi Philosof, brought tears to the eyes of many with her eulogy of her slain grandfather, given at his funeral on Mount Herzl in Jerusalem.

Forgive me if I do not want to talk about peace. I want to talk about my grandfather. You always awake from a nightmare but since yesterday I only awake into a nightmare — the nightmare of life without you and that is impossible to fathom.

The television does not stop broadcasting your pictures and you are so alive and real that I can almost touch you, but only just, because I can't anymore.

Grandfather, you were the pillar of fire in front of the camp and now we are just a camp left alone in the dark and we are so cold and sad.

I know they are speaking in terms of a national disaster. But how can you try to console an entire nation or let it share in your private pain when grandmother cannot stop crying and we are mute, feeling the vast emptiness now that you are gone?

Few really knew you. They can say many things about you but I feel they do not know at all the enormous extent of the pain and tragedy.

And yes, this is a holocaust — at least for us, the family and friends — because we are left without a pillar of fire.

Grandfather, you were and still are our hero. I wanted you to know that in everything I've done in life, I saw you before my eyes.

Your esteem and love were with us in every step we took and along every road we walked. We live in the light of your values, always.

You never abandoned us and now you have been abandoned. And now here you are, my eternal hero, cold and alone and I can do nothing to save you. You are so wonderful.

Great men have already eulogized you but no one has felt, like I have, the caress of your warm and soft hands, or your warm embrace which was reserved for us alone and your half-smile which always told me so much. That same smile, is no longer and froze with you.

I harbor no feelings of revenge because the pain and my loss are so great — too great. The earth crumbled under our feet and somehow we are trying to sit in the empty space that is left — but with little success.

I cannot finish but apparently a strange hand, a miserable hand has already finished for me.

Given no choice, I part with you, my hero, and ask you to rest in peace and think of us and miss us because here down below we love you so much.

Angels in heaven who are with you now, I ask you to protect him, and protect him well because you are deserving of this protection.

We love you, Grandfather, forever.

Rabin's View on Terrorism

"If you ask me what is the obstacle to the implementation [of the peace plan], it is terror. Arafat stopped the terrorism by the PLO. No

Israeli has been killed by them since the end of 1992. Terror is carried out mainly by the Hamas and the Islamic Jihad with the clear purpose of undermining the peace process. We face a unique kind of terrorism — the suicidal terror mission. There is no deterrent to a person who goes with high explosives in his car or in his bag and explodes himself. We find remnants of his body. Sometimes you can't identify him. Is the peace process reversible? It might be. But only if terror will succeed."

Little did anyone know or even think that Rabin would be struck down by a terrorist, not an Arab, but a fellow Jew.

Wider Conspiracy Theory

> There is a conspiracy of her prophets in the midst thereof, like a roaring lion ravening the prey; they have devoured souls; they have taken the treasure and precious things; they have made her many widows in the midst thereof (Ezek. 22:25).

Yigal Amir is a member of Eyal, a little known Jewish underground militant group. This accused assassin is now in custody in an Israeli prison. Daily we are learning more about his clandestine band. Other than in their discussion groups, they seem to have been involved in no overt terrorist activities prior to the killing of prime minister Yitzhak Rabin on November 4. Eyal seems to have only 12 members, who are described as Jewish religious extremists.

"They have secret meetings and maybe they hold (arms) training sessions, but they have never been linked to any serious terrorist activity," said Ehud Sprinzak, a professor at Hebrew University who has specialized in studies of Jewish militants. Iyal "was formed at the end of 1991 or beginning of 1992 by students at Tel Aviv University," according to Sprinzak.

Sprinzak said Eyal may have "offshoots" at Bar Ilan — a religious university near Tel Aviv where Rabin's accused killer Yigal Amir and Eyal head Avishai Raviv studied. He said, "They wanted to prove to the Kahanists it was possible to be more extreme, but except for a lot of rhetoric, they weren't," Sprinzak said.

According to Sprinzak, Avishai Raviv, the head of Eyal, in custody on suspicion of conspiring to kill Rabin, "wasn't needed because Amir seems like a serious guy, capable of planning and carrying out the killing by himself." Sprinzak expressed doubt that

Raviv was involved in a conspiracy. "But I wouldn't be surprised if they talked and talked and talked and finally somebody decided to do it," he said. Others now strongly disagree with the Sprinzak theory. Other very odd aspects to this "conspiracy" surfaced in the *Jerusalem Report* magazine.

Rabin Cursed by Kabbalist Black Magic

Saturday, November 4, 1995 — a day that will go down in history. It was early afternoon in Missouri. My pre-dated November 16 issue of the *Jerusalem Report* magazine had just arrived in the mail. As I sat in my bedroom chair, CNN was on the television, muted. I glanced up occasionally to see what was on. I started to read an article In the *Jerusalem Report* titled, "Invoking the Spirits." *What is this?* I mused. I could hardly believe my eyes as I read:

> Yitzhak Rabin does not have long to live. The angels have their orders. Suffering and death await the prime minister, or so say the Kabbalists who have cursed him with the pulsa denura — Aramaic for "lashes of fire" — for his "heretical" policies. "He's inciting against Judaism," says the Jerusalem rabbi who, clad in tefillin, read out the most terrifying of curses in the tradition of Jewish mysticism — opposite Rabin's residence on the eve of Yom Kippur.
>
> "And on him, Yitzhak, son of Rosa known as 'Rabin,' " the Aramaic text stated, "we have permission . . . to demand from the angels of destruction that they take a sword to this wicked man . . . to kill him . . . for handing over the Land of Israel to our enemies, the sons of Ishmael."
>
> The rabbi, who won't have his name published but identifies himself as a member of the far-right Kach movement, says the curse generally works within 30 days. That put the expiry date — for Rabin or the curse — In early November.
>
> For Jewish mystics of both North African and East European descent, curses taken from the tradition of "practical Kabbalah" are heavy weaponry — not to be used every day, but certainly available in wars, religious struggles, and even political battles. Not only the ultra-Orthodox but many traditional-leaning Israelis regard them with the utmost seriousness.

Invoking the pulsa denura is a perilous undertaking, for if the ceremony is not performed in a strictly prescribed fashion, it can strike the conjurers themselves.

Before Rabin, the last person so cursed was Saddam Hussein. One day during the 1991 Gulf War, as Scuds rained down on Israel, a minyan of fasting Kabbalists gathered at the tomb of the prophet Samuel just outside Jerusalem. There they entered a dark cave, where one of the holy men placed a copper tray on a rock and lit the 24 black candles he'd placed on it. As the mystics circled the candles, they chanted the curse seven times, calling on the angels not merely to visit death upon "Saddam the son of Sabha," but to ensure that his wife was given to another man.

That done, small lead balls and pieces of earthenware were thrown on the candles and the shofar was sounded. "The black candles," explains Yediot Aharonot journalist Amos Nevo, who documented the ceremony, "symbolize the person being cursed. When they're put out, it's as if the person's soul is being extinguished. Lead," he says, "is for the ammunition in the war against the cursed one, earthenware symbolizes death, and the shofar opens the skies so the curse will be heard.

With Saddam still in power, there would appear to have been a technical hitch. "Don't worry, his end will be bitter," says Moshe Nimni, aide to Rabbi Yitzhak Kadouri, the oldest and most prominent of the North African mystics in Israel, who was one of the curse-casters. "Besides," he says, "Saddam is plagued by an international boycott, and his daughters and their husbands have deserted him."

For Rabin and Saddam, the experience of Gershon Agron, Jerusalem mayor in the 1950s, should be sobering. When Agron initiated the first pool in the capital where men and women could swim together, he was cursed by rabbis of the extreme ultra-Orthodox Edah Haredit, says sect spokesman Yehudah Meshi-Zahav. Within a year. he was dead — smitten by hepatitis.

Or there's the case of archaeologist Yigal Shiloh, who excavated the City of David outside Jerusalem's Old City walls. After bones were found there, says Meshi-

Zahav, rabbis cursed the site. A year later, in 1987, Shiloh died of cancer.

In the smoke-filled rooms of politics, imprecations are also important weaponry. When Poalei Agudat Yisrael broke ultra-Orthodox ranks and took the then-unthinkable step of joining the government in 1960, curses flew. Soon after, party head Benjamin Minz was dead of a coronary. (By Peter Hirschberg, with reporting by Yuval Lion, the *Jerusalem Report*, November 16, 1995, page 17).

Kabbalah is thought by many to be a benign method of interpreting the Scriptures through numerics. This is a naive view. Kabbalah is occultism. Here we see the most evil possible face it could wear. The uttering of curses on others is similar to voodoo and witchcraft. It should be made clear that only a small minority of Kabbalists engage in this extremism, however. Only a small part of Jewish Orthodoxy is Kabbalistic. Regardless of what one thinks of curses, they fact that they are uttered by religious leaders can give a feeling of legitimacy to a potential assassin. One of the Ten Commandments is, "Thou shalt not kill [Heb. murder]," neither with swords, clubs, nor curses.

History Repeats

An ancient prophet recorded, "And the Lord said unto me, A conspiracy is found among the men of Judah, and among the inhabitants of Jerusalem" (Jer. 11:9).

"And they were more than forty which had made this conspiracy" (Acts 23:13).

Ill Winds Blowing for Bible Believers and Conservatives

Fallout from the news of Prime Minister Rabin's murder does not augur well for serious Bible-rooted religious people. It's the old problem of "getting tarred with the same brush." A "religious" fanatic performs some violent, outrageous act and lo, the secular media begins condemning those with a "Bible mentality," that has "no relationship to reality." After the tragic death of Prime Minister Rabin one could hardly watch TV news or talk shows without hearing the anti-Bible rhetoric.

I should not have been, but was amazed at what I heard from various commentators on television, blaming those with a biblical mindset for creating the climate that would lead to the assassination of a prime minister. Here are just a few of the outrageous statements I heard.

Thomas L. Friedman writes a column on foreign affairs for the Wall Street Journal. He has written a book, *Beirut to Jerusalem*.

When interviewed on CNN, Friedman was asked if he thought that Rabin's killer, Yigal Amir, had acted alone or if he had associates. He replied, "I have no doubt that he is a lone assassin, or he and his brother are the two assassins, but I don't think that is really the point to keep in mind. While their methods were outside the pale of any Israeli political party . . . Amir's objective in assassinating the Prime Minister, was a political end to destroy the peace process. And that is a political objective that is at the core of Israel's right wing Likud party and the other parties associated with it. He acted alone, but the political objective he was trying to achieve was widely shared."

Host: "Former Secretary of State James Baker was on our morning news just last hour and he said that this verbal violence, and he even called it verbal terrorism, needs to be cooled down. He said that there probably will be some changes in security as well as the political discourse. Do you see that happening?"

Friedman: "Well, I certainly think the political discourse has to be toned down."

Host: "Interior Minister Barak says he wants a crack down on extremists. Is that a possibility?"

Friedman: "I think it's a possibility, but again I think it's an illusion just to say that this guy is an extremist [and if] we crack down on them, the problem is over. The fact is you have a large segment of the Israeli political spectrum that shares the objectives that this man shared, which is to kill the peace process."

Host: "And so do you think this is not going to be the unifying, the assassination of the prime minister, [is] not going to unify the Israeli people?"

Friedman: "No, I don't think it's going to be unifying, I think it's going to be dividing. I think it should be dividing and that really was what King Hussein said in his eulogy to Yitzhak Rabin. He said, 'This is the time now for people who believe in the peace process to stand up and be counted.' Yitzhak Rabin was killed not because he was trying to unify the country, but because he was taking sides, the side in favor of the peace process."

Host: "And even so though do you think that Netanyahu the Likud leader and some of the other folks who disagree with that peace process will distance themselves from some of this rhetoric?"

Friedman: "Oh, they'll distance themselves from the act. They'll distance themselves from the most extreme rhetoric, but they will not distance themselves from the goal of killing the peace process." (CNN, 11-6-95).

Several guests commented on the "Larry King Live" TV program on CNN, November 6, 1995:

Abba Eban: "In this case it is not a problem of individual security in the technical sense. This comes off in a context of vigilance [sic] and hatred of fundamentalist thinking about Jewish history and about biblical memories which are entirely outside the scope of the context of reality, which have inflamed certain people and therefore there is an ideological background which is lacking in the case [of] other people."

King: "Michael, where does the anger come from?"

Michael Bar-Zohar: "From a very fanatical conviction that these leaders are going to give back part of the land of Israel which for those people is holy, so they are traitors and by all kind of certain Rabbis decisions, they deserve to die in order to keep the land of Israel they now have."

King: "As the accused said, 'God told him to do it,' right?"

Michael Bar-Zohar: "He tried twice to do it before."

James Baker: "There are people . . . as he just pointed out, that are saying, 'This is what you should do, because he is going to give away the land.' "

King: "And the Bible says to do it."

James Baker: "So its that kind of verbal violence that has to end and we've got to get back to a civil discourse."

King: "And how do you stop it?"

Michael Bar-Zohar: "I think you are outlawed, even in a democracy. I think there is a clear and present danger, in fact in our times and with regard to heads of state. And I think it is outlawed."

James Baker: "It is outlawed."

Other Points of View

Benjamin Netanyahu brought a balanced and insightful comment when he was interviewed on television on November 7, 1995: "I think everybody agrees that there weren't any of these manifestations inside my movement [Likud Party]. But the important thing is that such rhetoric, whether it comes from the right or from the left extremes of the political spectrum, wherever it comes from it should be, of course, put down."

Bryant Gumble: "Are you prepared to view this murder as an

isolated act then of an extremist, or is Jewish fundamentalism a real and ongoing danger to the security of Israel and its leaders?"

B. Netanyahu: "Look, there [are] obviously some pockets, they're quite small as we can see, in fact, very small. But you don't need much. You need one crazed individual. . . . But I think we should do our best to try to locate these people wherever they fester, and take preventive action. I believe that is true, by the way, internationally."

Mr. Gumble also questioned Attorney Alan Dershowitz: "[It] will end up being only an indictment against one individual because the Israelis have to understand the enormous distinction between moral responsibility on the one hand by some of the extremists and the Rabbis and the fundamentalists who called for this horrible crime and technical legal responsibility and they should be clear to make that distinction."

Israeli Conservatives Respond

The *Jerusalem Insider* faxed the following statements to us:

> "The following are three statements made by Likud leaders in the aftermath of the tragic murder of Israel's Prime Minister, Yitzhak Rabin:"

> 1. Benjamin Netanyahu, Likud Chairman: This is one of the most horrific tragedies in the history of the State of Israel and the history of the Jewish people.

> I am shocked to the depths of my soul by the murder of Yitzhak Rabin, one of the great warriors in the establishment of the State of Israel, the Commander of the Six-Day War and one of the important leaders of the State. This is an hour of deep mourning, shock and despair.

> We must banish from our society all those who violate the most basic principle of humanity, of the Jewish people and of democracy. This is also an hour of challenge for all of us, and I pray that we will maintain our reserve and unity in the face of one of the most grievous disasters to strike us since the establishment of the State." (Israel TV Channel One 11/4/95)

> A major disaster has befallen upon the people of Israel. Mr. Rabin, a human being, a warrior, and one of Israel's most significant and important leaders, has contributed immensely to the people of Israel.

The people of Israel have forsaken the dreadful phenomenon of political murder 2,000 years ago. This phenomenon was rejected due to a deep conviction that an internal strife was more dangerous than any external threat. I would like to state categorically: There will not be a recurrence of internal strife in Israel.

Democratic governments change by the ballot and not by the bullet. Therefore, the Likud will recommend that President Weizman entrusts cabinet formulation to the candidate of the Labor Party to the post of the Prime Minister. Likud will not oppose the cabinet introduced to the Knesset by Labor.

At this hour, it is incumbent upon us, and especially upon public servants, to display restraint and composure, in order to preserve the unity of the people at this critical time. (Israel Press Conference 11/5/95)

2. Former Prime Minister, Yitzhak Shamir: My reaction is characterized by deep mourning and astonishment. . . . One is required to calm down and to avoid internal strife. . . . The leaders of the country must act responsibly, and to avoid rhetoric which could trigger more disasters.

3. Uzzie Landau, M.K. and Chairman of Likud's Policy Committee: This is a most painful and troublesome moment for the late Prime Minister Rabin's family as well as for the people of Israel and the democratic institutions of the State.

One should condemn the murder and the murderer, and do the utmost to prevent further deterioration. It is incumbent upon everyone to display composure and restraint, in order to advance the cause of internal unity in face of the tough domestic and external challenges ahead. Political debates should be conducted keenly, pointedly, and responsibly. Moreover, all attempts to use the murder of Prime Minister Rabin as an instrument to incite against a prominent segment of the population, should be denounced in order to avoid further divisiveness.

The murderer is not a member of any significant or known political camp. He constitutes a pariah and a detestable phenomenon, which has been systematically, clearly, loudly, publicly and privately condemned by Likud's leadership and grassroots.

The Road to Peace

There is acrimonious debate going on in Israel over which path to peace the nation should follow in order, hopefully, to bring an end to intermittent wars and continuous terrorism. Rabin, head of the liberal Labor Party, showed himself ready to make concessions to the neighbors of Israel. Land for peace. Mr. Rabin was not the first to travel the "land for peace" road. Land for peace was tried before, with good results, and a peace treaty with Egypt that is still holding together.

Menachem Begin's Role

The process was actually started by a member of the Likud rightist party during the administration of Prime Minister Menachem Begin who invited Anwar Sadat, president of Egypt, to come to Israel and begin peace talks.

In one of many private conversations, Mr. Begin said to me, "David, my neighbors will be surprised at the concessions we will make if real peace can be achieved." Begin bargained away the Sinai Peninsula with the airfields built by Israel, the Gedi and Mitla Passes, and the Abu Rudis oil fields, discovered and developed by Israel. Sadat, honorably, signed a genuine peace treaty which, until now, has brought lasting peace between the two nations.

After the signing of a full peace treaty between Israel and Egypt, Moslem extremists in Egypt assassinated President Anwar Sadat, and the world mourned his passing.

The Oslo Plan

It is said that the Oslo convention was suggested by Johann Joergen Holst, foreign minister of Norway, whom some credit with being the architect of the peace plan between the PLO and Israel.

Other insiders claim that actually it was the wife of Joergen Holst who laid out the plan to him. At any rate he shared it with Yossi Beilin and Shimon Peres, foreign minister of Israel. Peres then presented the plan, already in motion, to a reluctant Yitzhak Rabin. It was hard for the old soldier, Rabin, to shake hands with his implacable enemy Yassir Arafat, but they did make the famous handshake on September 13, 1993, on the White House lawn in Washington, DC.

The world media revealed the astounding information that

secret negotiations had been conducted in Norway for over a year, led by the late Johann Joergen Holst, the Norwegian foreign minister. Holst presided over 14 secret meetings involving representatives of the Palestine Liberation Organization (PLO) and of Israel.

Peace is Desirable

Peace is not evil. It is good. Good treaties, honored by the parties thereto are not bad, they are good. It is better to have peace than war. But these are dangerous times for Israel, and for all of us. We walk a tightrope over chasms of unimaginable depth.

The Day of the Handshake

On September 13, 1993, Israel's prime minister, PLO leader Yassir Arafat, Israeli Foreign Minister Shimon Peres, along with U.S. President Bill Clinton and Secretary of State Warren Christopher, walked onto the White House lawn for the signing of one of the most incredible documents of our time, a peace accord between the PLO and Israel. It was the day of the incredible handshake.

It Was Expected

We fully expected the peace accord or something like it. We predicted it. In August 1993 we printed an article which referred to secret negotiations. We have prayed for the peace of Jerusalem, so if peace is achieved, thank God for it. We may think that Israel's leaders have taken unnecessary risks, but what is done is done, and even if Israel has made mistakes, we stand by her for our Lord's sake.

Oh brave New World Order! Have you brought us hope for mankind's survival, or do sinister agendas lurk in the shadows of international politics and pressure?

What manipulative tactics did you use on Mr. Rabin? What threats fell on his ears? What geo-political blackmail and arm twisting was exercised? Look at the distress in Mr. Rabin's face. What anguish has driven him as he comes to meet and shake hands, reluctantly, with his old enemy? All of this we observed in September 1993, but later that all changed. Rabin had entered into a strange partnership with Arafat. If it works, if it continues, if Arafat can bring his own terrorists under control, if the PLO Covenant can be revised, then it is good.

Peace Treaties With Enemies

We must remember, peace treaties are not made with your friends. Peace treaties are made with your enemies. Without enemies there is no need for peace treaties! Some conservative Israelis have taken offense at this concept, but it is true, nevertheless. As we examine various points of view, it is important to realize that the Bible is not a deck of Tarot cards. We know what the final outcome will be, but there is a lot of foggy bottomland to be traversed until Messiah comes. We simply do not know what is coming in this process, nor exactly where we are on the prophetic timetable. So while we see the peace process as being flawed, yet we hope, yet we pray for the peace of Jerusalem, and all her neighbors roundabout. We must all do the best we can to stay the ravages of anarchy and war as God gives us wisdom and strength.

We all want peace, but this is a wicked, greedy, and deceitful world that has shown negligible success in keeping peace through the long history of humankind. For all the efforts of sane and hopeful leaders we still live in a world steeped in war and violence. Jesus did not gloat when He said, "There shall be wars and rumors of wars." Rather He was weeping over the inability of rebellious humanity to solve its deepest problems.

Meeting in Ramallah

I participated in a meeting several years ago which was conducted in the Arab town of Ramallah, Israel. The meeting was set up at my request and involved an Israeli government official, Mr. Yitzhak Achia, myself, and several leaders of the Palestinian District Leagues (now defunct). There was anger around the conference table. Accusations were hurled. Finally, a sense of calm and reason prevailed. At the end of the day, all agreed that while there were many problems to work out, it is time to stop the killing and violence, and create a framework of communication in which Palestinians and Jews strive to find solutions to the problems of the area.

Follow Peace

Peace is good. God is the author of peace. William Tecumseh Shaman, a great Civil War general, declared, "War is hell." These words were part of his graduation address at Michigan Military Academy, June 19, 1879. "War is at best barbarism. . . . Its glory is all moonshine. It is only those who have neither fired a shot not heard the shrieks and groans of the wounded who cry aloud for blood, more vengeance, more desolation. War is hell." We are to "Follow peace with all men" (Heb. 12:14).

What good can come of the peace effort? Out of his deep pit of anguish the sufferer Job asked, "Who can bring a clean thing out of an unclean? not one" (Job 14:4). Wrong, Job. God can bring good out of evil, purity out of impurity. That is the theme of redemption. God can take a broken, ruined life and bring forth a new creation. "Therefore if any man be in Christ, he is a new creature: old things are passed away; behold, all things are become new" (2 Cor. 5:17).

One day, God will take this ruined planet and renew it. The thousand-year reign of Messiah is but the inauguration of an eternity of perfection. God brings good out of evil. Satan brings evil out of good. "By peace shall he destroy." Therefore it behooves us to "Be sober, be vigilant; because your adversary the devil, as a roaring lion, walketh about, seeking whom he may devour" (1 Pet. 5:8).

Evil is ever alert, unceasingly probing, continually watching, looking for an opening. We are not ignorant of the devil's devices.

We join the search for peace, but remember that "Hate is strong and mocks the song of peace on earth, good will to men." We are wary. We live in hope, but observe with caution.

When Messiah Reigns

Wars and violence will not completely cease until Messiah reigns from Jerusalem. Perhaps we can look forward to advancing peace in the Middle East and a time of relative peace in many parts of the earth. But the tide will turn for, "When they shall say, Peace and safety; then sudden destruction cometh upon them, as travail upon a woman with child; and they shall not escape" (1 Thess. 5:3).

"We looked for peace, but no good came; and for a time of health, and behold trouble!" (Jer. 8:15).

Israel's Guaranteed Survival

Only Israel, of all nations, is guaranteed survival. Only Israel resists the Antichrist. While the entire Gentile world bows to the Beast, Israel stands alone and bravely counterattacks his awesome forces. Judah takes up arms against the armies of hell. "And Judah also shall fight [Heb. make war] at Jerusalem" (Zech. 14:14). Great leadership arises in Judah! Israel declares of the Beast: he "shall tread in our palaces, then shall we raise against him seven shepherds, and eight principle men" (Mic. 5:5).

Listen devil, look out for the two mighty prophets, the seven shepherds, and the eight principle men. They are on your trail, oh loser of all time and eternity. Your evil intention will not prevail. For now we are commanded to pursue peace. "Let us therefore follow after the things which make for peace, and things wherewith one may edify another" (Rom. 14:19).

Prophetic Perspective

What does the peace effort mean in the light of Bible prophecy? When each of the World Wars ended it was said by some, "This treaty being signed is the beginning of the Tribulation of seven years, and one of the signers or sponsors of the treaty must be the Antichrist."

The peace accord of September 13, 1995, is not the Antichrist covenant. The peace treaty with Jordan is not that covenant with hell. We are not in the Tribulation. What we see evolving may be the framework that will develop into that agreement with hell (Isa. 28:18), but it is not in focus yet. One thing we have learned in recent years is that prophecy and world events can move at lightning speed. See the Berlin wall falling down! Observe the upheaval in the USSR and Eastern Europe. Watch how the European Community advances toward the formation of New Rome.

Let us always be alert to the signs of the times. We must also live our lives as responsible Christian citizens, ready to lend a hand in improving conditions here and now. We are aware that we are "polishing brass on a sinking ship," but this old ship has been slowly sinking since the fall of Adam and Eve, 6,000 years ago. Thank God that not all believers forsook the daily tasks of improving the quality of life here and now, even as we look for the coming of our Lord and anticipate the day when He will set it all in order. Real Bible prophecy never promotes irresponsibility.

North American Comparison

If the USA had been under terrorist attack from our northern neighbor, Canada, and our southern neighbor, Mexico, for the past 47 years we would be urging our leaders to make some kind of a treaty to end the slaughter. Any peace treaty, anywhere in the world that works, and is honored by the participants in the treaty is a good thing, even if it only works for a time.

Jesus advised, "Agree with thine adversary quickly, whiles thou art in the way with him" (Matt. 5:25). Moses wisely said, "When thou comest nigh unto a city to fight against it, then proclaim peace unto it" (Deut. 20:10). Making peace is better than going to war. In the Proverbs we read, "When a man's ways please the Lord, he maketh even his enemies to be at peace with him" (Prov. 16:7).

We pray for the peace of Jerusalem (Ps. 122:6) — and peace for all her neighbors.

13

Why We Watch

By Dr. John F. Walvoord

About one-fourth of the Bible was predictive when it was written, and obviously divine revelation is intended to alert us of future events with the intent of preparing believers for the events before they happen. Prophecy was never intended to be a contentious subject for people to argue over, but rather a practical subject to alert people to prepare for God's future plan. Much has been lost by misunderstanding and neglect of the prophetic Scriptures.

How Can Prophecy Be Correctly Understood?

In the history of the interpretation of the prophetic portions of the Bible, it is tragic that so many have misunderstood what the Bible teaches. This is first of all evident in the revelation in the Old Testament of the first and second coming of Christ. Though specifics of His coming to die, as well as His coming to reign are given in Scripture accurately as the writers were guided by the Holy Spirit, there is no evidence that anyone understood that there would be two comings, a first coming in which Christ would suffer and die and a second coming in which He would gloriously reign. Jewish interpreters of the Bible wrestled with this and were unable to come to a satisfactory solution. The tendency was, however, to gloss over the passages dealing with suffering and to emphasize the glorious prophecies of Christ's reign on earth such as is found in Psalm 2, 72, and 89, and Isaiah 2, 11, 65, and 66, to name a few.

Expectation was high in Israel that when the Messiah came, He would deliver them from the oppression of the Roman Empire and exalt Israel to be a leading nation of the world over whom the Messiah would reign in fulfilling the Old Testament prophecies. It is unquestionably true that the disciples followed Christ anticipating His glorious reign not His sufferings and death. If they had understood Christ's sufferings as preceding His glory, it is questionable whether they would have followed Christ but apparently nobody in the gospel period, except Christ himself understood that there would be a first coming in which He would suffer and die and a second coming in which He would reign gloriously.

In following Christ, the disciples confidently expected that He would exalt Israel and give them places of authority and honor. This was confirmed by the statement that they would sit on the throne judging the 12 tribes of Israel (Matt. 19:27-28). Christ made it plain that this would be when He sat on His throne of glory but they did not understand that this had to follow His second coming, not His first.

As the time approached when Christ would be crucified, they were repeatedly warned that Jesus would be crucified, die and be resurrected (Matt. 16:21-22; 17:22-23; 20:17-19; Mark 8:31-33; 9:30-32; 10:32-33; Luke 9:22,44-45; 18:31-34). The disciples did not receive this announcement with understanding, and so thoroughly erased it from their minds that when Christ actually died, they did not remember His predictions or that He would rise from the dead. By contrast, His enemies remembered and sealed the tomb and sent the soldiers to prevent anyone stealing His body and claim that He was resurrected. It is doubtful that the disciples ever really understood that there was a first coming in which He suffered and died separated by a long time period before His second coming until actually they saw Christ ascending to heaven (Acts 1). That reinforced that His sufferings and death were past and His second coming would feature His glorious reign.

This misunderstanding concerning the difference between the first and second coming and the time interval between is perpetuated in the New Testament in the confusion over whether the second coming includes the rapture or whether the rapture is an earlier event separated from the second coming by a time period.

In the history of the church, it was recognized that the Rapture, the truth that Christ was coming for His saints, is presented as an imminent event but that the Second Coming had certain very specific prophecies that had to be fulfilled first. They struggled with this and the Early Church fathers frequently on one page would say that He could come any day and on the next page that something had to happen first without resolving the problem. There is no clear record of the concept that the Rapture and the Second Coming are two events until the emergence of Ephraem of Nisibis (306-373). A prolific writer, he was copied by others who claimed to be him who stated that the elect will be gathered before the Tribulation and taken to be with the Lord. Though controversy raises some question about this quotation, it seems that there were a few who caught the idea that the Rapture was a separate event. Later this was given widespread interpretation in the Bible conference movement of the nineteenth and twentieth centuries. Accordingly, the idea of a pre-Tribulation Rapture separated from the Second Coming by probably more than seven years has been followed by a large number of premillennial interpreters.

From a practical standpoint, however, if Christ is not coming before the Tribulation, His coming is not imminent because obviously there is still Tribulation ahead and prophecies to be fulfilled before the Second Coming. If however, the Rapture is before these events, then it takes on the concept of an imminent return which many believe the Bible teaches. The question of looking for the Lord's return however is therefore preceded by other questions which must resolve the problem of the place in the future events that the rapture of the Church occupies.

Causes for Confusion in Prophetic Interpretation

Because of widespread disagreement as to when the Rapture occurs and what its true nature is, a great deal of confusion is evident in prophetic literature. Many books have been written describing in graphic terms the great Tribulation, climaxing in the second coming of Christ as if the world is already in the process, often totally ignoring the passages dealing with the Rapture. If the Rapture precedes the Tribulation it becomes one of the most prominent, important prophecies which a believer today can understand.

The cause for confusion goes back in the history of the Old Testament as has been previously mentioned, in which the first and Second Coming were considered one event. There is a similar confusion with the Rapture and the Second Coming today. The immediate cause however was the rise of non-literal interpretation of prophecy due to the influence of a school of theology which sprang up in Egypt to Alexandria about A.D. 190. They attempted to harmonize the Scripture with a pure idealism of Plato and the only way this was possible was by taking the entire Scripture as a great allegory and not interpreted literally. The Early Church rose up and defended the interpretation of grammatical, literal, and historical interpretation and for the most part succeeded in erasing the non-literal interpretation from most areas of theology. Because eschatology is different in depending on future fulfillment, they were less successful in this and the result was that premillennialism was largely put aside in favor of amillennialism, namely the teaching that we were already in the millennium or at least that there was going to be no literal millennium following the second coming of Christ. This became the predominant doctrine of the church and was standardized somewhat by Augustine in the fourth and fifth centuries and it became the accepted doctrine of both the Roman Catholic Church and the Protestant reformers. Obviously, the matter of the Rapture could not be studied or clarified until the issue of whether the premillennial view was correct or not. This did not occur until the last few centuries when the Bible conference movement rescued premillennialism from this obscurity and made it one of the prominent doctrines of conservative Christianity today. If there is a literal Millennium then there is also a literal Tribulation and the concept of the church going through this as those who deny the pre-Tribulation Rapture hold, becomes far less tenable.

In the history of the Church, the doctrine of the literal Second Coming is incorporated in all of our major creeds whether Protestant, Roman Catholic, or Greek Orthodox, and for this reason even the secular world understands that Christ said that He would bodily come again to judge the world as these doctrinal statements declare. While this is a clear interpretation of prophecy literally, confusion arises when the events which lead up to it are not taken literally and the events that follow are not taken literally as is true particularly of the amillennial point of view.

There has been considerable development in this since World War II, because prior to this it was customary for the amillennialist to ignore the Tribulation completely as something that has already been fulfilled in the sufferings of the Church. After World War II, they made a complete U turn and recognized that there is a time of Tribulation preceding the Second Coming and so took away the doctrine of imminency of the second coming of Christ. It also made less tenable the idea that the Church could go through this period of trial unscathed. This was accomplished by watering down the Tribulation and taking it in less than its full description as it is portrayed in the Bible prophecies of the end times.

The Rapture as Presented in the Bible

The rapture of the Church is a New Testament doctrine not found in the Old Testament. There is no indication in the Old Testament that God would take a whole generation of believers out of the world prior to the final time of trouble. The first indication of this is found in John 14 the night before His crucifixion when Christ announced that He would come back to take His disciples to the Father's house. This was incomprehensible to the disciples who were looking for a kingdom on earth and was not explained until later when the apostle Paul was given special revelation on this subject. This became part of his missionary message and, as in the case of the Thessalonians, he preached not only the death and resurrection of Christ but also the fact that Christ promised to come back to take His church to heaven. As presented in 1 Thessalonians 4, it was given to the Thessalonians as an imminent event and something that would end their bereavement for loved ones who had died.

The Thessalonians apparently had followed Paul's teaching on the Rapture so closely that they anticipated the Rapture could occur at any time. When some of their number died however, this presented a new problem as to when they would see their loved ones again. There were some apparently who postulated that there might be a delay and though this is not clear, they may have had in mind that they would not be resurrected until the Second Coming which would climax the Tribulation. When this problem of interpretation was brought to Paul's attention by Timothy, he wrote 1 Thessalonians and described in detail what would happen when the Rapture occurs. A careful study of 1 Thessalonians 4:13-18 reveals the Rapture as an imminent event.

Verse 13 indicates that God wants us to know the wonderful hope we have in Christ. In verse 14, he states that the Rapture is just as sure as the death and resurrection of Christ even though it is still future. He further states that on the occasion of the Rapture, God would bring back from heaven the souls of Christians to the earthly sphere who have died, because He would resurrect their bodies and the soul will re-enter the body. The exact process is described in verse 15-17 in these words:

> For the Lord Himself will descend from heaven with a shout, with the voice of an archangel, and with the trumpet of God. And the dead in Christ will rise first. Then we who are alive and remain shall be caught up together

with them in the clouds to meet the Lord in the air. And thus
we shall always be with the Lord. Therefore comfort one
another with these words (1 Thess. 4:15-18;NKJ).

The order of events involve Christ descending bodily from
heaven to the air above the earth, His shout of command ordering
Christians who have died to be resurrected and living Christians to be
instantly changed attended by the shout of the archangel and rejoicing
in this event and what is described as the trumpet of God. When this
occurs all over the world, Christians will be instantly resurrected and
living Christians will be instantly changed according to 1 Corinthians
15:51-53. After being caught up from the earth, they will go to the
Father's house as indicated in John 14:3. In answer to the Thessalonian's
questions, they will not have to wait for their loved ones to be
resurrected as it will occur a moment before their translation. The
promise is that after this, they will be with the Lord forever wherever
He is, whether on earth, the millennial earth, or the new heaven and
new earth. The message is intended to be a comfort and an encouragement to the Thessalonians who were facing the loss of their loved
ones.

It should be noted that there is not a word here about any
intervening event. The Thessalonians are not told that they have to go
through the Tribulation first before they will see their loved ones.
Here as in all the passages on the Rapture, there is implication that the
Rapture could occur any day. As far as Scripture revelation is
concerned, there are no intervening events. This coincides with the
pre-Tribulation Rapture but does not make room for the post-Tribulation view or other views.

The question remains as to how soon the Rapture will occur.
After all, almost two thousand years have passed since this prophecy
was given. How does a believer know that there will not be many more
years before the Rapture is fulfilled?

The Timing of the Rapture

Many attempts have been made to date the Rapture and all of
them have been false because the Bible does not give this information.
However, there are indications that the Rapture could occur very
soon. This seems to be a contradiction, because if the Rapture has no
signs, how can one say that there are signs of the Rapture approaching.

The answer is found in the sequence of chronological events that
occur before the Second Coming. If prophecy is taken literally, the

Bible describes in detail exactly what the world situation will be at the Rapture and how events will unfold that finally climax in the Second Coming. These events can be stated in order.

At the time of the Rapture, there apparently will be a revival of the ancient Roman Empire that was in power when Christ was on earth. Today that empire is dead and gone but the Scriptures imply that there will be a resurrection of this empire in the end time. This is indicated in Daniel 7:7-8 where the ten horns of the beast represent ten kingdoms according to Daniel 7:25, and apparently anticipates that there will be revival of the Roman Empire in the form of ten countries. Under these circumstances, it is very significant that developments in the world today seem to pave the way for this. When these ten nations get together in a voluntary political union, a dictator will arise who will conquer three as indicated in Daniel 7:8 where the little horn, the ruler, uproots three of the ten horns representing conquering three countries. From then on, the Scriptures regard him as the ruler of all ten nations. From this position of power, he is able to attempt to solve the major problem of the Middle East, namely the place of Israel.

According to Daniel 9:24-27, Israel's total prophetic history is embraced in 490 years, the last 7 years of which have never been fulfilled. A reasonable explanation is that this ruler will impose a covenant on Israel for 7 years offered as a covenant of peace. According to Daniel 9:27, it will be observed for three and one-half years and then will be broken and a time of desecration and destruction follow. This coincides with prophecies in the Book of Revelation that there will be 42 months of Great Tribulation (Rev. 7:14, 13:5), a title which Daniel, Christ, and the Book of Revelation give this final three and one-half years leading up to the second coming of Christ (Dan. 12:1; Matt. 24:21; Rev. 7:14). In this period, the dictator of the ten nations becomes a world ruler dominated by Satan (Rev. 13:7) and reveals his own atheistic background as he claims to be God himself (2 Thess. 2:4). Because he tries to eliminate from the world all who would not recognize him, God pours out the terrible judgments described in the Book of Revelation, and the world is decimated in its human population and destroyed in its physical properties leading up to the second coming of Christ. Christ himself said in Matthew 24 that if He did not terminate the process of the Great Tribulation, there will be no people left (Matt. 24:22).

In summary, the events are as follows: the revival of the Roman Empire approximately at the time of the Rapture, emergence of a ruler who conquers the first three, and then all ten countries, the imposition of a seven-year covenant upon Israel according to Daniel 9:27, the observance of a peace treaty for the first half of the seven years, the breaking of the treaty at the time of the Great Tribulation, the last half in which a world ruler would take over dominated by Satan, the terrible judgments of the Tribulation time both from God and from the world ruler, and then the second coming of Christ.

When this sequence of events is clearly understood, the fact that Europe is at peace today becomes tremendously significant. For centuries, the major nations of Europe have fought each other and when each war ended, they would start arming for the next. This was true for hundreds of years up to the time of the Second World War. At the conclusion of the Second World War however, a strange change took place. Due to the atomic bomb, it was recognized that if another war broke out, each side would be able to destroy the other which would not make the war profitable. Accordingly, they abandoned efforts to fight each other and adopted a friendly stance where the common market was made possible and today Europe is an economic unit with more than ten nations involved. While this unification of Europe economically is not the political union which the Bible predicts, it is obviously the soil in which such a political union could take place. Even the secular press frequently refers to the possibility of the United States of Europe uniting Europe in a political union. Because this is precisely what would happen if the ten nations of the Roman Empire were revived, it makes it clear that we are now for the first time precisely at the moment in history where the Roman Empire could be revived and if this is connected with the rapture of the Church, it also helps us to date it.

Probably a sensible conclusion is that while the date of the Rapture is not revealed, for the first time, we have some solid evidence that the Rapture could be very soon. This leads to practical conclusions about what we Christians should do in the light of these prophesied events.

Are We Ready for the Rapture?

The reason Christians should be watching for the Rapture rather than the Second Coming is that the Second Coming is not imminent but the Rapture is. If Christ may come any day and Christians who have died will be resurrected and living Christians changed, it obviously puts a challenge before those who are living today to make every day count for Christ. In other words, our opportunities should be maximized in doing the things that we want to do if Christ were coming very soon.

There is no ground in Scripture for frantic efforts, but obviously the first question is are we ready in the sense of are we born again — for only Christians who are born again and part of God's family will be raptured. They have to be in Christ by the baptism of the Spirit which occurs at the moment of their faith in Christ. Undoubtedly, many church members will be left behind who fell short of a vital, personal relationship to Jesus Christ.

A second, very practical lesson is that we should be concerned about those around us who are not Christians whether they are loved ones or strangers. Christians should get behind every effort to win people for Christ and they should be engaged in personal evangelism and prayer for the lost, supporting the church and evangelistic efforts in trying to win others to Christ. Certainly, this is a crucial time in history if the Rapture could be very soon.

It should be noted that the Bible does not outline frantic or extreme efforts in preparation for the Lord's return. The Bible does not indicate that Christians should give all their money away as some have tried to do who have dated the Rapture. Instead, however, Christians should be wise stewards giving as much as they can because obviously if the Rapture occurs, they will leave behind whatever physical wealth they have. It is also obvious that we have many opportunities for service for God in recognition of His plan and program and we should order our lives especially as they are related to eternal values, things that will really count as we stand before Christ, the judgment seat of rewards, which the Bible describes as following the Rapture. Accordingly, we watch because it could be soon but watching is not enough. We must be serving and making the most of our remaining time.

14

Rapture: Three Fascinating Discoveries!

by Grant Jeffrey

Over the last 30 years I have been fascinated with Bible prophecy because it authenticates the Scriptures as God's inspired Word and it points to the imminent return of Jesus Christ to usher in the Messianic kingdom. I am always delighted when God leads me to new information that confirms His Word. In my ongoing research into recent archaeololological discoveries and into writings of Early Church leaders I have made several exciting new discoveries that I want to share with my readers. In this chapter we will explore a number of interesting discoveries about the following subjects: the finding of a teaching about the pre-Tribulation Rapture from the first centuries of the Early Church; the archaeological discoveries of the tombs of Mary, Martha, and Lazarus that prove the historical accuracy of the Gospels; and the proof that miraculous healings, raising of the dead, and the charismatic gifts were common among believers during the first three centuries following the resurrection of Christ.

The Pre-Tribulation Rapture Was Taught by the Early Church

Obviously, the truth about the timing of the Rapture will

ultimately be found only in Scripture. The Protestant Reformation was based essentially on this return to the authority of the Bible. The Latin phrase *Sola Scriptura*, meaning "Scripture Alone," became the rallying cry of the reformers who ignored centuries of tradition and church councils in their insistence that truth could only be discovered in the Word of God. While the ultimate resolution of this discussion must be based on our interpretation of Scripture, it is important to answer the errors of our opponents who disparage "the blessed hope" of the Rapture with misinformation about the modern rediscovery of the truth about the pre-Tribulation Rapture.

Many post-tribulationist writers have attacked the pre-Tribulation Rapture doctrine by claiming that it cannot be true because no Church writer or reformer ever taught this doctrine until approximately 170 years ago. While the real question for sincere students of Scripture must be whether or not the Bible truly teaches this doctrine, the argument that no one ever saw this "truth" throughout the 1,800 years of Church history has been very effective, causing many Christians to abandon their belief in the pre-Tribulation Rapture. The only problem with their argument is that they are totally wrong.

Many contemporary writers claim that the pre-Tribulation Rapture theory first originated around A.D. 1820. They ascribe the theory's initial creation to either Emmanuel Acumza (Ben Ezra, 1812), Edward Irving (1816), or Margaret Macdonald (1830), and finally to John Darby (1830). For example, Dave MacPherson in *The Incredible Cover-Up*, written in 1975, stated, "Margaret Macdonald was the first person to teach a coming of Christ that would precede the days of Antichrist."[1] Before 1830 Christians had always believed in a single future coming, that the catching up of 1 Thessalonians 4 will take place after the Great Tribulation of Matthew 24 at the glorious coming of the Son of Man when He shall send His angels to gather together all of His elect." Reverend John Bray, in *The Origin of the Pre-Tribulation Rapture Teaching* (1980), declared, "People who are teaching the pre-Tribulation Rapture today are teaching something that never was taught until 1812. . . . Not one of those Early Church fathers taught a pre-Tribulation Rapture. . . . I make the offer of five hundred dollars to anybody who will find a statement, a sermon, article in a commentary, or anything, prior to 1812 that taught a two-phase coming of Christ separated by a stated period of time, such as the pre-Tribulation rapturists teach."[2]

Those writers, among others who despise the teaching of the

pre-Tribulation Rapture, dogmatically assert that it was taught for the first time in 1830 by John Darby and the Plymouth Brethren or one of the other individuals mentioned above.

A number of these authors will have to drastically revise the next edition of their books based on two remarkable textual discoveries that conclusively prove that a number of Christian teachers, centuries before John Darby rediscovered this biblical teaching, clearly taught that the Rapture would occur before the tribulation period. During the summer of 1994, after more than a decade of searching, I discovered several fascinating manuscripts that contain clear evidence of the teaching of the pre-Tribulation Rapture in the Early Church.

Ephraem's Teaching on the Pre-Tribulation Rapture

"For all the saints and Elect of God are gathered, prior to the Tribulation that is to come, and are taken to the Lord lest they see the confusion that is to overwhelm the world because of our sins" (*On the Last Times, the Antichrist, and the End of the World,* by Ephraem the Syrian, A.D. 373).

The early Christian writer and poet, Ephraem the Syrian (who lived from A.D. 306 to 373), was a major theologian of the early Byzantine Eastern Church. He was born near Nisbis in the Roman province of Syria, near present-day Edessa, Turkey. Ephraem displayed a profound love of the Scriptures in his writings as illustrated by several of his written comments quoted in *Works of Nathaniel Lardner* (vol. 4, 1788). "I esteem no man more happy than him who diligently reads the Scriptures delivered to us by the Spirit of God, and thinks how he may order his conversation by the precepts of them." To this day his hymns and homilies are used in the liturgy of the Greek Orthodox and Middle Eastern Nestorian Church. While the 16-volume Post-Nicene Library includes a number of homilies and psalms by Ephraem the Syrian, the editors noted that he also wrote a large number of commentaries that have never been translated into English.

Ephraem's fascinating teaching on the Antichrist has never been published in English until now. This critically important prophecy manuscript from the fourth century of the Church era reveals a literal method of interpretation and a teaching of the pre-millennial return of Christ. More importantly, Ephraem's text revealed a very clear statement about the pre-tribulational return of Christ to take His elect saints home to heaven to escape the coming Tribulation. In addition, Ephraem declares his belief in a personal, Jewish Antichrist, who will rule the Roman Empire during the last days, a rebuilt temple, the two witnesses, and a literal Great Tribulation lasting 1,260 days. It is also fascinating to note that he taught that the war of God and Magog would precede the tribulation period. I discovered another text by Ephraem called *The Book of the Cave of Treasure* that revealed he taught that Daniel's seventieth week will be fulfilled in the final seven years at the end of this age that will conclude with Christ's return at the Battle of Armageddon to establish His kingdom.

The following section includes key passages from Ephraem's important text, written about A.D. 373, and translated by Professor Cameron Rhoades of Tyndale Theological Seminary at my request.

On the Last Times, the Antichrist, and the End of the World

1. Most dearly beloved brothers, believe the Holy Spirit who speaks in us. Now we have spoken before, because the end of the world is very near, and the consummation remains. Has not the first faith withered away in men? . . .

2. *We ought to understand thoroughly therefore, my brothers, what is imminent or overhanging.* Already there have been hunger and plagues, violent movements of nations and signs, which have been predicted by the Lord, they have already been fulfilled, and there is not other which remains, except the advent of the wicked one in the completion of the Roman kingdom. Why therefore are we occupied with worldly business, and why is our mind held fixed on the lusts of the world or the anxieties of the ages? Why therefore do we not reject every care of earthly actions and prepare ourselves for the meeting of the Lord Christ, *so that He may draw us from the confusion, which overwhelms the world?* Believe you me, dearest brothers, because the coming of the Lord is nigh, believe you me, because the end of the world is at hand, believe me, because it is the very last time. . . . ***Because all saints and the Elect of the Lord are gathered together before the tribulation which is about to come and are taken to the Lord, in order that they may not see at any time the confusion which overwhelms the world because of our sins*** [italics added]. And so, brothers, most dear to me, it is the eleventh hour, and the end of this world comes to the

harvest, and angels, armed and prepared, hold sickles in their hands, awaiting the empire of the Lord. . . .

3. When therefore the end of the world comes, there arise diverse wars, commotions on all sides, horrible earthquakes, perturbations of nations, tempests throughout the lands, plagues, famine, drought throughout the thoroughfares, great danger throughout the sea and dry land, constant persecutions, slaughters and massacres everywhere. . . .

6. When therefore the end of the world comes, that abominable, lying and murderous one is born from the tribe of Dan. He is conceived from the seed of a man and from a most vile virgin, mixed with an evil or worthless spirit. . . .

7. But when the time of the abomination of his desolation begins to approach, having been made legal, he takes the empire. . . . Therefore, when he receives the kingdom, he orders the temple of God to be rebuilt for himself, which is in Jerusalem; who, after coming into it, he shall sit as God and order that he be adored by all nations . . . then all people from everywhere shall flock together to him at the city of Jerusalem, and the holy city shall be trampled on by the nations for forty-two months just as the holy apostle says in the Apocalypse, which become three and a half years, 1,260 days.

8. In these three years and a half the heaven shall suspend its dew; because there will be no rain upon the earth . . . and there will be a great tribulation, as there has not been, since people began to be upon the earth . . . and no one is able to sell or to buy of the grain of the fall harvest, unless he is one who has the serpentine sign on the forehead or the hand. . . .

10. And when the three and a half years have been completed, the time of the Antichrist, through which he will have seduced the world, after the resurrection of the two prophets, in the hour which the world does not know, and on the day which the enemy or son of perdition does not know, will come the sign of the Son of Man, and coming forward the Lord shall appear with great power and much majesty, with the sign of the word of salvation

going before him, and also even with all the powers of the heavens with the whole chorus of the saints.... Then Christ shall come and the enemy shall be thrown into confusion, and the Lord shall destroy him by the Spirit of his mouth. And he shall be bound and shall be plunged into the abyss of everlasting fire alive with his father Satan; and all people, who do his wishes, shall perish with him forever; but the righteous ones shall inherit everlasting life with the Lord for ever and ever.

To summarize the key points in Ephraem's text on the last days:

1. Ephraem's manuscript lays out the events of the last days in chronological sequence. Significantly, he began with the Rapture, using the word "imminent," then he described the Great Tribulation of three and a half years duration under the Antichrist's tyranny, followed by the second coming of Christ to earth with His saints to defeat the Antichrist.

2. Significantly, at the beginning of his treatise in section 2, Ephraem used the word "imminent" to describe the Rapture occurring before the Tribulation and the coming of the Antichrist. "We ought to understand thoroughly therefore, my brothers which is imminent or overhanging."

3. He clearly described the pre-Tribulation Rapture: "Because all saints and the Elect of the Lord are gathered together before the tribulation which is about to come and are taken to the Lord, in order that they may not see at any time the confusion which overwhelms the world because of our sins."

4. He then gives the purpose of God rapturing the Church "before the tribulation" so that "they may not see at any time the confusion which overwhelms the world because of our sins." Ephraem used the word "confusion" as a synonym for the tribulation period.

5. Ephraem described the duration of the "great tribulation" (the last half of the seven-year tribulation period) in sections 7, 8, and 10, as follows: "forty-two months" and "three and a half years," and "1,260 days."

6. He summarized: "There will be a great tribulation, as there has no been since people began to be upon the earth," and described the Mark of the Beast system.

7. He declared that Christ will come to the earth after the "three and a half years" tribulation period in section 10: "And when the three and a half years have been completed, the time of the Antichrist,

through which he will have seduced the world, after the resurrection of the two prophets . . . will come the sign of the Son of Man, and coming forward the Lord shall appear with great power and much majesty."

Dr. Paul Alexander, perhaps the most authoritative scholar on the writings of the early Byzantine Church, concluded that Ephraem's text on the Antichrist taught that the Lord would supernaturally remove the saints of the Church from the earth "prior to the tribulation that is to come." Ephraem wrote that the saints will be "taken to the Lord lest they see the confusion that is to overwhelm the world because of our sins." Dr. Alexander believed this text was written by some unknown writer in the sixth century, but he concluded that it was derived from an original Ephraem manuscript (A.D. 373). Other scholars, including the German editor Professor Caspari, who wrote a German commentary on this Latin manuscript in 1890, believed that Ephraem's manuscript was written by the genuine Ephraem in A.D. 373. Professor Cameron Rhoades translated Ephraem's Latin text into English at the request of my friend Dr. Tommy Ice and myself.

Ephraem and Daniel's Seventieth Week
— the Tribulation Period

A question naturally arises in the mind of Bible students about how long Ephraem believed the Tribulation would last. While Ephraem correctly describes the "great tribulation" as three and a half years, his other writings revealed that he believed the whole tribulation period, "that sore affliction," would last "one week" of seven years. Ephraem's book, *The Book of the Cave of Treasures*, taught about the genealogy of Christ. He wrote that the sixty-ninth week of Daniel 9:24-27 ended with the rejection and crucifixion of Jesus the Messiah. He stated, "The Jews have no longer among them a king, or a priest, or a prophet, or a Passover, even as Daniel prophesied concerning them, saying, '*After two and sixty weeks Christ shall be slain,* and the city of holiness shall be laid waste until the completion of things decreed' (Dan. 9:26). That is to say, for ever and ever" (italics added, *The Cave of Treasures*, page 235). In Daniel's prophecy he foretold that Jerusalem would be rebuilt "even in troublesome times" during the initial period of "seven weeks" of years (49 years). Daniel's prophecy declared that this initial period of seven "weeks" of years would be immediately followed by a further period of 62 "weeks" of years ending with the cutting off of the Messiah (483 years). The combined total of 69 weeks of years (7 weeks plus 62 weeks) was to conclude with the rejection of Christ. As quoted above, Ephraem taught that Jesus Christ was slain at the end of the combined 69 weeks of years.

However, in the section of his book dealing with the future war of God and Magog, Ephraem wrote about the final (seventieth) week of Daniel as follows: *"At the end of the world and at the final consummation* . . . suddenly the gates of the north shall be opened. . . . They will destroy the earth, and there will be none able to stand before them. *After one week of that sore affliction [Tribulation], they will all be destroyed in the plain of Joppa.* . . . Then will the son of perdition appear, of the seed and of the tribe of Dan. . . . He will go into Jerusalem and will sit upon a throne in the Temple saying, 'I am the Christ,' and he will be borne aloft by legions of devils like a king and a lawgiver, naming himself God. . . . *The time of the error of the Antichrist will last two years and a half,* but others say *three years and six months"* (italics added). Although there are some curious elements in his description of prophetic events, it is clear that Ephraem believed that the seventieth final week of Daniel's prophecy of the 70 weeks will finally be fulfilled during the final seven years of this age when the Antichrist will appear. This evidence of a belief in a "gap" or "parenthesis" between the sixty-ninth and seventieth week of Daniel 9:24-27 from the fourth century of the Christian era is significant. It is worthwhile to note that the teaching that there would be a "gap" or parenthesis between Daniel's sixty-ninth week and the seventieth week of years was also taught by others in the Early Church, including the epistle of Barnabas (A.D. 110) and the writings of Hippolytus (A.D. 220).

Dr. John Gill Taught the Pre-Tribulation Rapture in 1748

Dr. John Gill, a famous eighteenth-century Baptist theologian, published his commentary on the New Testament in 1748. He is considered a serious Calvinist scholar who wrote many volumes on theology. In his commentary on 1 Thessalonians 4:15-17, Dr. Gill points out that Paul is teaching a doctrine that is "something new and extraordinary." Gill calls the imminent translation of the saints "the rapture" and calls for watchfulness because "it will be sudden, and unknown before-hand, and when least thought of and expected." This is a clear, detailed 1748 teaching on the imminent pre-Tribulation Rapture (80 years prior to John Darby in 1830).

"For this we say to you by the word of the Lord, that we which are alive and remain unto the coming of the Lord shall not prevent them which are asleep" (1 Thess. 4:15). Gill's commentary on this passage is: "The Apostle, having something new and extraordinary to deliver concerning the coming of Christ, the first resurrection, or the resurrection of the saints, the change of the living saints and *the Rapture both of the raised, and living in the clouds* to meet Christ in the air expresses itself in this manner" (italics added).

"Then we which are alive and remain shall be caught up together with them in the clouds, to meet the Lord in the air; and so shall we ever be with the Lord" (1 Thess. 4:17). In commenting on this verse Gill revealed that he understood there would be an interval of time between the Rapture and the return of saints with Christ at Armageddon.

Suddenly, in a moment, in the twinkling of an eye, and with force and power; by the power of Christ, and by the ministry and means of the holy angels; and to which *rapture* will contribute the agility, which the bodies both of the raised and changed saints will have; and *this rapture of the living saints* will be together with them; with the dead in Christ, that will then be raised; so that the one will not prevent the other, or the one be sooner with Christ than the other; but one being raised and the other changed, they'll be joined in one company and general assembly, and *be rapt up together: in the clouds;* the same clouds perhaps in which Christ will come will be let down to take them up; these will be the chariots, in which they'll be carried up to Him; and thus, as at our Lord's ascension a cloud received Him, and in it He was carried up out of the sight of men, *so at this time will all the saints ride up in the clouds of Heaven: to meet the Lord in the air; whither He'll descend . . . here Christ will stop* and will be visible to all, and as easily discerned by all, good and bad, as the body of the sun at noonday; *as yet He will not descend on earth, because not fit to receive Him; but when that and its works are burnt up, and it is purged and purified by fire, and become a new earth, He'll descend upon it, and dwell with His saints in it:* and this suggests another reason why He'll stay in the air, and His saints shall meet Him there, and whom He'll take up with Him into the third heaven, till the general conflagration and burning of the world is over, and to preserve them from it: and then shall all the elect of God descend from heaven as a bride adorned for her husband,

and He with them . . . *then they shall be with Him, wherever He is; fist in the air, where they shall meet Him; them in the third heaven, where they shall go up with Him; then on earth, where they shall descend and reign with Him a thousand years;* and then in the ultimate glory to all eternity.

To summarize Dr. Gill's 1748 pre-Tribulation Rapture teaching about the sequence of prophetic events it is vital to note that he declared:

1. The Lord will descend in the air.

2. The saints will be raptured in the air to meet Him.

3. Here Christ will stop in the air and will be visible to all.

4. As yet, He will not descend on earth, because it is not fit to receive Him.

5. He'll take up the saints with Him into the third heaven, till the general conflagration and burning of the world is over.

6. He will preserve them from it.

7. And then shall all the elect of God descend from heaven to earth with Christ.

Gill then summarizes the sequence:

1) They shall be with Him, wherever He is; first in the air, where they shall meet Him, then

2) In the third heaven, where they shall go up with Him; then

3) On earth, where they shall descend and reign with Him a thousand years.

Therefore, in addition to Ephraem's pre-Tribulation teaching from the fourth century, we have another clear statement of this doctrine from Dr. John Gill, more than 80 years before John Darby in 1830. Those who have stated that the pre-Tribulation Rapture was never taught throughout the entire history of the Church until 1820 are simply ignorant of these important Christian texts. The French writer Joubert once wrote, "Nothing makes men so imprudent and conceited as ignorance of the past and a scorn for old books."

Why is it important to teach the doctrine of the pre-Tribulation

Rapture? The apostle Peter warned that many people would challenge our Lord's promise of His second coming in the last days. "Knowing this first; that scoffers will come in the last days, walking according to their own lusts, and saying, 'Where is the promise of His coming?' " (2 Pet. 3:3-4).

What does the Bible teach us about the proper attitude of a Christian on the subject of Christ's return? Paul tells us, "So that you come short in no gift, eagerly waiting for the revelation of our Lord Jesus Christ" (1 Cor. 1:7).

One of the distinguishing characteristics of a true follower of Jesus is that of a faithful, waiting, and watching servant. Dr. Klink, one of the great students of the faith of the Early Church, wrote, "This constant expectation of our Lord's second coming is one of the characteristic features of primitive Christianity." Paul also commends a constant expectation of the Rapture in Philippians 3:20 where he said, "For our citizenship is in heaven; from which we also eagerly wait for the Savior, the Lord Jesus Christ."

The great reformer John Calvin wrote of the vital importance of the hope of the Second Coming: "It ought to be the chief concern of believers to fix their minds fully on His Second Advent." Martin Luther, in his *Sermon of Consolation,* declared that the hope of Christ's return is an absolute necessity for a Christian: "If thou be not filled with a desire after the Coming of this day, thou canst never pray the Lord's prayer, nor canst thou repeat from thy heart the creed of faith. For with what conscience canst thou say, 'I believe in the resurrection of the body and the life everlasting,' if thou dost not in my heart desire the same? If thou didst believe it, thou must, of necessity, desire it from thy heart, and long for that day to come; which, if thou doest not desire, thou art not yet a Christian, nor canst thou boast of thy faith."

Throughout the New Testament we read continual exhortations to hold the hope of our Lord's soon return as the focus of our spiritual life. Far from being an unimportant issue, interesting only to students of prophecy, the "blessed hope" of the Rapture should be a cornerstone of every Christian's spiritual life.

The message and hope of the imminent second coming of Christ to rapture the saints has the following purposes:

1. It calls us to constant watchfulness for His return (1 Thess. 5:4-6).

2. It motivates Christians to witness to unbelievers in

light of His imminent coming (John 9:4).

3. It reminds us to walk in holiness in an immoral world while we await His return (1 John 3:3).

4. It comforts the saints by reminding them of their eternal destiny with Christ (John 14:1-3).

5. It warns of the coming judgment on those who reject His salvation (2 Thess. 1:8-9).

6. It inspires us to persevere against opposition in light of His reward (2 Tim. 4:1-8).

7. It encourages sinners to repent and accept the Lord while there is still time (Acts 3:19-21).

The promise in the Scriptures of the imminent second coming of the Messiah, Jesus Christ, is the last best hope of mankind. It is the promise of the ultimate vindication of God's plan to redeem mankind and the earth from the curse of sin and death. The final realization of Jesus Christ's claim that He is the promised Messiah, and the fulfillment of prophecies about the coming kingdom of God will culminate when the heavens open to reveal Christ coming in all His glory at the Battle of Armageddon. However, the Scriptures teach that another event will occur before Christ comes to defeat the Antichrist and the armies of the world at Armageddon at the end of the seven-year tribulation period. This separate and earlier event is often called the Rapture. Throughout the Bible the passages that detail the revelation of Christ at the end of the tribulation period describe a totally different event than those passages describing the coming of Christ in the air to take the saints home to heaven.

The longing for the Rapture and the return of Christ has motivated generations of Bible students to examine the Scriptures in a search for clues as to the exact timing of His glorious appearing. Unfortunately, despite clear scriptural warnings against date-setting regarding the time of His return, many have indulged in unhelpful speculation about the time of the Rapture. Harold Camping's book *1994*, for example, claimed that Christ would return on September 17, 1994. Millions of followers of these writings have been deeply disappointed when their foolish predictions proved false. However, despite these disappointments, we must not abandon our hope for an imminent Rapture. We must simply be obedient to Christ's command that "Now when these things begin to happen, look up and lift up your heads, because your redemption draws near" (Luke 21:28).

John Wesley de Fletcher wrote a fascinating letter to Charles

Wesley in 1755 that expressed the proper attitude we should have toward the return of Christ. "I know that many have been grossly mistaken as to the year of His return, but, because they were rash, shall we be stupid? Because they say 'Today!' shall we say, 'Never!' and cry 'Peace, peace,' when we should look about us with eyes full of expectation?"

The Bible warns us to live in holiness because Christ could return at any moment, without warning. Jesus, in Luke 12:37 and 40, admonished, "Blessed are those servants, whom the master, when he comes, will find watching. . . . Therefore you also be ready, for the Son of Man is coming at an hour you do not expect." Peter, in his second epistle, said, "You therefore, beloved, since you know these things beforehand, beware lest you also fall from your own steadfastness, being led away with the error of the wicked" (2 Pet. 3:17). We must live in a dynamic spiritual balance. While we are commanded to live in holiness and urgently witness as though He will return before the dawn, we are called to plan and work to fulfill the Great Commission as if He will tarry for another hundred years. We are to "do business ['occupy' in the Authorized Version] till I come" (Luke 19:13), fulfilling Christ's Great Commission to "go therefore and make disciples of all the nations, baptizing them in the name of the Father and of the Son and of the Holy Spirit, teaching them to observe all things that I have commanded you" (Matt. 28:19-20).

This discovery of texts written before 1820 brings us to the conclusion that a remnant of the faithful, from the beginning of the Early Church until today, have upheld the great precious biblical truth of pre-Tribulation Rapture. Ephraem the Syrian's A.D. 373 manuscript *On the Last Times, the Antichrist, and the End of the World*, along with Dr. John Gill's 1748 *Commentary on the New Testament* refute the dogmatic declarations of a post-Tribulation Rapture. In my earlier book, *Apocalypse,* I quoted from the early Christian writing called *Shepherd of Hermas* (A.D. 110), proving it taught the pre-Tribulation Rapture as the hope of the Church.

The Discovery of the Tombs of Mary, Martha, and Lazarus

Some writers have claimed that there is virtually no archaeological evidence to back up the historical claims of the Gospels. The truth is that tremendous archaeological evidence has been discovered in Israel that proves the accuracy of the New Testament!

Over a century ago a French Christian archaeologist, Charles Claremont-Gannueau, wrote a little-known report, dated November

13, 1873, from Jerusalem to the Palestine Exploration Fund. In this report he told of his monumental discovery, in a sepulchral cave near Bethany, of a group of Jewish ossuaries (stone coffins) from the first century of the Christian era. To his great surprise, Claremont-Gannueau found that these ancient Jewish stone coffins contained the names of numerous individuals mentioned in the New Testament as members of the Jerusalem Church. Despite its importance, this report was not published in the newspapers of the day. As a result, it was virtually lost to history. Several years ago I purchased a book, from a rare book dealer in London, which contained this obscure report by Charles Claremont-Gannueau. The 1874 report, published by the Palestine Exploration Fund, included his translation of several of these inscriptions, which indicated that he had discovered the tombs of Mary, Martha, and Lazarus, as well as numerous other Christians from the first-century church. A Christian newspaper from Israel, the *Jerusalem Christian Review*, has carried several fascinating articles in the last few years about the wonderful archaeological discoveries that confirm the historical accuracy of the Gospel account.

In the spring of 1873, Effendi Abu Saud, while constructing his house on the eastern slopes of the Mount of Olives near the road to ancient Bethany, accidentally discovered a cave that proved to be an ancient burial catacomb. Inside, he found 30 ancient stone coffins. Professor Charles Claremont-Gannueau examined the ossuaries in this ancient family sepulchral cave carved out of limestone rock. The Jews in the first century buried their dead either in the ground or in a tomb. Several years later they would clean the bones of the skeleton and re-bury these bones in a small limestone ossuary, often 45 inches long, 20 inches wide, and 25 inches high. The lids of these ossuaries are triangular, semi-circular, or rectangular. Inscriptions containing the name and identification of the deceased were painted or engraved on the sides or on the lids of the ossuaries, in Hebrew or Greek. Claremont-Gannueau was excited to note that several ossuaries were inscribed with crosses or the name "Jesus," proving that these Jewish deceased were Christians. Although he was unable to take photographs, he did take squeezes with a special cloth of the ornamented surfaces as well as of the inscriptions.

Engraved on the sides of three of these ossuaries from this cave were the names of "Eleazar" (the Hebrew form of the Greek name "Lazarus"), "Martha," and "Mary." These names were followed by the sign of the cross, proving they were Christian. In the Gospel of

John we read the touching story of Christ raising His friend Lazarus from the dead. "Now a certain man was sick, Lazarus of Bethany, the town of Mary and her sister Martha" (John 11:1).

Claremont-Gannueau noted that this was one of the most important archaeological discoveries ever made concerning the origins of the early New Testament Church. He wrote, "This catacomb on the Mount of Olives belonged apparently to one of the earliest families which joined the new religion of Christianity. In this group of sarcophagi, some of which have the Christian symbol and some have not, we are, so to speak, [witnessing the] actual unfolding of Christianity. Personally, I think that many of the Hebrew-speaking people whose remains are contained in these ossuaries were among the first followers of Christ. . . . The appearance of Christianity at the very gates of Jerusalem is, in my opinion, extraordinary and unprecedented. Somehow the new [Christian] doctrine must have made its way into the Jewish system. . . . The association of the sign of the cross with (the name of Jesus) written in Hebrew alone constitutes a valuable fact."

The 1874 report contained the following additional inscriptions found on ossuaries:

Hebrew Inscriptions:

1. *Salome, wife of Judah*, engraved in very small characters . . . a cruciform sign.

2. *Judah,* with the cross +. Perhaps the husband of Salome.

3. *Judah the Scribe.* On another face of the sarcophagus, Judah, son of Eleazar the Scribe.

4. *Simeon the Priest* (Cohen).

5. *Martha, daughter of Pasach.* Perhaps the name is Jewish as well as Christian.

6. *Eleazar, son of Nathalu.* The form "Nathai" for Nathan is not uncommon.

7. *Salamtsion, daughter of Simeon the Priest.* The name of the woman, Salam Sion, is of the greatest interest. It is the name Salampsion of Josephus (daughter of Herod).

Greek inscriptions:

1. *Jesus,* twice repeated, with the cross +.

2. *Nathaniel,* accompanied by a cross.

It is interesting to note that Claremont-Gannueau also found in one of the ossuaries "three or four small instruments in copper of bronze, much oxidized, consisting of an actual small bell, surmounted by a ring. The Arabs thought they were a kind of castanets. Can we trace here the equivalent of the bells hung on the robe of the high priest? And do these ornaments come from the sarcophagus of our Simeon?"

The French archaeologist realized that there is a high degree of probability that these tombs belonged to the family of Mary, Martha, and Lazarus, the close friends of Jesus. Claremont-Gannueau wrote, "What gives additional value to these short inscriptions is that they furnish a whole series of names found in the Gospels, in their popular and local Syro-Chaldaic forms. The presence of the names of Jesus and Martha, of which we only knew historically that it was the feminine form of the Aramaic, would alone be sufficient to make this collection important from an exegetic point of view. By a singular coincidence, which from the first struck me forcibly, these inscriptions, found close to the Bethany road, and very near the site of the village, contain nearly all the names of the personages in the Gospel scenes which belonged to the place: Eleazar (Lazarus), Simon, Martha . . . a host of other coincidences occur at the sight of all these most evangelical names."

In addition, the Italian scholar P. Bagatti discovered another catacomb holding 100 ossuaries on the western side of the Mount of Olives, opposite the Temple Mount, near the Catholic chapel called Dominus Flevit. Coins minted by Governor Varius Gratus (A.D. 16) proved that these tombs were used for burial of Christians before the fall of Jerusalem in A.D. 70. Several of the coffins in the cave belonged to a family of priests buried in the first century. Based on the inscribed crosses and the name "Jesus," Baggati concluded that several of these priests were followers of Jesus Christ. Bagatti found many ossuaries containing the following names inscribed on their sides, together with the sign of the cross or the name of Jesus: Jonathan, Joseph, Jarius, Judah, Matthias, Menahem, Salome, Simon, and Zechariah. Many of these names appear in the New Testament records of the Early Church at Jerusalem. One ossuary contained the Greek inscription "Iota, Chi and Beta," which read "Jesus Christ, the Redeemer."

Without question, the most fascinating ossuary was the one inscribed with crosses and the name "Shappira." This is a unique name which has not been found in contemporary Jewish literature outside the New Testament passage of Acts 5:1. Luke recorded the death of this woman and her husband when they lied to God and the Church (Acts 5:1, 5-10). "But a certain man named Ananias, with Sapphira his wife, sold a possession. . . ."

During the fall of 1945, Dr. Eleazar Sukenik of Hebrew University investigated another first century Jewish catacomb at the southern end of the Kidron Valley on the road to Bethlehem. He found several ossuaries with the sign of the cross, Greek inscriptions, a coin minted in A.D. 41 for King Herod Agrippa I, proving the tomb was sealed by A.D. 42. Professor Sukenik concluded that the ossuaries "contain almost the whole dictionary of names in the New Testament."[3]

One coffin had a surprising dedication in Greek to "Jesus" followed by the exclamation "Y'ho," meaning "Jehovah" or "the Lord." The inscription reads: "[To] Jesus, the Lord." In light of the A.D. 42 date for the sealing of this tomb, the presence of this dedication to "Jesus, the Lord" attests to the acceptance by Christians of Jesus Christ as God within ten years of the death and resurrection of Jesus. Christian theologian Professor Alexander Hopkins commented on this significant inscription as follows: "The inscription which was hidden for almost 2,000 years and inscribed at least two decades before any part of the New Testament was written . . . bears a personal testimony of faith . . . a message from the past with a very modern meaning for the present."[4]

Several years ago they found another Jewish Christian ossuary in Jerusalem that contained the inscription "Alexander, son of Simon of Cyrene." The Gospel of Mark refers to this person as follows, "Now they compelled a certain man, Simon a Cyrenian, the father of Alexander and Rufus, as he was coming out of the country and passing by, to bear his cross" (Mark 15:21).

Miracles, Healing, and the Gifts of the Holy Spirit Continued for Centuries

Many Christians have been told that the miracles, healings, and charismatic gifts of the Holy Spirit, enumerated in 1 Corinthians 12, were given to the early Christians solely to launch the Church, and that these supernatural signs ceased when the apostles died. Several writers have declared that a search of the writings of the Early Church confirms that there are no references to these "gifts" continuing in operation beyond A.D. 100. I recently acquired a CD-ROM computer disk that contains the writings of the Early Church writers from the time of Christ until the Council of Nicea in A.D. 325, known as the Ante-Nicene Fathers. After an exhaustive search of these early Christian writings, I can confirm that God continued to manifest His supernatural power in the display of miraculous healings, raising from the dead, and other charismatic gifts of the Holy Spirit for the next three centuries following the resurrection of Christ.

There are brief references to these gifts still continuing in the Early Church manual known as the *Testimony of the Apostles — the Didache* (11:10-13, 11:20) composed in A.D. 110. Additional references are found in the *Letter to the Corinthians* (2:1-5) by Clement, bishop of Rome, written in A.D. 100, and the *Shepherd of Hermas* (43:9; 24-33; 52-54), written in A.D. 110. However, in addition to those above there are a number of significant references to these supernatural gifts continuing in the Church for centuries following Christ's resurrection.

Irenaeus — *Refutation and Overthrow of Knowledge Falsely So Called*

The Christian teacher Irenaeus wrote a treatise called *Refutation and Overthrow of Knowledge Falsely So Called* in A.D. 185 that mentioned the continued operation of miraculous powers that were exercised by believers in his day. He demonstrated clearly that right down to his own time, manifestations of divine and supernatural power were witnessed in some churches. "Some drive out demons really and truly, so that often those cleansed from evil spirits believe and become members of the Church; some have foreknowledge of the future, visions, and prophetic utterances; others, by laying-on of hands, heal the sick and restore them to health; and before now, as I said, dead men have actually been raised and have remained with us for many years. In fact, it is impossible the gifts which throughout the world the Church has received from God and in the name of Jesus Christ crucified under Pontius Pilate, and every day puts to effectual use for the benefit of the heathen, deceiving no one and making profit out of no one." In addition, Irenaeus wrote, "Similarly, we hear of many members of the Church who have prophetic gifts and by the Spirit speak with all kinds of tongues, and bring men's secret thoughts to light for their own good, and expound the mysteries of God."

Justin Martyr — *Dialogue with Trypho*

Justin Martyr wrote his Dialogue with Trypho in A.D. 165 and referred clearly to many gifts of the Holy Spirit appearing in the daily life of the second century Church (chapter XI). In chapter XXXIX he wrote, "Daily some of you are becoming disciples in the name of Christ, and quitting the path of error; who are also receiving gifts, each as he is worthy, illumined through the name of this Christ. For one receives the spirit of understanding, another of counsel, another of strength, another of healing, another of foreknowledge, another of teaching, and another of the fear of God."

Tertullian — *The Passion of Perpetua and Felicitas*

Tertullian was a major theologian and Christian writer from Carthage, North Africa. In A.D. 215 he described these supernatural visions and prophetic gifts of the Holy Spirit as operating normally in the third century Church: "And thus we who both acknowledge and reverence, even as we do the prophecies, modern visions as equally promised to us, and consider the powers of the Holy Spirit as an agency of the Church for which also He was sent, administering all gifts in all, even as the Lord distributed to every one."

Origen — *Against Celsus*

Origen was a Christian theologian who lived and taught in Alexandria, Egypt, from A.D. 185 to 254. In his book *Against Celsus*, written in A.D. 250, Origen described the gifts of the Holy Spirit as still appearing, but he notes that these miraculous signs are beginning to diminish. "Traces of the Holy Spirit who appeared in the form of a dove are still preserved among Christians. They charm demons away and perform many cures and perceived certain things about the future according to the will of the Logos" (book I, chapter XLVI, 2,8).

In book VII, chapter VIII of his book *Against Celsus*, Origen noted that these charismatic gifts were diminishing, although some "traces of His presence" are still evident. "Moreover, the Holy Spirit gave signs of His Presence at the beginning of Christ's ministry, and after His ascension He gave still more; but since that time these signs have diminished, although here are still traces of His presence in a few who have had their souls purified by the Gospel and their actions regulated by its influence."

Novatian — *Treatise Concerning the Trinity*

In A.D. 270, Novatian of Rome wrote a strong defense of the doctrine of the Trinity and died as a martyr during the second last wave of persecutions of the pagan Roman emperors. Novatian wrote toward the close of the third century of the Church Age about the key role of the Holy Spirit in empowering the Church. "They were henceforth armed and strengthened by the same Spirit, having in themselves the gifts which this same Spirit distributes, and appropriates to the Church, the spouse of Christ as her ornaments. This is He who places prophets in the Church, instructs teachers, directs tongues, gives powers and healings, does wonderful works, offers discrimination of spirits, affords powers of government, suggests counsels and orders, and arranges whatever other gifts there are of charismata; and thus make the Lord's Church everywhere, and in all, perfected and completed."

These documents from the first three centuries of the early Church Age tell us that God continued to empower the saints with supernatural gifts and healing miracles to demonstrate that the Holy Spirit's power was undiminished.

How You Can Be Assured of Eternal Life in Heaven

Someday each of us will meet Jesus Christ face to face: "It is appointed for men to die once, but after this the judgment" (Heb. 9:27). God declares that "all have sinned and fall short of the glory of God" (Rom. 3:23). It is impossible for a Holy God to allow an unrepentant sinner into a sinless heaven. In light of the many signs that His return is very near, each of us must make our final choice. Every day their sinful rebellion is leading men and women inexorably toward hell and an eternity without God. "For the wages of sin is death, but the gift of God is eternal life in Christ Jesus our Lord" (Rom. 6:23). However, God loves us so much that He sent His Son Jesus the Messiah to suffer the punishment for our sins for everyone who would confess his sin and ask forgiveness. In the Gospel of John the prophet declared: "But as many as received Him, to them He gave the right to become children of God, even to those who believe in His name" (John 1:12).

Final Warning — Final Choices

The Holy Scriptures declare that the choice regarding eternal salvation is very clear. Who will be the god of your life? Jesus Christ or you? Either you will admit you are a sinner in need of a pardon and will accept Jesus to become your Lord, or you will insist on remaining the god of your life, even though that decision will lead you to hell. If you insist on being your own god, you will succeed, but at the awful cost of an eternity in hell. Pride is the first and greatest sin. Sinful pride is displayed in the stubborn attitude of many people who insist on having their own way, even at the cost of an eternity without God.

Milton declared in his epic poem, "Paradise Lost," that in the end, either we shall say to God, "Thy will be done," or in the end God will say to us, "Thy will be done." Finally, it is your choice. Ultimately, you must choose heaven or hell as your eternal destination. If you choose to commit your life to Jesus Christ you will be assured that you will meet Him at the Rapture as your Saviour. If you reject His claims to be the Lord of your life, you will have chosen to meet Him as your final judge at the end of your life. The apostle Paul quoted Isaiah when he said, "Every knee shall bow to Me, and every tongue shall confess to God" (Rom. 14:11; Isa. 45:23).

The New Testament recorded the crisis which prompted the jailer of the Philippian prison where Paul and Silas were imprisoned, to make his final choice. God used an earthquake to break the chains that bound the two preachers and to open the prison doors. When the jailer awoke he was afraid that the prisoners had escaped. As he drew his sword to commit suicide, the apostle Paul announced that the prisoners were still there. The frightened jailer recognized the power of Jesus Christ to save His servants. He called out, "Sirs, what must I do to be saved?" Paul gave him the key to eternal life: "Believe on the Lord Jesus Christ, and you will be saved, you and your household" (Acts 16:30-31). The Bible confirms that this man and his family found faith in Christ. "He rejoiced, having believed in God with all his household" (Acts 16:34).

Jesus Christ's invitation to salvation remains open to anyone who is willing to repent of their sins. There is still time to accept Jesus as your personal Saviour. "Behold, I stand at the door and knock. If any one hears My voice, and opens the door, I will come in to him, and dine with him, and he with Me. To him who overcomes I will grant to sit with Me on My throne, as I also overcame and sat down with My Father in His throne. He who has an ear, let him hear what the Spirit says to the churches" (Rev. 3:20-22).

For those who have already chosen to follow the Lord, I encourage you to obey the Great Commission of our Lord and Saviour. In Matthew 28:19-20 Jesus commanded, "Go therefore and make disciples of all the nations, baptizing them in the name of the Father and of the Son and of the Holy Spirit, teaching them to observe all things that I have commanded you; and lo, I am with you always, even to the end of the age."

Our knowledge of the nearness of the return of Jesus Christ should awaken a renewed love of Christ and a passion to witness to those around us while there is still time. The purpose of this book is to introduce non-believers to faith in Christ and to encourage Christians in their faith. In addition, my goal is to provide believers with prophecy material that they can give to their friends and neighbors who do not yet have a personal faith in Christ. The incredible events of the last decade are causing many to ask what lies ahead for the earth. There is a growing fascination in North America with Bible prophecies regarding the last days. This tremendous interest provides us with the greatest opportunity to witness in our lifetime.

The Lord has not left us in darkness concerning the general time of Christ's return. Although we cannot know "the day nor the hour in which the Son of Man is coming" (Matt. 25:13), the fulfillment of three dozen prophecies in our generation indicate that He is coming back to earth in our generation. Someday soon the heavens will open "with a shout, with the voice of an archangel, and with the trumpet of God" (1 Thess. 4:16) announcing to the Church the awesome news that our time of waiting is finally over. At that moment Jesus Christ will appear in the clouds to receive His bride, His faithful Church, rising supernaturally in the air to meet their Lord and King.

Despite the dangers that lie ahead for mankind, those who love Jesus Christ as their Saviour can rest in the knowledge that all these events are in the Lord's hands. The apostle John concluded his prophecy with the great promise of Christ. "He who testifies to these things says, 'Surely I am coming quickly.' Amen. Even so, come, Lord Jesus!" (Rev. 22:20).

Conclusion

Millennial Fever

by William T. James

This generation of earth's inhabitants rushes eagerly toward the turn of the Millennium. Fabulous opportunities await in a New Age, cyberspace world of fantastic advances in most every field of human endeavor. Internet and the Worldwide Web will bring all people together in an interconnectedness that will cause to come to fruition the many things that are wrapped up in the apothegm "it's a small world."

Feverishly, the titans of international commerce position themselves to best take advantage of what they anticipate will be incredible revenue-producing frontiers. Lesser mortals brace against the buffeting winds of change while being siphoned through the time funnel's vortex into a new century and the enigmatic year A.D. 2000.

Much is being said and written about what it all means, this humanity-coalescing wind of destiny, and where it will take civilization. While bright optimism prevails among futurist forecasters, there is the looming shadow of doubt that tinges their thinking. The apprehension stems in part from the foreboding they sense many of their fellow human beings harbor.

An article titled, "Apocalypse Soon: Approaching Millennium Produces a Kind of Fever" reflects data collected on the attitudes of people as the year 2000 approaches, which is apparently at the root of the future watchers' shadow of uncertainty. The writer of the article says in part:

> "For the Lord himself shall descend from heaven with a shout, with the voice of the archangel, and with the trumpet of God. And the dead in Christ shall rise first; then

we who are alive and remain shall be caught up together with them in the clouds to meet the Lord in the air" (1 Thess. 4:16-17).

"The twentieth century is almost over," Johnny Cash sang some 15 years ago, his rough bass introducing a hint of menace into what had been a whimsical little Steve Goodman sing-along.

The approaching Millennium is producing a kind of fever in Americans. As we wait for the zeroes in that celestial odometer to click into alignment we imagine that our system of marking time means something to the cosmos. In our hubris, we imagine something portentous in the changing of a century that is also a thousand-year benchmark.

It is historically reasonable to expect an increase in apocalyptic fervor as we approach the arrival of the twenty-first century. It's bound to get crazy at the end of a Millennium, whose spell is as inexplicable and real as the dark charms of the full moon.

The term itself — Millennium — has several definitions. Most of them are fraught with secular and religious anxiety about the future. . . .

Americans have cultivated an especial fondness for apocalyptic lore since William Miller's followers gathered in the fields to await the return of Christ in the mid-nineteenth century. But interest in the end times has been heightened once again by current events and the approach of the Christian era's third Millennium.

Great interest in the future world ruler called the Antichrist and swift development of certain technologies add to the fear of the future, according to the writer of the article.

The Antichrist will seek power over all humanity by requiring that every person wear a mark or number (probably 666) in order to engage in commerce. Those who refuse this mark will either starve or be slain, while those who do accept it will be forever damned. No wonder the talk of a cashless society — and the further speculation that we might someday have financial information encoded on our very skin — disturbs some people.

Indeed, signs of the imminent apocalypse are manifest, if you believe the movies, heavy metal music, or a particular strain of evangelical teachings. For some the question is not so much whether the end is near but whether we have already entered the period some refer to as the end times.

Some believe the whole thing is about to wrap up; that the year 2000 might just be the last time any of us have any use for a calendar. All over America a growing number of Bible-believing Evangelicals have expressed an interest in apocalyptic prophecy, and the fin de sicle seems a natural hook on which to hang the cataclysmic end to the present age.

Hollywood and the entertainment industry has cashed in on the public's frenzied interest, according to the article's author.

In the middle of Mike Leigh's brilliant 1993 film *Naked*, actor David Thewlis, portraying the damaged drifter Johnny, delivers a chilling monologue about the signs of the approaching Millennium that precisely describes the beliefs of millions of fundamental Christians — bar codes on cereal boxes and the emergence of the United Nations are signs the end is nigh.

Of course, pop culture has found all kinds of uses for the symbolism and poetry of eschatology; Hollywood chronically loots the Bible for plots and nifty bits of business. Countless horror films, some intelligent (Roman Polanski's *Rosemary's Baby,* Michael Tolkin's brutal *The Rapture)*, some entertainingly camp (the string of Damien films that began with *The Omen* in 1976), some irredeemable (the Demi Moore vehicle *The Seventh Sign)* have made use of various aspects of the Book of Revelations.

But for many, the Book of Revelations is a deadly serious business, not the stuff of pulp entertainment.

The writer concludes the article with a brief analysis of David Koresh's disturbed interest in matters involving prophecies about the apocalypse and the ensuing debacle that led to many deaths within the Davidian cult's compound at Waco, Texas. Unfortunately, like so many within the so-called mainstream press, the article's author all but links evangelical Protestants with David Koresh's unbiblical lunacy.

Most mainline Protestant denominations approach Revelations cautiously, and consider its symbolism almost impenetrable.

Yet in Protestantism's fundamentalist wing, Revelations is seen as not only prophetic, but as perhaps the most vital book in the Bible. Koresh himself declared that "all the books of the Bible begin and end in Revelations."

And while the Davidians, with their belief in the personal divinity of David Koresh, were (and continue to be) well outside the mainstream of religious thought, the standoff and subsequent firestorm at Waco have raised questions about threats to the religious freedom of any fringe group. One needn't think Koresh was the second coming of Jesus Christ (actually Koresh thought of himself as the third "Christ") to wonder if government ignorance of, and indifference to, their beliefs didn't contribute to the tragedy at Waco.

In his recent book, *The Ashes of Waco,* Texas writer Dick Reavis reports that an Alcohol, Tobacco and Firearms agent assigned to infiltrate the Davidian compound was so religiously illiterate he had to call his priest to help him locate Revelations in the Bible.

"Had anyone paid close attention to what Koresh had been preaching, or even to the history of Mt. Carmel," Reavis writes, "the agency would have known not to launch a raid."

A little ignorance is never a good thing.[1]

Agreed, a little ignorance is never a good thing, whether it involves an ATF agent who has such limited comprehension of the Bible that his ignorance contributes to a tragedy that causes the death of many men, women, and children, or whether it involves a so-called mainstream journalist whose basic ignorance of his topic is manifest in the fact that he does not know that the last book in the Word of God is Revelation, not Revelations.

The journalist's calling the Book of Revelation, *"Revelations"* in every instance within his article points to the profound truth in his closing statement, *"A little ignorance is never a good thing."* The

Book of Revelation is not about a group of "*revelations*" pertaining to apocalypse. The sixty-sixth book of God's Holy Word is the *Revelation of Jesus Christ*. Indeed, it is not a good thing to be ignorant of Jesus Christ. As a matter of fact, it is a deadly matter to deliberately shun knowledge of the only begotten Son of the Living God!

This present world system, according to the staggering events of our time which point to Christ's second coming, appears to be on the very brink of raging into apocalypse. Jesus is the Saviour of the world. Therefore, to leave Him out of the picture when considering the future means desperation and doom for mankind individually and collectively.

Millennial fever is on the rise while the world system grows sicker by the hour. The Great Physician's prescription for the terminal illness called *sin* is His invitation to believe totally in His wonderful Son who shed His blood for you on Calvary's cross almost 2,000 years ago. Humbly confess that you are a sinner and ask Jesus to save you and become the Lord of your life. You can then be certain, based upon the absolute integrity of Almighty God himself, that you are forever safe in the arms of Jesus, in life, in death, or when He comes suddenly to catch His children up from Planet Earth.

He is coming again. Even so, come, Lord Jesus!

Notes

Introduction

[1] Kenneth L. Woodward, "God Gets the He-ho," *Newsweek* Sept. 11, 1995, page 76.

[2] George Plagenz, NEA religion writer, "Interest in Second Coming Is Growing with Americans," *Benton Courier* Feb. 10, 1995, page 7A.

[3] Geoffrey Cowley with Joseph Contreras, Adam Rogers, Jennifer Lach, Christopher Dickey, and Dusarsan Raghavan, "Outbreak of Fear," *Newsweek* May 22, 1995, page 48.

[4] Cowley with Contreras, Rogers, Lach, Dickey, and Raghavan, "Outbreak of Fear," page 51-52.

[5] Theres Luthi, "Neue Zurcher Zeitung," Zurich, Oct. 26, 1994, "The Global Village of Germs," *World Press Review* May 1995, page 39.

[6] Peter LaLonde, *Point of View,* October, 1995.

Chapter 1

[1] Henry Morris, *The Long War Against God: The History and Impact of the Creation/Evolution Conflict* (Grand Rapids, MI: Baker Book House, 1989).

[2] J.R. Newman, editor, *What is Science?* (New York, NY: Simon and Schuster, 1955) page 272, 278.

[3] Paul Kurtz, Preface to the re-publication of *Humanist Manifestos I* and *II*, booklet distributed by the American Humanist Association.

[4] "Tenets of Humanism," *The New Humanist,* May/June 1933.

[5] Isaac Asimov interview by Paul Kurtz in *Free Inquiry,* Spring 1982, page 9.

[6] Colin Patterson interview by Peter Franz on BBC program produced by Brian Leek, March 4, 1992.

[7] Duane T. Gish, *Evolution—The Fossils Still Say No!* (El Cajon, CA: Institute for Creation Research, 1996).

[8] Stephen J. Gould, *The Panda's Thumb* (New York, NY: W.W. Norton & Co., 1989).

[9] Andrew Carnegie, "Wealth," *North American Review* (Vol. CXL VIII, 1989), page 46.

[10] Andrew Carnegie, *Autobiography* (Boston, MA: Houghton-Mifflin, 1920) page 327.

[11] Daniel Gasmann, *The Scientific Origins of National Socialism* (New York, NY: American Elsevier, 1971), page 168.

[12] Elie A. Schneour, "Abortion Foes Err in Setting Conception as the Starting Point," *Los Angeles Times,* Jan. 29, 1989, Part V, 5.

[13]Aldous Huxley, "History of Tension," *Scientific Monthly,* July 1957, page 9.

[14]Teilhard de Chardin, *The Phenomenon of Man* (New York, NY: Harper and Row, 1965), page 219.

[15]Teilhard de Chardin, *The Heart of the Matter* (New York, NY: Harcourt, Brace and Jovanovich, 1979), page 92.

[16]Kristin Murphy, "United Nations' Robert Muller — A Vision of Global Spirituality," *The Movement Newspaper,* September 1983, page 10.

[17]Paul Vitz, *Sigmund Freud and the Christian Unconscious* (New York, NY: Guilford Publications, 1988).

[18]Richard Wurmbrand, *Marx and Satan* (Wheaton, IL: Crossway Books, 1986), page 12.

[19]Alfred Russell Wallace, *The Wonderful Century* (New York, NY, 1898), page 139.

[20]Alfred Russell Wallace, *My Life* (London, 1905), page 362.

[21]Wallace, *The Wonderful Century,* page 140.

[22]Loren Eiseley, "Alfred Russell Wallace," *Scientific American,* February 1959, page 81.

[23]Milton Munitz, *Space, Time and Creation* (Glencoe, IL: The Free Press, 1957), page 13.

Chapter 2

[1]Hal Lindsey, *Week in Review*, June 10, 1995.

[2]Dr. James Dobson, Focus on the Family Speech to the National Radio Broadcasters, February 1994.

[3]"Sex, Death, and Videotape," *Newsweek,* May 29, 1995, page 53.

Chapter 3

[1]Vernon McGee, "Thru the Bible With J. Vernon McGee," audiotape, vol. 5 (Pasadena, CA: Thru the Bible Radio, 1983).

[2]McGee, "Thru the Bible with J. Vernon McGee" audiotape, vol. 3.

[3]McGee, "Thru the Bible With J. Vernon McGee," vol 5.

[4]Dave Breese, "John Ankerberg Show," Dallas, TX, March 1995.

[5]J. Dwight Pentecost, *Things to Come: A Study in Biblical Eschatology* (Grand Rapids, MI: Academie Books, an imprint of Zondervan Publishing, 1964) page 203-204.

[6]Hal Lindsey, "The Rapture Factor," audio/video, Hal Lindsey Ministries.

[7]Charles Stanley, "Message on the Rapture," audio/video, In Touch Ministries, March 1995.

[8]David Jeremiah, "Turning Point," audio message on the Book of Daniel, March 1995.

[9]Renauld Showers, "The John Ankerberg Show," audio/video, 1995.

[10]Peter LaLonde, "The John Ankerberg Show," audio/video, 1995.

[11]John Walvoord, "The John Ankerberg Show," audio/video, 1995.

Chapter 4

[1]Will Durant, *Caesar and Christ* (New York, NY: Simon & Schuster), vol. 3 from series "The Story of Civilization," 1935-1967.

Chapter 5

[1]Josephus, *Against Apion*, I, 18, 21.

[2]Josephus, *Antiquities*, VIII, 13, 1.

[3]Bradlee, H.W., *A Student's Course on Legal History* (Boston, MA: Suffolk Bar, 1929).

[4]S. Cope, *Mystery Babylon* (Anchorage, AK: Masada Publications, 1994), page 25.

[5]Joseph Wechberg, *The Merchant Bankers* (New York, NY: Simon & Schuster, 1966), page 261 and cover note.

Chapter 6

[1]Richard DeHaan, *Israel and the Nations in Prophecy* (Grand Rapids, MI: Zondervan, 1977), page 11-12.

[2]*Thru the Bible with J. Vernon McGee,* audiotapes, vol. 5 (Pasadena, CA: Thru the Bible Radio, 1983).

[3]Hal Lindsey, Steeling the Mind of America Conference, Denver, CO, 1993/1994.

[4]"Deteriorating Arsenals Pose Hidden Threat," *Insight*, November 23, 1992.

[5]"Arms Sales," *CQ Researcher,* December 9, 1994.

[6]"Arms Sales," *CQ Researcher*, December 9, 1994.

[7]Billy Graham, *Approaching Hoofbeats: The Four Horsemen of the Apocalypse* (Minneapolis, MN: Grason, 1983), page 78, 84.

[8]DeHaan, *Israel and the Nations in Prophecy,* page 53-54.

[9]*Thru the Bible with J. Vernon McGee*, audiotapes.

[10]"When Will the End Come?" The Christian Jew Hour, 1995.

[11]*U.S. News & World Report,* July 3, 1995, page 40.

[12]Steeling the Mind of America Conference, Denver, CO, 1993.

[13]*Week in Review*, Seattle, WA, July 22, 1995.

Chapter 7

[1]This chapter has been taken from a summary of *The Magog Invasion* by Chuck Missler, (Palos Verdes, CA: Western Front, Ltd, 1995). This book clearly establishes the various parties, details the key features of the Ezekiel text, and includes a comprehensive review of the current intelligence profile of Russia and the Middle East, and the advanced weapons being positioned.

Chapter 8

[1]Hal Lindsey, *The Late Great Planet Earth* (New York, NY: Bantam Books), page 57.

[2]Merrill C. Tenney, *The Zondervan Pictorial Encyclopedia of the Bible* (Grand Rapids, MI: Zondervan Publishing House, 1979).

[3]J.R. Church, *Guardians of the Grail* (Oklahoma City, OK: Prophecy Publications, 1989).

Chapter 9

[1]R.J. Rummel, *Death by Government* (New Brunswick, NJ: Transactions Publ., 1994).

Chapter 14

[1]Dave MacPherson, *The Incredible Cover Up* (Medford, OR: Omega Publications, 1975).

[2]John Bray, *The Origin of the Pre-Tribulation Rapture Teaching* (Lakeland, FL: John L. Bray Ministry, Inc.).

[3]Jean Gilman, "Search for First Century Christians," *Jerusalem Christian Review,* vol. 7, issue 1.

[4]Jean Gilman, "Dedication to 'Jesus, the Lord,' in First Century Tomb," *Jerusalem Christian Review,* vol. 7, issue 6.

Conclusion

[1]Philip Martin, "Apocalypse Soon? Approaching Millennium Produces a Kind of Fever," *Arkansas Democrat-Gazette,* August 20, 1995, sec. E: 1-2.

William T. James

William T. James, "Terry," as he is addressed by those who know him, prefers to be thought of as an intensely interested observer of historical and contemporary human affairs, always attempting to analyze that conduct and those issues and events in the light of God's Holy Word, the Bible. He is frequently interviewed in broadcasts throughout the nation.

James has authored, compiled, and extensively edited three previous books, *Storming Toward Armageddon: Essays In Apocalypse, The Triumphant Return of Christ: Essays in Apocalypse II,* and *Earth's Final Days: Essays in Apocalypse III.* Each book presents a series of in-depth essays by well-known prophecy scholars, writers, and broadcasters.

As public relations director for several companies, he has written and edited all forms of business communications, both in print and electronic media. Prior to that he worked as creative director for advertising agencies and did extensive political and corporate speech writing as well as formulated position papers on various issues for the clients he served. In addition to writing, he worked closely with clients and broadcast media in putting together and conducting press conferences and other forums.

As with all his books, Terry James' overriding desire for this book is that Jesus Christ be magnified before the world so that all people might be drawn to the Saviour, that the lost might be redeemed, and that the child of God might be persuaded to faithfully work to sow the gospel message while expectantly watching for the soon return of the Lord.

Dave Breese

David Breese is an internationally-known author, lecturer, radio broadcaster, and Christian minister. He ministers in church and area-wide evangelistic crusades, leadership conferences, student gatherings, and related preaching missions.

He is president of Christian Destiny, Inc., of Hillsboro, Kansas, a national organization committed to the advancement of Christianity through evangelistic crusades, literature distribution, university gatherings, and the use of radio and television.

Dr. Breese is active in a ministry to college and university students, speaking to them from a background of theology and philosophy. He graduated from Judson College and Northern Seminary and has taught philosophy, apologetics, and Church history. He is frequently involved in lectures, debates, and rap sessions on university campuses.

Breese travels more than 100,000 miles a year and has spoken to crowds across North America, Europe, Asia, the Caribbean, and Latin America. His lectures and debates at universities in the United States and overseas center on the confrontation of Christianity and modern thought.

Breese is also the author of a number of books, including *Discover Your Destiny, His Infernal Majesty, Know the Marks of Cults, Living for Eternity,* and the latest, *Seven Men Who Rule from the Grave.* His books, booklets, and magazine articles have enjoyed wide readership across the world. He also publishes *Destiny Newsletter,* a widely-circulated periodical presenting the Christian view of current events.

J.R. Church

J.R. Church is widely recognized as among the foremost prophecy teachers in America. He has authored numerous books on the subject, among them, *Hidden Prophecies in the Song of Moses, Hidden Prophecies in the Psalms,* and *Guardians of the Grail,* which tells of European political intrigue and the move toward a New World Order. His books have sold hundreds of thousands of copies worldwide, having been translated into a number of languages.

In 1964, he organized a church in Lubbock, Texas, where he pastored for over 17 years, building a large bus ministry and a Christian school. He moved to Oklahoma City in 1979, and over the years has developed the ministry, Prophecy in the News.

The ministry publishes a monthly newspaper on prophetic research entitled *Prophecy in the News* and presents a syndicated television broadcast by the same name, which airs on stations across the country and by satellite network to the entire western hemisphere.

Converted at age seven, he set out with one main goal in life — to win people to Jesus Christ. He and his wife, Linda, have been married 35 years. They have two children, a daughter, Teri, and a son, Jerry, Jr.

J.R. Church is in wide demand as a speaker and lecturer on matters pertaining to biblical prophecy, appearing at national and international prophecy conferences and seminars. In addition, he is often seen and heard on various television and radio shows throughout the nation.

His latest books include *They Pierced the Veil,* a commentary on the 12 minor prophets, and *The Mystery of the Menorah.*

Grant Jeffrey

Internationally recognized prophecy researcher Grant R. Jeffrey and his wife, Kaye, have been serving the Lord in full-time ministry since the 1988 publication of Grant's first book, *Armageddon.* That book became an instant bestseller, as did his five successive books, *Heaven, Messiah, Apocalypse, Prince of Darkness,* and the most recent, *Final Warning,* released in May 1995. Since 1988, Grant has reached readers with the message of Christ's soon return through the worldwide sales of more than one and a quarter million copies. Sales of the book support the Jeffreys' ministry activities, which include conferences in North America, Europe, Kenya, Barbados, and Singapore.

Grant, who resides in Toronto, Ontario, was a professional in the pension and insurance brokerage field for 18 years prior to entering the ministry. During the 1970s and 1980s, he taught eschatology part-time at L.I.F.E. Bible College and Christianview Bible College in Canada. Bible prophecy has fascinated him since he was 14; that keen interest has led him to acquire more than 5,000 volumes on eschatology, theology, and archaeology.

In 1994, Grant received an honorary Doctor of Literature degree from Louisiana Baptist Theological Seminary for his research in eschatology.

The material in chapter 14 is included in Grant Jeffrey's excellent book, *Final Warning: Economic Collapse and the Coming World Government.* To order, call 1-800-883-1812. Grant Jeffrey's address is: Frontier Research Publications, Inc., Box 129, Station U, Toronto, Ontario, M8Z 5M4.

David A. Lewis

David A. Lewis is a clergyman, author, lecturer, researcher, publisher, and is active in national and international circles in promoting the welfare of the Church, of Israel, and the Jewish people. His ordination has been with the Assemblies of God for over 35 years.

Dr. Lewis speaks at churches, conferences, minister's seminars, colleges, camp meetings, district events, etc. He has taught short courses in eschatology and apocalyptic literature in both secular and theological colleges, also short-term seminars and spiritual life emphasis in Bible colleges.

He has traveled to the Middle East over 50 times. He has visited and done research in Israel, Egypt, Turkey, Syria, Lebanon, Jordan, and Cyprus. He has also ministered in Hong Kong, Kowloon, Barbados, Virgin Islands, Iceland, Mexico, Canada, and has traveled to mainland China and many European countries.

David Lewis has conferred on numerous occasions with heads of state including Prime Ministers Begin, Peres, and Shamir of Israel, as well as members of Israel's Parliament, Mayor Teddy Kolleck of Jerusalem, Moderate Palestinian Arab leaders, various U.S. senators, congressmen, and has met with former President Reagan.

He was invited and appeared as a witness on the Middle East before the Senate Foreign Relations Committee in Washington, DC.

He has strong contacts with religious leaders in a broad spectrum of churches, with many Jewish religious and political leaders, and in diverse disciplines of the scientific communities.

Books by Lewis include *Prophecy 2000, Smashing the Gates of Hell, Magog Cancelled 1982, Dark Angels of Light, Coming Antichrist,* and *Holy Spirit World Liberation.*

Chuck Missler

As an expert on Russia, Israel, Europe, and the Middle East, Chuck Missler gives intriguing behind-the-scenes insight to his audiences. His more than 30 years in the corporate world as CEO of four public corporations contracting with the U.S. Department of Defense has left him with an extensive network of overseas contacts. With affiliates and associates in nine countries, Missler is a major contributor to several international intelligence newsletters. He has also negotiated joint ventures in Russia, Israel, Malaysia, Japan, Algeria, and Europe. In addition, Missler is an authority on advanced weapons and strategic resources and has participated in projects with SAMCOM-USSR, DSL, JCS, USACADA, DOJ, CCIA, and SDI. A member of the International Press Association, he is an honors graduate from the U.S. Naval Academy.

For 20 years, Chuck Missler taught a Bible study in southern California that grew to more than 2,000 attendees. In 1992, he moved to Coeur d'Alene, Idaho, where he founded Koinonia House to distribute his books, lectures, and tapes. His dynamic style, conservative values, and adherence to biblical principles have made him a highly acclaimed speaker and critic.

His newsletter, *Personal UPDATE,* a 32-page Christian prophecy and intelligence newsletter, has grown to reach more than 50,000 monthly subscribers and he has more than 8 million tapes in circulation worldwide.

If you wish to receive a 12-month complimentary subscription to *Personal UPDATE* contact:
Koinonia House
P.O. Box D
Coeur d'Alene, ID 83814
1-800-546-8731

Henry Morris

Morris, who founded the Institute for Creation Research in 1970, directed that organization until his retirement in 1995. With a distinctive professional and educational background that spans many facets of civil engineering, mathematics, and the sciences, he has steadfastly defended biblical inerrancy in more than 60 books on scientific topics.

Morris' best-sellers *The Genesis Flood*, *The Genesis Record*, and *Scientific Creationism* have become must-read material for serious Bible students. He has lectured in 45 states and 10 foreign countries, including meetings in more than 400 churches, 180 colleges and universities, and 160 conferences and conventions.

Gary Stearman

Since 1987, Gary Stearman has been affiliated with J. R. Church, founder and president of Prophecy in the News. There, he is occupied with the continuing work of research in Bible prophecy. In conjunction with J.R. Church, he is co-author of *Mystery of the Menorah and the Hebrew Alphabet.* This groundbreaking work is devoted to showing that the Bible has a large-scale alphabetic plan that extends across the entirety of its 66 books. The plan presents redemption and prophecy as an alphabetic series.

As a writer/researcher, he feels called to pursue the scriptural bypaths that put Bible prophecy in contemporary terms. Along with many others, he is of the opinion that the prophetic landscape is rapidly moving toward its culmination. As a result, he believes that the Lord is now revealing many of Scripture's hidden themes, symbols, metaphors, and timelines to watchful men of faith.

He appears with Mr. Church on a weekly 30-minute television broadcast that brings these and many other subjects into a public forum. Together, they underscore the nearness of Christ's appearance at the end of this age, and they witness His saving power, to win as many viewers as possible to the Lord.

Since 1984, Mr. Stearman has pastored *Grace Community Bible Church of Oklahoma City.* There, his primary concern is scripturally-based, expository Bible teaching, with an emphasis on Christian maturity and discipleship. He believes that the Lord Jesus Christ provides the only hope for an increasingly destabilized world that has lost its moral, ethical, and spiritual compass.

Dr. John F. Walvoord

Chancellor of Dallas Theological Seminary, Dr. Walvoord is recognized as one of the leading conservative evangelical theologians of America. A specialist in the field of biblical eschatology, he has an extensive ministry in Bible conferences.

Dr. Walvoord, who has served in his current position since 1986, is an extensively published author. His most recent work includes *Prophecy* (1993) and *Major Bible Prophecies* (1991). He is a regular contributor to *Bibliotheca Sacra*; contributor to numerous published symposiums and reference works; author of frequent articles in Christian magazines, and a member of the revision committee for the New Scofield reference edition of the Holy Bible.

David F. Webber

Dr. David Webber, a speaker for more than 35 years on Southwest Radio Church, a long-running radio broadcast ministry founded by his father, E. F. Webber, in the 1930s, is a well-known author of a number of significant books on prophecy. He has conducted tours to Israel and to other regions of interest to Christians. He is an internationally-known conference speaker and publishes a monthly newsletter, *David Webber Reports.* David Webber Ministries produces a daily radio broadcast and a weekly shortwave radio program heard worldwide.

During his many years of Christian broadcast work, David has interviewed most every prophetic scholar of note from around the world. Additionally, he himself is often sought out for interviews on biblically prophetic matters as they relate to current events and issues.

Dr. Webber attended Oklahoma City University, where he obtained a B.A. in theology, and Belen Memorial University in Chillicothe, Missouri, where he received an honorary doctorate.

His published books include *The Image of the Ages* and *The Mark is Ready,* which is scheduled to be released in early 1995.

issues and events

from prophetic perspectives

The William T. James monthly briefing paper that presents analysis of current issues and events in the words of the world's best-known writers, speakers, and broadcasters

For a free issue of "i.e." simply fill in, then clip the coupon below and send to:

James Informarketing
P.O. Box 1108
Benton, AR 72018-1108

Please include with the coupon a self-addressed, business-sized envelope stamped with first-class postage.

Please send me a free issue of "i.e." I have enclosed, along with this coupon, a business-sized envelope stamped with first-class postage.

Name _____

Address _____
       (Street)

_____
(City)   (State)   (Zip)

Essays in Apocalypse I

Storming Toward Armageddon

David Breese • Ray Brubaker • Joseph Carr
Joseph R. Chambers • Tim LaHaye • David Allen Lewis
Robert Lindsted • Texe Marrs • with William T. James

- Wonder what the last years of the 1990s hold for you, your children, and the world?
- Baffled by the sequence of end-time events?
- Want up-to-date facts without a lot of speculation?
- Wish someone would explain in laymen's terms what the Bible says about the last days?

Get ready to be:
Startled by news reports from around the world.
Shocked by the terrifying trends in our society.
Challenged to make a difference today!
$10.95 • 336 pages • 0-89221-228-4

Available at bookstores nationwide or contact
New Leaf Press • P.O. Box 726 • Green Forest, AR 72638

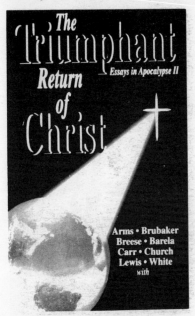

Essays in Apocalypse III

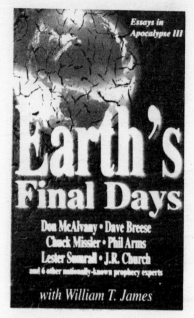

Earth's Final Days

**Bob Anderson • Phil Arms • John Barela • Dave Breese
Steve Butler • J.R. Church • Don S. McAlvany
D.A. Miller • Chuck Missler • Lester Sumrall
David F. Webber • John Wesley White
• with Wm. T. James**

Is this the last generation before the Lord's return? The group of essayists gathered for *Earth's Final Days* explore the possibility that we are living in the last days. Read about these issues for our time:

- Wars and rumors of wars
- Government: keeper of law or champion of the lawless?
- The murder of values in a once-great nation.
- How close is economic disaster?
- What did Jesus say about the last days?

$11.95 • 368 pages • 0-89221-279-9